KNOWING

KNOWING THE FACE OF GO...

THE FACE OF GOD

TIM STAFFORD

NAVPRESS

BRINGING TRUTH TO LIFE

NavPress Publishing Group

P.O. Box 35001, Colorado Springs, Colorado 80935

The Navigators is an international Christian organization. Our mission is to reach, disciple, and equip people to know Christ and to make him known through successive generations. We envision multitudes of diverse people in the United States and every other nation who have a passionate love for Christ, live a lifestyle of sharing Christ's love, and multiply spiritual laborers among those without Christ.

NavPress is the publishing ministry of The Navigators. NavPress publications help believers learn biblical truth and apply what they learn to their lives and ministries. Our mission is to stimulate spiritual formation among our readers.

Library of Congress Catalog Card Number: 95-26663
ISBN 08910-99344

Previously published as *Knowing the Face of God* © 1986, 1989 by Tim Stafford, Zondervan Publishing House.

Some of the anecdotal illustrations in this book are true to life and are included with the permission of the persons involved. All other illustrations are composites of real situations, and any resemblance to people living or dead is coincidental.

Unless otherwise identified, all Scripture quotations in this publication are taken from the *HOLY BIBLE: NEW INTERNATIONAL VERSION* ® (NIV®). Copyright © 1973, 1978, 1984 by International Bible Society. Used by permission of Zondervan Publishing House. All rights reserved.

Stafford, Tim.
    Knowing the face of God / Tim Stafford.
        p.   cm.
    Originally published: Grand Rapids, Mich. : Zondervan, c1989.
      ISBN 0-89109-934-4
      1. Christian life. I. Title.
    [BV4501.2.S7145 1996]
    231.7—dc20   95-26663
                       CIP

Printed in the United States of America

2 3 4 5 6 7 8 9 10 11 12 13 14 15 / 00 99 98 97 96

CONTENTS

PART ONE: A PERSONAL RELATIONSHIP   9

  1   A PERSONAL PREFACE   11
  2   DOUBLE VISION   20
  3   AN INTRODUCTION TO A PERSONAL RELATIONSHIP   29
  4   EXCHANGING NAMES   34
  5   THE COMMITMENT OF LOVE   41
  6   CONVERSATION   55
  7   A HOME   69
  8   FAMILY   78
  9   MEALS   89
 10   WORK   99
 11   TOUCH   108
 12   STORIES   119
 13   PRAISE   127
 14   FORGIVENESS AND SACRIFICE   137
 15   SUFFERING   150
 16   THREE DANGERS   163

PART TWO: THE FACE OF GOD   167

 17   SEEING IS BELIEVING   169
 18   THE GLORIOUS APPEARANCE   173
 19   VISION OR REALITY?   180
 20   THE PROBLEM OF INVISIBILITY   185
 21   WHAT DO WE MAKE OF JESUS?   191
 22   THE DARKNESS OF THE LIGHT OF JESUS   196
 23   THE DARKNESS OF THE HOLY SPIRIT   201
 24   THE AGE TO COME   208
 25   WAITING IN HOPE   219
 26   UNTIL THEN   225
 27   FROM HERE FORWARD   232
 28   WAKING TO THE LIGHT   240

APPENDIX: THOUGHTS ON THE HISTORY OF SPIRITUALITY   244

To my mother and father,
who taught me what matters

ACKNOWLEDGMENTS

Since this book comes out of a long search, and since its scope is as broad as life itself, I would need pages to thank all those whose insights and example were crucial to its development. I would like to acknowledge the help of a few, however, including one whom I only know through her writing: Helen Oppenheimer. Her *Incarnation and Immanence* was a great help to me.

Philip Yancey assisted me not only as an editor who knows my writing as well as he knows Chicago streets, but also as an encouraging fellow-seeker. He believed in the importance of this book.

My brother Bill, along with his wife, Barbara, steered me out of some terrifying theological tangles.

My wife, Popie, more than anybody, cheered me through the long writing and revising process and offered a great deal of shrewd, reliable advice.

A number of people read all or part of this book in manuscript, making comments and suggestions. In addition to the friends named above, they are David and Carol Andersen, Randy and Carrie Bare, Harold Myra, Fred Prudek, Chase and Harriette Stafford, Mike and Lesley Van Dordrecht, Paul and Elizabeth Wrightman. Judith Markham not only read the manuscript, she edited it well. I owe all of them great thanks.

I know that my Redeemer lives,

and that in the end he will stand upon the earth.

And after my skin has been destroyed,

yet in my flesh I will see God;

I myself will see him

with my own eyes — I, and not another.

How my heart yearns within me!

—Job 19:25-27

PART ONE

A PERSONAL RELATIONSHIP

How shall I call upon my God,

my God and my Lord,

since, in truth, when I call upon him,

I call him into myself?

What place is there within me

where my God can come?

How can God come into me,

God who made heaven and earth?

O Lord my God,

is there anything in me that can contain you?

—Augustine, *Confessions*

1

A PERSONAL PREFACE

~

More than a few times as I read and thought and prayed in preparation for writing this book, I doubted whether I had any business with it. In truth, I never felt so small and incoherent as while reflecting on the immensity of my subject. What drove me on was desire to understand my relationship with God and to grow in it. And as I opened the subject with others, I felt I touched something live and tender in them, something they rarely spoke of and perhaps even seldom thought of, but something that, when brought into the light, rose up huge and hungry.

I was conscious that my friends and my family, those who had worked with me or grown up with me, would remember me as they read my words. Not everything they remembered would prove me qualified to write boldly on this subject. More crucially, God would read this book—was reading it even as I wrote. It was more than a little unsettling to have such a Presence looking over my shoulder as I wrote about him.

No one in the Bible earned more scorn from God than the false, though very religious, prophets who spoke confidently of things they knew nothing about. As I prepared to write and as my mind spread out (very thinly) over God's astonishing range, I had reason to fear being like those men in their well-meaning blather about the Lord. I echoed Augustine: "How can God come into me, God who made heaven and earth?" I do not want to be among those he dismisses: "Go away. I never knew you."

Yet a verse has comforted me considerably: "The man who thinks he knows something does not yet know as he ought to know. But the man who loves God is known by God" (1 Corinthians 8:2-3).

This allows no room for arrogance. Prideful certainty, in fact, is a certain sign of knowledge gone astray. "But the man who loves God is known by God." His knowledge of me, not mine of him, is the crucial certainty. It is the only foundation I can stand on to search into a subject too great for me. In fact, I cannot resist. I would rather speak of him in faltering, uncertain words than keep silent about the very foundation of my life.

A CONFESSION

I find it impossible to write about knowing God except as a confession. To want to know someone is intensely personal. It is no less so to want to know God. This book is not the story of my life by any means; yet if you are to understand why I am where I am now on this matter, you must understand where I came from.

I grew up in an evangelical Christian home where I was taught to pray and read the Bible. My parents cared that their children learned to love God and didn't care about anything else nearly so much. Early in life I saw very clearly that they were right, and so I followed them in faith, essentially without trauma.

I was and am by temperament a stable person, not prone to ecstasies or paralyzing depressions. But I was lonely. Until I reached college I didn't know anyone outside my family who was spiritually on my wavelength. This was largely my own fault; I was a very private person.

At college I found a small Christian fellowship with no more than two dozen students in the core group. It was a difficult period for Christians on a university campus; to our peers we seemed narrow and outmoded. But that was hardly what I experienced. For the first time in my life I was with believers my own age who read and thought, who were unafraid of any subject, but who also studied the Scriptures and prayed without embarrassment. There was a warmth between them I had never experienced. It was like falling in love. I felt as though the fog had lifted off heaven just a little.

I did not make the connection at the time, but I now think it was this very delight in Christian fellowship that made me look at my life with increasing despair. I had awakened to a deep enjoyment of Christian brothers and sisters, and I could not help longing for the same awakening with God. I was supposed to "hear his voice" in a two-thousand-year-old book. I was supposed to "talk with him in prayer." But when I read the Bible I heard no voices, and my prayers often seemed more like talking to myself. My sense of his presence was never intense enough to form absolute proof of God. And other people's experiences were—other people's.

One inky, blustery night when the wind blew the trees' arms high into the air, I walked for miles, asking God again and again to simply show himself to me. I shouted to heaven to shatter the silence. I did not want to "work up" a feeling of God; I wanted God to break in on me.

He did not.

I heard no voice, saw no lights in the sky. I went home to my dorm room and went to bed. And I survived. I did more than survive; I grew. But I did not stop longing for God to be unquestionably real—real to me.

I doubt that my friends ever dreamed such things were stirring in me, although I do remember taking my heart in my hands and talking to one friend, renowned in my circles for his spiritual wisdom. (One is never so renowned for anything as while a senior in college.) I said to him, "If only I could be absolutely certain that Jesus is here in this room with us, hearing every word we say. I believe he is, but at the same time I don't believe it. If I did, I would be able to act differently. I wouldn't dare sin in his presence."

My friend seemed puzzled. He said Jesus did seem real to him, but he couldn't find a way to make him more real to me.

On another occasion I felt this emptiness as it affected someone else. We were shocked when word circulated that a stalwart member of our fellowship had decided to quit being a Christian. I, along with some others, went to see him. In the small tinny trailer where he lived, we broached the subject gingerly, in the somber way you edge up to a topic you know you are going to disagree on.

To my surprise our friend did not produce an intellectual argument against the existence of God. His parents were missionaries; he did not deny the validity of their faith. He did not deny that Jesus was the way, the truth, and the life. He said simply that Jesus was not working for him. He had done everything possible to "make it work," and nothing did. He did not want to argue. He was glum but resolute. He mentioned predestination. "Maybe God hasn't chosen me," he said. He was not closing the door on God. He was simply tired of working so hard at getting God to come in.

If I were Augustine, addressing my confessions directly to God, I might ask, "O God, where were you while that miserable conversation went on? Were you there as you are everywhere? Were you close as the air we breathed, the air we used to make our words? How could you tolerate such misery, misery in him for not believing, misery in us for not being able to answer him? You could have answered him in a flash by writing on the wall as you did for Belshazzar, by appearing visibly as you did for the disciples. Lord, why did you hide yourself while you were there? I believe, Lord, but I want to understand."

I don't want to give the impression that my faith was utterly dry. Sometimes emotions and glimmerings streaked through me—not things of substance I could show off to a skeptical psychologist, but things that were meaningful to me. I thought they came from God. I didn't lack for intellectual satisfaction or for demonstrations of God's power. I saw him changing lives. My questions and doubts were only a footnote, a silent interjection into an exhilarating story. On a human level, Christianity was more than I had hoped for. It was the human-to-God level I felt shaky about. I wanted more.

I have come to realize that I was not alone in my longing. It's just that such questions usually aren't voiced. When they are—when the conversation moves to the subject of knowing God—listeners grow suddenly quiet and attentive. For a long time I thought this was a disapproving silence. I now know it is the silence that falls on a room of hungry people when someone talks of food.

KNOWING GOD OR KNOWING ABOUT GOD?

Some years ago Dr. J. I. Packer published an excellent book called *Knowing God*. It sold, to the surprise of some, like life insurance on a sinking ship. The sales were surprising because *Knowing God* did not contain a dramatic testimony or personal anecdotes; it was essentially a theology of the attributes of God. Theology books do not usually sell so well, even very good theology books.

My theory is that the title and introduction sold the book. A vast, unfed hunger hides just below the surface of our churchly activities, a hunger to know God intimately and personally. Even suffering to read theology would be worth it, if in the end your hunger to know him were satisfied. Dr. Packer's introduction whets our appetites: "Not many of us, I think, would ever naturally say that we have known God. The words imply a definiteness and matter-of-factness of experience to which most of us, if we are honest, have to admit that we are still strangers. . . . A little knowledge of God is worth more than a great deal of knowledge about Him."

I have the greatest admiration for Dr. Packer and his book. Yet I find it obvious that *Knowing God* is filled with a great deal of knowledge *about* God. It is so reverent and wise that I am sure few people feel disappointed when they finish it. But it does not directly satisfy the hunger the book began with, the hunger to know God himself, not just about him.

In Dr. Packer's defense it must be said that no book can do that; you cannot bring Christ personally into ink and paper. A book or a sermon is at best a doorway through which Christ may come. It is not his substance. And also, there may be no more essential means of knowing God than knowing about him. You cannot divorce a person from his personality, his history, his words, and his promises. I have no doubt that *Knowing God* has led many to Christ himself.

My point is simply that a book entitled *Knowing God* is more accurately *Knowing About God*, but few notice the discrepancy. There has been so little discussion within the evangelical movement of "knowing God" that people do not even have a defined idea of what this subject covers. Yet they have the hunger. That is why they bought Packer's book.

A PERSONAL RELATIONSHIP WITH GOD

There is another strand in this book, one I did not initially connect with my hunger for God. It too began during my college years, and I vividly remember its beginning.

Two friends were talking. One had grown up in church; the other was a recently born-again Christian. The new Christian was trying to convince the other that he needed to be converted—that earnest prayers and religious duties were not enough for salvation. The born-again Christian finally blurted out, "I'm not talking about religion. I'm talking about a *personal relationship with God!*"

I had heard that phrase a thousand times; it was part of growing up in an evangelical environment. But I heard it anew that day, perhaps almost the way nonevangelicals hear it, and I caught the slight edge of arrogance: "I've experienced it. It may be theory to you, but not to me."

In the film *Sleeper* Woody Allen plays a character who wakes up in another century, having been frozen in a scientific experiment. He is given a stack of photographs from our century to identify, which prompts a series of hilarious one-liners. Billy Graham's picture comes up. Allen pauses, then says, "Billy Graham . . . claimed to have a personal relationship with God." The audience, of course, cracks up. That is how absurd the idea sounds to some.

Indeed, it is an astonishing claim. When you say you have a "personal relationship" with a famous person, it means you can get to that person outside official channels; you can call him at home. Other people may know him by reputation, but you know *him*. You are not just associates; you are *friends*. Was that what my born-again friend meant? If we examined his life under a microscope, minute by minute, would we find such intimacy with Christ?

Perhaps he meant only that he was *trying* to create intimacy with God and expecting to realize it through his praise and prayers and Bible reading. If so, how exactly did this differ from some ordinary church-attender's sense of faith as a list of God-related duties? Where was the intimacy with God?

I thought I could partly grasp the meaning of the phrase—for I was convinced it did mean something—by thinking of what a personal relationship was not. Perhaps my friend was trying to say that he did not relate to God institutionally, as we relate to banks or mortgage companies or the Republican Party. Or perhaps he was trying to say that he did not relate to God intellectually, as a set of propositions, as a force or a cosmic idea.

Or perhaps my friend was saying that the center of the Christian faith is Jesus Christ himself. He is a person. If we relate to him at all, it must be personally.

But where did he find this person? Was there a single thing in the born-again Christian's life he could have pointed to and said, "There! That's it! You certainly can't have *that* without a personal relationship"?

I never breathed a word of these questions because in my circles, having a "personal relationship with God" was synonymous with being a Christian. I didn't want word to circulate, "Have you heard about Stafford? We really need to pray for him. He's doubting his relationship with God."

I worked for three months washing dishes in a Connecticut restaurant. Most of my fellow workers were Italians whose version of nominal Catholicism seemed to have inoculated them against any temptation to take God or morality seriously. So a conversation with one waitress, a bone-thin divorcee with too much eye shadow, shocked me. George Harrison's song "My Sweet Lord" came on the radio in the back room. Hearing the song with its recurring words, "My sweet Lord, I really want to know you . . . but it takes so long, my Lord," the waitress immediately told me of a religious experience she had had the day before. As she had been listening to this same song, she had burst helplessly into tears. She was bewildered. "Why do you think I did that?" she demanded.

I would like to be able to say that I told her that her heart was aching for the love of Jesus, but I can't. I was as bewildered as she was. Maybe if she had been a "nice person" I would not have been so surprised, but I classed her with the tough kids I had left in high school: the boys who took auto shop and went off to fight in Vietnam, and the pasty, unhealthy girls in short skirts who swore. Was it possible that such people too were hungry for God? The song moved me, but I had not expected it to move anybody else in that restaurant. And I did not know how those stirrings related to Christian faith— whether a longing that the songwriter applied to Krishna could be legitimate and not devilishly deceptive. Later, reflecting on the experience, I began to suspect that my longing was shared by many unlikely characters—perhaps by everyone.

Eventually my hunger for God and my questions about a "personal relationship" merged into a single quest: I hungered for a personal God. And so, I realized, did many others—even those who had no idea that they did.

In my quest I never strayed from the evangelical Christian path, nor was I tempted to. It was my heritage and I stuck to it. Regardless of its faults, the evangelical tradition had one quality that drew me irresistibly: it spoke openly and often about a personal relationship with God. If religion didn't offer God full strength, I wasn't interested.

If anything, evangelicals spoke too confidently of God. They could see him at work and talk with him without difficulty. For them miracles were not out of date nor incredible; "God led me to . . ." was a common phrase. Evangelicals peered at the world around them, straining to discern exactly what God was doing. Some read books on prophecy to understand the hidden meanings in their newspapers, meanings of God's powerful activity. Others even claimed to hear God's audible voice. Well-known evangelists reported reassuring visions related to their finances. When the "God is dead" theology made *Time* magazine, preachers made a joke out of it: "I read in *Time* that God is dead. I was quite surprised. I turned to my wife and said, 'That's odd. I talked to him just this morning!'" Evangelical hymns reinforced the idea of a vividly present God: "He walks with me, and He talks with me, And He tells me I am His own; And the joy we share as we tarry there, None other has ever known."

Furthermore, I never heard anyone raise a word of caution about these claims. If someone said, "God led me to stop and see my friend Mary," no one asked whether God did, indeed, prompt that and how. I never heard any pastor say, "We're going to sing 'He Touched Me,' and then we'll talk about the questions it raises." Some people certainly must have had their doubts, but they never voiced them.

Everyone acted as though this way of talking was the most natural in the world. Indeed, I wanted to be where this kind of conversation *was* the most natural thing in the world. Yet there was a considerable gap between the talk and my experience. I had two questions:

1. Just what could be personal about a relationship with God? Being as clear-eyed and realistically truthful as possible, what could I claim? What could I hope for?
2. How could I more fully know the personal God, not just know about him?

As Augustine asked, "What place is there within me where my God can come? How can God come into me, God who made heaven and earth? O Lord my God, is there anything in me that can contain you?"

In this book I have tried to address these questions and to show you the answers I have found. For I have come to believe that God's personality does crowd the world around me, even inside me. I believe I can know him with the same faculties and in many of the same ways that I know my friends.

If the Bible carries one repeated message about God, it is that *he wants to be known*. But it has taken me a long time to understand how.

2

DOUBLE VISION

~*~

I am convinced that evangelical Christians have adopted the phrase "personal relationship with God" largely because it is evangelistically effective. You will not find the phrase in the Bible, and as far as I know, it was not much used by Christians in earlier generations. Yet for us it has become synonymous with "genuine faith." For instance, I have heard evangelical leaders refer to a Roman Catholic Christian by saying, "I'm convinced that he has a real personal relationship with Jesus Christ." By this they mean that he has a genuine Christian faith, that they accept him as a Christian.

Our forefathers were more legal-minded, concentrating on sin and its forgiveness through the cross. We have switched our emphasis to loneliness and alienation. The reason, I suppose, is that our generation has done what would seem impossible: denied the reality of sin.

People don't want to hear that they are sinners, but they do not object to being told that they are lonely. In our mass-production society people crave personal contact. So Christians emphasize loneliness instead of sin. They preach that alienation is cured by a personal relationship with God. He fills, as we say, our God-shaped vacuum.

I do not disagree with this. But because our emphasis on personal relationship has grown mainly from evangelistic experiences, without considerable biblical reflection, it leads many people into confusion and disappointment. We need to think more deeply.

NO ORDINARY FRIEND

What is, or can be, personal about a relationship with God? Can we claim honestly to have such a thing? Or are such words just blue sky and Santa Claus?

Obviously God is not my personal friend in the ordinary way. I cannot play tennis with him or invite him for dinner. I cannot ask a question and expect a straight answer. My relationship with him may be *like* a friendship in certain respects, but it is also unlike it. There is only one God, and ultimately no one and nothing is "like" him. My relationship with him must also be unique.

If I am to understand this uniqueness, I must disabuse myself of jargon and half-thought-out ideas that feel, from long usage, as comfortable as old jeans. I must poke at things I would rather leave alone and stir up questions that get subconsciously repressed.

I take no pleasure in this. Daring to ask uncomfortable questions about such a personal matter as one's faith seems to carry a risk, like trying to catch snowflakes on a warm hand. In seeking to illuminate will we destroy?

But hard questions about Christian faith, though they seem life-threatening, are not. We live not by our own health but by the health of the gospel, and we cannot knock the real gospel down with a few clumsy questions. Only our illusions will crumble so that truth stands out more clearly.

❦

Suppose someone—call him Joe—goes to an evangelistic crusade. He finds himself deeply moved by the sermon; he hardly knows why. He may not have a deep sense of sin or separation from God; in fact, before he wandered into this meeting, he may have thought his life was just fine. But the preacher's confidence in God catches him. If he were able to articulate what he feels, he would say that he has suddenly realized something is missing from his life and only God can fill the emptiness. Proper theology, the fellowship of the church, moral standards, a coherent and compassionate world view never even cross his mind as he rises from his seat and stumbles forward. The preacher's pounding words have said that God wants him and will fill his life. Now he wants God.

When Joe reaches the front, a counselor holds a brief, biblical discussion with him about the barrier of sin to fellowship and then asks him to pray a simple prayer inviting Jesus to enter his heart, to live there forever. When Joe at last lifts his head and opens his eyes, the counselor assures him that God always answers a prayer of that kind; Jesus has entered his heart if he has prayed sincerely. He is now a new creature. He has a relationship with God forever.

The counselor then issues some warnings. "Some people feel lightning bolts when Christ enters their life," he says, "and that's wonderful when it happens. But you can't rely on feelings. Some people don't feel any different at all. The main thing is to have faith in Christ, to believe in his promises. He has promised to come into your life, and since it is impossible for him to lie, you must simply believe that Jesus is in your heart whether you feel anything or not."

Naturally, the counselor points out, Jesus will want to make some changes in his new home, and it is important for Joe to be prepared for these. He must grow in Christ. To do this, he must read the Bible and pray every day. He must also join a church. If Joe is not already a member of a church, the counselor will be happy to point him toward a good one.

In a somewhat dazed condition Joe leaves the meeting, rejoining happy (or dubious) friends and family members. He is flushed with success, awed by the dramatic choice he has made. He has "done it." He may feel a dramatic sense of relief and freedom. He will very rarely feel disappointed, that some trick was played on him. He is in no mood to question small discrepancies. But something did get switched without his notice. He walked down front expecting a personal relationship with God. He left with the understanding that he must read the Bible and pray every day. No one has explained very precisely the connection between the two.

So Joe digs out a long-forgotten Bible; he even finds some Bible study materials at a local Christian bookstore and begins to discipline himself to read. He struggles to concentrate his thoughts into prayer, although his mind tends to wander and he occasionally wonders if he is just talking to himself. He joins a church where joy permeates the worship service and a sincere and thoughtful pastor teaches from the Bible.

Gradually Joe's morals and world view are re-formed. He finds genuine warmth in the family of faith. Of course there are times of frustration and periods of flat boredom. The church is not ideal and neither is Joe.

But underlying everything, joys and complaints, is a great, sneaking disappointment: the discrepancy between what he was offered — a personal relationship with God — and what he actually experiences. He goes to church. He meets his friends. He hears interesting and encouraging sermons. But everything is on a human level: ideas, friendships, activities. Where is God? What is so personal about singing songs? Or talking into the air? Or looking into events to see whether they are coincidences or so-called "answers to prayer"? It was the personal God he wanted, not church or "the Christian life." He knows he should trust God; he believes God will somehow "meet" those who truly seek him. But he is unsure whether he is supposed to be content with his current experience or whether he should expect something more. Is he missing something?

Occasionally, fleetingly, God seems almost to appear. Something in the church service moves a lump to his throat — a hymn, a prayer that embodies his need. He hears a talk that gives him exhilarating new hope. On some days his own Bible study strikes straight to his heart. But are these experiences what was meant by "a personal relationship"? Can he even be sure that God is responsible for them? After all, he sometimes feels the same way when he hears the national anthem.

⌐⌐

What do we say to people like Joe? Do we give them a pat on the back and tell them (in so many words) that the talk about a personal relationship with God is just rhetoric? "This is all there is. Just follow the rules and you'll be all right."

When the fever of salvation cools and the new believer begins to ask questions, evangelical Christians are rarely much help. "You ask me how I know he lives? He lives within my heart," they sing. One of the most popular Christian songs of my generation encourages us to sing, "Then by faith I met him face to face, and I felt the wonder of his grace." What kind of truth is this? The apostle Paul, after all, wrote, "Now we see through a glass darkly, but *then* face to face" (1 Corinthians 13:12, KJV, emphasis added). If truth at all, this song offers the kind of truth that sees a business opportunity and immediately says, "I've just become a millionaire." But such subtle distinctions rarely get into the Sunday sermon.

The questioner may even be made to fear something is wrong with him. He receives suggestions about how he can improve his spiritual life—the underlying assumption being that he must be failing somehow. (Indeed, he certainly is failing somehow—but that is not the whole explanation of the problem.) He may notice too that his questions make some pastors and leading laypeople quite nervous.

This lack of serious explanation, combined with flamboyant language implying that "you could just feel the Spirit move," reinforces the disappointment for many people. By harping on the very point about which many of us feel confused, then changing the subject the moment someone asks a pointed question, the evangelical movement seems determined to make us feel worse than we already do. Many of us would eagerly echo Isaiah's prayer, "Oh, that you would rend the heavens and come down" (Isaiah 64:1), although indeed we have in mind something quite different from what Isaiah longed for.

We do not usually look for God to break triumphantly into history, but to do something individual—to provide a personal vision of himself.

DOUBLE VISION

Evangelicals are not the only ones with this longing. Anyone who reads the Bible will feel it, for in the Bible the personal reality of God is unquestionable. The Old Testament God shows up unbidden. He forces people to account for him. Moses was no wilderness philosopher-monk dreaming of ethical monotheism. During his forty years of tending sheep he had started no rebellions, had written no theological tracts. God interrupted his tranquility and said, "Take off your sandals." Throughout the Old Testament God's miracles of salvation and judgment are strewn as freely as desert sand. God initiates; humankind responds. The prophets did not begin their messages, "Having observed our current situation and meditated on its meaning, I feel constrained to say. . . ." They began, "This is what the Lord says."

The New Testament brings God considerably closer. God is *our*

Father; the church is *married* to Christ; every Christian is "in Christ" and he is in us as though not even the barrier of skin separates us any longer. Could any more intimate images be chosen? And while these images are filled with comfort and encouragement, they also produce pain. What sort of son has never seen his father? What sort of wife has no feeling for her husband's arms?

We are forced toward an uncomfortable double vision. The stories and promises of the Bible offer a banquet to fill our hunger; yet we live underfed lives. We drag out of bed in the morning, force our eyes to focus on the words of Scripture, mumble words into space, and get moving toward work, where God may not even be mentioned, where he certainly does not appear. We are so numb we hardly notice our poverty. Occasionally tragedy forces us to see our lack of satisfaction, and we pray more forcefully with the psalmists, "Lord, show me your face." But the clock ticks on, one day rolls over into the next, and we cannot spend forever asking speculative questions about the whereabouts of God.

We are forced to live with double vision.

Not all feel the split intensely or voice their doubts dramatically. Many people seem happy, content, and grateful for God's mercy to them; they don't worry about what they lack. But I am concerned about them, too, for they may have adapted to the problem of split vision by stuffing one half of it into a bin labeled "inspiration." God did not make promises in order to have them consigned to such a bin.

Different people adapt to double vision in different ways, depending on their personalities. To give you a general impression of what I mean, I have lumped them into four categories: the dropouts, the joiners, the enthusiasts, and the hard-liners.

DROPOUTS, JOINERS, ENTHUSIASTS, AND HARD-LINERS

One: Dropouts

Dropouts are those who, like the missionaries' son from my college days, suffer acutely from the double vision—so much so that they finally give up trying to reconcile it. They do not make speeches or lead groups out of the church. They just disappear. They joined the church with aching hearts; they disappear with aching hearts. They may put the blame on hypocrisy or legalism or fundamentalism or other catchwords, but they leave because they did not find in church what they hoped for. It didn't work, and nobody in the church seemed to even recognize their problem. *Either all those people are phonies,* the dropout thinks, *or something is wrong with me. For some reason God has not chosen to make himself real to me.*

If you think I exaggerate, go door-to-door in your neighborhood and find out why people do not go to church. Or count up the people who have disappeared from your church and ask them why.

Two: Joiners

If dropouts are idealists, joiners are entirely practical. *Religion is a good thing,* a joiner thinks in his heart, *like Rotary.* They believe in participation, and they stay in the church as stalwart members. They believe, but they have managed to ease the pinching hunger for God that probably drew them in the first place. Perhaps they look nostalgically back to those early, passionate believing days much as they look back to first dates.

Joiners are as easy to overlook as dropouts, for they make no waves. They contribute money and time; they are good and faithful people. Often they are activists, trying to stir the church into motion. The trouble is that by blocking off one half of their double vision, they have made themselves and their faith almost entirely earthbound. Nothing draws them to God himself; they are only religious. If the Lord were to appear in the clouds today, it is questionable whether they would be pleased at the interruption. They have adapted but it is a deathly adaptation. They miss out on the full joy of their Christian faith because they have written off their heart's cry and no longer feel and hear the radical, uncompromised promises of Jesus.

One can never be certain to what degree someone else fits this description, for there are many sincere Christians who are simply reluctant to trumpet their deepest convictions. But I suspect the breed is extensive, as it was in Jesus' day when thousands followed him to the public feeding, but none followed him to the cross.

Three: Enthusiasts

Some people forever expect the answer to turn up. Every new movement, organization, speaker, or book catches them. *This,* they think, *is the missing ingredient.* Perennially optimistic, they are also extraordinarily patient. They are the ones who buy all the new books and records, attend all the conferences, know all the latest lingo. Every time you meet them they offer to lend you a cassette tape.

If you look at their past you find it a record of moving from one thing to another. The humdrum local congregation can never contain their search for the missing ingredient. They can never settle down to live the ordinary Christian life with the same people year after year, and thus they miss the true power of the Spirit. Enthusiasts can be led astray into sects or cult groups.

Four: Hard-Liners
Hard-liners feel intensely the double vision of the Christian life, but their temperament does not let them admit ambiguity or uncertainty. They appear super-confident, though under the surface they may be terribly in need of affirmation and prominence. They are like the enthusiasts except they never (or seldom) move on to the new thing. Rather, they settle down to defend their narrow status quo from any charge that it fails to ultimately satisfy. They may be fundamentalists or tongues-speakers. They may trumpet the Victorious Christian Life, or they may find God among the poor or in nuclear protests. They may insist that the way to experience the fullness of the kingdom is to witness every day, using a certain booklet. If you feel any discrepancy between life as it is and life as you think it ought to be, they have the answer. Hard-liners form the backbone of new movements and new denominations, and sometimes old ones as well.

Hard-liners cope with double vision by denying the reality of the messages they receive from their dull everyday lives in favor of a heavenly vision.

~⊷

Clearly, I am painting with a broom. But I think you will recognize some of the portraits I have drawn. And while these types may seem to differ greatly, may even represent denominations or groups that squabble with each other, they do share a common problem. We all do.

It is by no means our only problem or even our greatest problem, but it is a problem seldom acknowledged and thus it contains a grave hidden danger. For a great deal of our flurrying talk and activity dodges around an unspoken question: Where is God?

If we are to answer this question, we must voice it as boldly as the psalmists did: "How long, O LORD? Will you hide yourself forever?" (Psalm 89:46).

Now the question is on the table, and we can move on to answering it. In doing so, however, we must remember that we are dealing with an awesome and incalculable God who may at any moment turn silly questions back on us with a blast, as he did with Job (who had a better right to be confused than we do). We must center our hopes not on our efforts, but on his own gracious showing of himself. He, and not we, holds the key to the problem. "His divine power has given us everything we need for life and godliness" (2 Peter 1:3).

CHAPTER 3

AN INTRODUCTION TO
A PERSONAL RELATIONSHIP

D id you ever hear of a ten-year diet? I never have. Six weeks is usually the most anybody will commit to self-improvement. We're creatures of the here and now.

That's true for spiritual improvement as well as physical improvement. We have limited interest in what can be accomplished in a lifetime. We're more interested in what can be changed on a single night.

We live in the present, and we judge the potential of our relationship with God by what others tell us is possible in the present. If a speaker describes his intimate conversations with God, we feel challenged (or depressed), judging that we are not living up to our potential. If, on the other hand, our input comes from more ordinary Christians, we may rate our spirituality as satisfactory—humdrum, perhaps, but satisfactory.

This is the view of an ant, toiling across the deck of a supertanker. All he can see is flat and hard, so he concludes that the universe is flat and hard. He doesn't realize that beyond his vision is life in a completely different medium. Nor, perhaps, does he realize that the supertanker is moving somewhere.

I have two answers to the question, "Where is God?" One is meant to expand our antlike view of reality. It particularly expands our view of time. Someday, Scripture says, Christians will see God face to face, and will be transformed by that sight.

This perspective is crucial. It puts our religious experience—and our lack of it—in perspective. In part two of this book I will consider this biblical perspective in some detail.

The ant on the deck of the supertanker, however, has a hard time seeing the importance of what lies over his horizon. He is more interested in his life here and now. So that is where I begin. Christianity is not merely a matter of waiting for the Second Coming. It is enjoying life in Jesus here and now. But how, within what we know as everyday reality, may we encounter him personally? That is my concern in the rest of part one.

WHAT IS A PERSONAL RELATIONSHIP?

What is so personal about "a personal relationship with God"? When I first began to ask this question, I could not answer it. I could see very little that was "personal" in my ordinary Christian life of prayer and Bible study and church involvement.

So I backed up a step. Instead of asking what a personal relationship with God might be, I asked what a personal relationship might be—*any* personal relationship. When I asked the question that way, I made a fundamental discovery: Personal relationships are a peculiar phenomenon. We know people in a way entirely different from the "impersonal" way we know objects and forces and ideas.

What the phrase "personal relationship with God" claims, most basically, is that God is a person. Since I am a person, I must therefore know him through means peculiar to persons.

I admit that this does not seem, at first glance, like a very dramatic discovery. But it led me to a train of thought that has transformed my search for deeper intimacy with God.

I sometimes pose this question to a group: Suppose a young woman is dating a man ten years older than she. Although she is extremely attracted to him, she is not sure she really knows him. Because of their age difference he seems unlike any of her friends. How should she get to know him?

Each group has given me a long list of ways people get to know each other: by talking together, sharing activities, meeting each other's friends and family, exchanging life histories, reading and discussing the same books or movies or television shows, working together, and so on. Some may emphasize one means over another, but no one has ever suggested that just one of these means is all that is needed. Everyone agrees that we get to know people by seeing them from many different angles.

Contrary to this, many spiritual programs emphasize only one avenue to God: a type of Bible study, a method of prayer, a style of social activism, a form of corporate worship. "Do this," they seem to say, "and you will know God." They create, I think, a mechanical image of God. It is as if our spiritual life were a machine with one crucial piece missing or broken. If only we could get that piece going (speaking in tongues or yielding to God's power or reading the Bible daily or witnessing regularly), our spiritual life would start up and take off like a lawn mower.

Personal relationships do not work that way. While it is true that a missing or broken area of life can mar a relationship, it is also true that if we want to grow closer to someone, we do not usually hunt through the past for some crucial missing ingredient. We look to make better use of the many opportunities we already have.

In our relationship with God we sometimes have to put right one thing that has gone wrong. And sometimes one new experience brings a sense of ecstatic communion with him. But if we stick to that one point exclusively, we will end up terribly disappointed. Our future with God lies not in some one thing, but in many things expressing the full range of his character.

In some ways, then, we know God "personally" as we know our friends "personally." Yet knowing him is also, in some ways, like another kind of personal relationship: our relationship with ourselves.

We don't usually think about how hard it is to know ourselves, but anyone who has seriously tried to understand why he does what he does, what influences have made him as he is, why he is happy or unhappy, will admit there is no darker tangle of secrets. Paul, examining a piece of this puzzle, wrote, "I do not understand what I do. For what I want to do I do not do, but what I hate I do" (Romans 7:15).

This relationship with self deserves examination because it illuminates an aspect of our relationship with God that is quite unlike our relationship to friends and family members. God does not relate to us only from the outside, as our friends do. Through the Holy Spirit, God gets inside us and forms a unity with us. He is there as an active and personal influence. The Spirit teaches us about God and also creates in us the faith that makes us love that knowledge. Theologians have been driven near to despair by this fact: We cannot speak objectively about God; only through the eyes of faith may we speak truly of him. To know him we must be dependent on him. His own Spirit is the light in which we see him.

This is clearly parallel to our difficulty in knowing ourselves. In describing ourselves, we are something like fish describing water: it is all we know, and it is also the medium through which we see everything else. We cannot know ourselves from the outside, only from the inside. But we know God from the inside as well as from the outside, for we are "in Christ," and he is in us.

WAYS TO KNOW GOD

For the next twelve chapters, I want to track the means we have for knowing persons, with the assumption that, since God is personal, the ways I know human beings will often resemble the ways I know God. I will take up one way per chapter, and for each I will ask, "Do we have any parallel means for relating to God?"

True, some aspects of human relationship are yet unavailable with God—sight, for instance. But most are quite obviously available. For myself, though, I had never recognized these opportunities for what they are. I had carried on in my religious way, never quite realizing the closeness of God's personality. I can echo Jacob: "Surely the LORD is in this place, and I was not aware of it" (Genesis 28:16).

In exploring ways to know God, there is one mistake we must not make. We must not portray knowing God as too difficult or complicated. It is not. He is very near. We can reach him merely by opening our mouths. And he is near because he wants to be near. If it were up to us to find God, it would be hopeless. Were he to hide himself, our detective work would be in vain. But God chooses to "open up" to each of us. He does it individually, in a different way for each person, but within certain inevitable patterns. These are the patterns I intend to track. We can call them "means of grace," for they are the means he has used to relate to us without our deserving it. They include such familiar means as the sacraments, prayer, and Bible reading. Others, such as storytelling, are less familiar.

When we speak of "means of grace," we are really talking about "means of personality." Most of us more readily think, quite impersonally, about the "right way to do things." For instance, we argue over whether it is best to praise God spontaneously or through a prepared liturgy, by kneeling or lifting hands, through traditional hymns or contemporary music. Basically, though, we need to see how all kinds of praise help form personal relationships. If we do not understand this at the outset, we will evaluate praise by how it makes us feel, by our aesthetic preferences, rather than by its lasting contribution to our relationship with God.

My concern is not with a failure of technique but a failure of understanding. We may know all about the right way to carry on religiously, but do it so mechanically that we forget a personal relationship is at stake. We make God a machine, not a person. I want to reclaim the sense that God's personality fills the earth. He is everywhere we turn, holding himself out to us, asking to be known, but we are so busy looking at techniques that we fail to look up and see him.

I do not expect to teach you a whole new way to pray. I hope to wake you up, to make you lift your head and open your eyes. Jesus is all around you. If you can begin to see that his personality is spilling out on every side, is available not as some "power" or "holiness" but as *himself*, I think you will pursue the means of grace with clearer eyes and greater excitement. Perhaps you will even be moved to try again at things you gave up on long ago because you could not see the point.

4
EXCHANGING NAMES

ڊ

Go into what is known as a "California-style" restaurant and you will probably be greeted like this by your waiter: "Hi! My name is James, and I will be your waiter tonight. Our specials are. . . ." James the waiter has been told to greet you this way because giving his name supposedly makes your exchange more personal. "James," however, will never bother to ask for your name. I do not think I would like it if he did, for there is no real personal relationship between waiters and diners. The restaurant is merely trying to create a "personable" atmosphere, in the same way they hang ferns in a room without windows to create a "garden" atmosphere.

By clear though unwritten rules we exchange names in certain situations and not in others. With waiters, bank tellers, and telephone operators, we ordinarily do not because we don't expect to become friends with them; we are conducting business. But whenever we hope to go beneath the surface with someone, to even the slightest degree, we tell each other our names.

It is a strange procedure. Smiling at you, I utter a short sound which has no meaning in English. You eagerly take it up, repeating it to be sure it sticks in your memory. You may comment if you like its sound or find it unusual. Then, in exchange, you utter a similarly meaningless sound, which I must remember. Why? Names help with identification, as do license plates on cars. But there is much more in a name than identification; otherwise we could exchange social security numbers. We do not like it when computers reduce us to numbers, and we would be outraged if people did. Names are personalized little sounds that belong to us. They offer access to our personality. They afford a means of approaching us personally.

In trying to understand how a mind filters the overwhelming information the senses provide, psychological experiments have been done where people are given two voices to listen to at once. Through earphones they hear, in the left ear, a lecture on nuclear physics. At the same time, in the right ear they hear someone reading a newspaper article on government agricultural policy. If told to listen to one ear only, most people can screen the other ear out entirely. If told to listen to the lecture on physics, they will learn nothing whatsoever about agricultural policy—not even the subject of the article. If in the course of the newspaper article their name is mentioned, however, they will invariably hear that. Apparently, the mind monitors all sounds, even those it is not listening to. At the mention of its name, it immediately gives its attention. Obviously, our name is subconsciously as well as consciously precious to us.

We want our names to be important to others too. Those teachers or politicians who are good at remembering names are usually popular; people feel they care, that they have "the personal touch." It is very irritating to find, in telling another person about a treasured friend, that you have momentarily forgotten that friend's name. Who will believe that you really care about someone whose name you forget?

Where do we get these short, meaningless sounds? They are not chosen arbitrarily. A name cannot be formed from just any sound. I may legally name my next child "Plake" or "IBM," but I will meet the determined resistance of his grandparents if I do. We have powerful unwritten rules about which sounds may constitute names. I remember an elementary school teacher who had taught in Turkey. When she told us the names of some of her students there, we all broke into incredulous laughter. Every culture has a limited pool of sounds that may be used for names, and these limits ensure that we name each child for someone. Some names are explicitly for a grandparent or aunt or friend. Others are not named with a particular individual in mind, but we don't choose the name out of the air. We like the sound—which usually means we liked someone else who went by that name. The name must, in any case, sound like a name, that is, like a human being, a member of our human family.

If names were only meant to differentiate individuals, we would strive for names no one ever heard before, the more unusual the better. No one would ever be named Susan Smith. But names have a subtler purpose than mere differentiation. They establish us as part of a large body of people, past, present, and future. My name, Timothy Chase Stafford, is a mass of information about the family and culture I come from. "Stafford" is of course my father's name, and presumably I could trace it all the way to England. "Chase" is my grandmother's maiden name. "Timothy" links me to Greece, to Palestine, and to the New Testament Christian community. It also links me, no doubt, to various Timothys my parents knew. By my name alone you can prove that I am not an island but part of a vast family tree spreading out through space and time. A kind of immortality speaks through names, a perpetuation of beloved people through their children and grandchildren and even their friends' children. You can hardly give a handsomer compliment than naming your child after a friend.

On the other hand, when someone changes his name he hopes to lose himself, to obliterate his old self. There is something pitiable about government informers who must be given new identities; it seems they can never be quite whole people again. But a new name can also be a symbol of hope. In the Bible it symbolized a new character in new relations: Abram became Abraham, Simon became Peter, and Saul became Paul. Since then people have often taken new names upon their conversion to Christianity, a practice that led to the term, still used in Europe, "Christian name." Our Western Christian heritage continues to glow dimly in our names, which remain largely borrowings from the Bible or from saints.

Some cultures give secret names; to know these is to have power over the person. We have something resembling "secret" names in nicknames or even first names. To be on a "first-name basis" implies intimacy. To use someone's nickname is to join a small company who know the person that way — sometimes a company so small that you are the only member. Lovers and intimate friends seem irresistibly drawn to nicknames; they invent a steady supply of new pet names as though the repeated naming process presses them into the very substance of the person they love.

I could go on and on multiplying examples that prove the mysterious and deeply personal nature of names. The Bible, throughout, betrays a great sensitivity to names: their hidden meanings, their links to a person's character, the way they join people together so that a whole mass of people may be called by the name "Israel" hundreds of years after Israel's death. Names represent the uniqueness of the person and the interrelatedness of the human family. Names establish us as persons and as persons in relationship. Most critically, names open the door for relationships. They are the beginning, the first sign of our willingness to give of ourselves to another person.

THE NAME ABOVE ALL NAMES

God, like us, has a name. When God introduced himself to Moses from the burning bush, he called himself Yahweh. God was not speaking to an atheist who needed to be convinced that God existed. Rather, God sought to convince Moses, and through him all of Jacob's children, that he cared for them personally, that he was attuned to their agony, that he would personally accompany them out of Egypt. God wanted to establish a permanent personal relationship. By giving Moses his name, God was inviting Moses and his people into a personal encounter.

Scholars worry about what God's name means in Hebrew, to the extent that they sometimes overlook the larger point. "Yahweh" is a personal name, like "Bill" or "Susan." Its Hebrew derivation matters less than the fact that, like "Bill" or "Susan," it offers access to a personality. It is, I think, a great misfortune that this personal name has been rendered, in most English translations, impersonal. "Yahweh" has been turned into "Lord God" or the like, which is not primarily a name but a title. Anybody, even the Egyptians, knew enough to call God "God." In "Yahweh" God's chosen people were presented with an unprecedented privilege. Yahweh did not give his name to just anyone; he gave it to people with whom he planned on forming a relationship.

The Israelites came to the point where they respected God's name so much they would never actually say it. I suspect the evolution of their usage followed a track something like this: If by some chance I met the president of the United States, and he, taking a specific liking to me, said, "Call me Bill," I would want to respect that privilege. In speaking to outsiders I would not refer to him as Bill, but as "the president." Because he had told me I *could* use his first name, I might become more cautious about using it in any context other than the proper one. Similarly, out of respect the Israelites came increasingly over the centuries to treat "Yahweh" as an unspeakable name. They substituted euphemisms, such as "the Name above all Names." Because it was such a remarkable invitation to intimacy, Yahweh became an awesome, forbidden word. By an odd quirk of human nature, God's most personal offerings to man are often turned into things so holy and rarefied that they end up quite impersonal.

If this were the whole story, I think we would want to go back to using "Yahweh" in our prayers. It would sound odd to us at first, as unfamiliar names do (our grandparents used "Jehovah," which is merely another rendering of the Hebrew "Yahweh"), but it would be a striking improvement over addressing God as "God." "God" may, like any word, become a name through repeated personal use, but there is nothing intrinsically personal in it. The word "Yahweh" cannot be anything less than personal.

I do not insist on praying to "Yahweh," however, because God did not stop offering personal names to his people. We were given another name: the name of Jesus. Unlike the unique name "Yahweh," this name was not unusual. Joshua, who led Israel into the promised land, had it before our Savior, and so did Jesus Justus and others after him (Colossians 4:11). "Jesus" was a name like "Jim" or "Bob." By its commonness, "Jesus" emphasized God's full participation in the Jewish family.

People in Jesus' time thought of Joshua when they met Jesus; they thought of the name's root meaning: "Savior." But Jesus' life and character have transformed the meaning of his name so that it is bound not by its history before him but by its history in him. In that name is embodied the visible image of the invisible God who came to earth and gave his life for us. His wisdom, his courage, his compassion, his love are bound up in it. When we address God by that name, all the Gospels come tumbling out of our mouths, as do all his acts through the Holy Spirit in the years since he rose into heaven.

Millions of Christians mumble "in the name of Jesus" at the end of every prayer. Most of them miss the point, I suspect. "In the name of Jesus" is not some magic formula but a reference to a friend who has given us his name to use when we conduct his business. We pray in Jesus' name so that our prayers may be heard by our Father as his prayers were. When the first Christians baptized "in the name of Jesus" (as all did in the book of Acts), this was not a mere initiation to a club; it was an introduction into the personal life of Jesus. It indicated acceptance in the inner family, taking the family name of the people who spoke to God on a first-name basis. Ironically, praying "in the name of Jesus" has acquired a formal, technical, and purely functional importance—some words you must say at the conclusion of every prayer, rather than a uniquely personal address. To pray "in the name of Jesus" means we know whom we are talking to. God is not just a power. He is an all-powerful *person*. He has through Jesus introduced himself to us, given us his name.

But there is another, even more intimate name by which we may address God, because Jesus gave us permission to do so. We may call God "our Father."

"Father" is not in itself a name; it is a title. It is a name only to one small group: the father's children. Putting "our" in front of "Father" transforms it into something even more intimate than a personal name. For a father is inescapably bound to his children. They may leave him, as did the prodigal son, but the father cannot abandon them if he is any kind of father at all. He must feed and care for them, tenderly love them, and give them a share in the family business whether they are good or bad, strong or weak. A father cannot change his mind and return his child to sender. Once in the family, the child deserves his care forever. Thus, "Father" is a uniquely personal name for God that emphasizes his unqualified commitment to us. Nobody in the Old Testament had the nerve to address God as "Father," though they regarded him as the Father of Israel. Only of the Messiah did God say, "He will call out to me, 'You are my Father'" (Psalm 89:26).

Which is just what Jesus did. Nobody has ever spoken with such absolute conviction about his intimate family connection with God. His only interest was "to do the will of my Father." He passed on to his disciples only what his Father had given him. Most stunningly, when someone asked to see the Father, he said, "Don't you know me, Philip, even after I have been among you such a long time? Anyone who has seen me has seen the Father" (John 14:9). When Jesus taught us to pray, "Our Father," he had in mind his own intimate, personal privilege of family. And in case anyone missed the point, he himself spoke to God with the more familiar, babyish term, "Abba." This term, Paul says in Romans 8:15, is a testimony to our intimate, personal relationship with God.

GOD KNOWS OUR NAMES

If there were any doubt that God has opened himself personally to us, it would be eclipsed by the offer of his personal names. What else can they mean, except that he wants to be known? He not only tells them to us; he asks us to use them. I confess that most of the time I have only the barest idea of the power of this privilege. The name of Jesus, which I am permitted to use whenever I feel like it, will someday stun the universe into submission: "At the name of Jesus every knee should bow, in heaven and on earth and under the earth" (Philippians 2:10).

Yet God has gone even further than this privilege. A relationship must have two sides. God does not only hand out his name; he knows our names. He addressed Moses personally while Moses still thought him a curious physical phenomenon, a burning bush. He called Samuel by name while Samuel was too young to know who was calling. Yahweh knows my name and he calls me by name. He has written it in his records, in the book of life. When my name comes up before God, Jesus will acknowledge it (Revelation 3:5).

God has given his name as an invitation to enter an intimate, family relationship with him. Yet immediately the question comes: "After I call him by name, what do I say to him?"

5

THE COMMITMENT OF LOVE

~

Not too long ago I was in a corporate office headed by an old friend. I was doing some business with mid-level executives who, not knowing of this friendship, began talking about their boss. I listened with some alarm, because it seemed that they misunderstood my friend. They had facts to back up their assessment of his personality, yet I was sure, and am sure today, that they did not really understand him. They had all the facts, but because they did not love him as I do, they could not put those facts into perspective.

People whose friends or family members run for public office often have the same experience. When they see negative coverage by the media, they are incensed at the unfairness of it, charging that the news media are obsessed with finding fault. To an outsider their objections usually don't seem to have much merit. But from one point of view they are quite right. When we love someone, we know him or her in a way that an "objective" view fails to achieve.

This "loving knowledge" is at the heart of personal relationships. We may comprehend a complex subject, like nuclear physics, through study, but persons reveal themselves fully only to those who love them. This is how we want to know God. Yet the growth of deep, heartfelt, giving love is not easy to produce. Many people take it as an accident: they either "fall in love" or they don't. And if they don't fall in love with God, what can they do about it?

Where does love come from? How does it begin? I have several friends to whom this matter seems an impenetrable darkness. They want to fall in love and be married, yet it doesn't "happen." They have friends of the opposite sex but no chemistry. "The male mind continues to be a complete mystery to me," a young woman wrote me recently. "Any clues?"

I do not, unfortunately, know how to make love begin. I think I can describe the process, but I am unable to make it occur. Biologists are in a similar position; they know everything about the tomato, except why. They can tell you how to improve or preserve one but not how to create one.

Love is a living thing. Its raw materials are common interests, physical attraction, shared values, and so on, but these no more make love than tomato purée makes a tomato. The seed from which love grows is always specific, often small, and rarely predictable. Why does a father love his children? Nobody knows. They have little in common, but love grows like a weed with or without encouragement. A deep friendship may grow from something as insubstantial as Chinese food. One friend of mine confesses that he was first attracted to his wife because she had beautiful teeth. I fell madly in love when I heard my wife laugh at a ridiculous television commercial. Such specificity may seem silly and irresponsible, but love is like that. Nobody knows why it starts. We can only say that something beyond us, or beyond our control, opens our eyes and our hearts to another person.

Sometimes love is planted without our knowledge or permission. I have a friend who when she was single was pursued by a determined young man. He had fallen in love with her, but she was not at all interested. In fact, as he persisted she found herself decreasingly attracted. She had liked him as a friend, but now she could hardly stand to see him. One night she had a bad dream, and in the morning she told it to the women who shared her house. (My wife was one of them.) In the dream God had changed her heart so that she fell in love with the young man in question. When she woke up, she was horrified at the thought. Nonetheless, the dream told more about her than she knew herself, for in less than a year she had fallen desperately in love with the persistent young man, and they were married. You do not need a degree in psychology to know that she had been growing in love with him for some time but would not accept it.

Love grows gradually and secretly, but it is realized in sudden leaps of recognition. Here we have a responsibility, and a crucial one.

We cannot make love begin, but we can nurture it by recognizing it. This applies to all kinds of love—love between friends, between parents and children, between brothers and sisters—but most obviously in romantic love.

TELL THE WORLD

I had known Popie for some time when we fell into conversation one afternoon, and she seemed to glow in a different light than she had before. I didn't express this to her, but to myself I admitted, "I'm quite attracted to her." It was a tiny but dramatic plunge toward love. After that I looked on her with different eyes.

I made a further leap when, sometime later, I told her of my attraction. I was still not committing myself to anything, yet I paced and fretted before writing that letter. When we admit love, we pass through a one-way door; we cannot simply change our minds and back out as directly as we went in. We find ourselves in a new place with each other, a place to explore.

I made a third leap on my wedding day when I said to Popie (before an audience), "I do." What changed on that day? My love did not increase. Rather, I recognized and expressed a love that had already grown. But by recognizing it I went through another door. Once in I could not get out. I didn't want to. Beyond that door we could explore each other physically and mentally without restrictions. We could know each other as it had been impossible to do before. If we had never gone through that door, our love would have gradually wasted away to nothing.

Love always grows with these two strands intertwined: the passion and the recognition, the attraction and the avowal, the spirit and the form. The passion grows like a wild plant, often without our intention, sometimes without our knowledge. We wake up one morning and it is there; it has been there, for all we can tell, for some time. We have no control over it. But passion requires some kind of recognition, some avowal of acceptance and fidelity.

Here we play an active role. First we admit to ourselves, "I love her." Then we admit it to the one we love, "I love you." Finally, we admit it to the world: "We love each other and will do so until death." The vow without the underlying passion would be superficial or manipulative, as when a boy tells a girl, "I love you," to get what he wants. But the passion without a vow would be joy unfulfilled. Love could not be savored, shared, enjoyed. It could not grow. Even in non-romantic contexts this is so: Two people who work together may feel deep mutual admiration, but if they do not express this, verbally or nonverbally, they will miss the full joy of friendship. In the case of marriage, this avowal is so crucial that virtually all cultures (not just "Christian" cultures) regard love as unreal and illegitimate unless and until public avowal is made.

The avowal of love creates a secure circle in which two people can reveal themselves to each other. In it they can be open and unashamed. When someone cheats on that avowal, the circle is broken and real intimacy becomes impossible. Adultery destroys marriage, gossip destroys friendship, abandonment destroys parent-child love, idolatry destroys our relationship with God.

Within the unbroken circle, love grows while keeping these leaps of recognition as a reference point. Friends reminisce about their past. Married couples celebrate their anniversaries. They remember the day they first said, "I love you." When they fight, they refer back to their wedding as to a rock on which they stand: "I married you. However bad things may seem, I committed myself to you. We will weather this storm." The avowal of commitment is so crucial to ever-deepening love that it cannot be done and forgotten. The mind must travel back to it again and again, as though to recall the shape of that foundation.

PUBLIC COMMITMENT

What compels us to love Jesus? Nobody can say. Love for him is unique in each person, and the attraction—or lack of it—unpredictable. A person we felt certain would never be interested in anything religious suddenly becomes, passionately, a Christian. On the other hand, that nice girl who grew up in a strong Christian home is completely disinterested in Christ.

Love rarely grows from a logical root. Some people come to commitment to Christ because of their hunger for truth, but more often they develop a passion for Christ because of things that later seem insubstantial: the way light shone through stained glass on a particular morning, or a sudden scare, or an emotional message by a traveling evangelist, or the memory of a gentle Christian grandmother. Later on, Christians who started with such flimsy reasons may develop a stronger rationale. But at the beginning reason is often on the sideline, watching.

Is this an embarrassment to us? It need not be, unless we are equally embarrassed by the reasons people fall in love. The church is not a philosophical society any more than a marriage is. Christian faith involves the mind, but it is primarily a climate of personal love. Love has its own reasons.

The Holy Spirit—the Teacher, the Counselor, the Person who comes alongside us—plants this seed of love in us. "By him we cry, 'Abba, Father.' The Spirit himself testifies with our spirit that we are God's children" (Romans 8:15-16). There is nothing irrational about calling out to God as "Daddy"; we are like small children before God. But only the Spirit enables us to love him for it, rather than resent him.

Our choice, then, is what to do with this love we feel. The first step is to admit it to ourselves. We have, as the emblem of sin, deep resistance to God and his love, and a tremendous capacity to deceive ourselves. People can quite successfully ignore the pressure of God's Spirit if they like—ignore it as though God were not a factor to them at all and they had no longing for his light. They do not have to admit it, even to themselves. Only when they do—when they say to themselves, "I must know more about him"—can love begin to grow.

The second step is to admit our love to the object of that love. Such a simple act and yet how hard it is to do! People clear their throats and look at the floor while admitting their feelings to a new friend or new lover, even though their attraction has been obvious for some time to everybody. In the same way, those who have begun to love God do not find it easy to pray their first prayer of love, to say the simple words, "Father, I don't know what this means or where it will lead, but I have to tell you I love you." Something happens to the relationship when that step is taken. We feel new freedom to explore the dimensions of God's character. We also hear, quite clearly, the sound of the door closing behind us. We are in this relationship now. There is no simple way to back out.

As a love relationship develops, "I love you" will be communicated many times. It is not enough, however. At some time a public commitment must be made. This third step is final. The stakes are high, but the rewards of complete freedom and intimacy make public commitment desirable. In doing this, we publicly bind ourselves to God and he to us. Now we can begin to really know and enjoy love without uncertainty. The courtship is over. We belong to him.

If evangelical Christians have stressed anything about a personal relationship with God, it is this third step of public commitment. We usually use it to divide people into two classes: the saved and the unsaved, Christians and nonChristians. If someone admits to God and to the world his need for Christ and invites Christ "into his heart" to live forever, he is in evangelical eyes a new creature. Someone else may be found in church every Sunday, may know the Bible and profess to believe it, may be moral and kind in every aspect of his life, but until we know of his personal avowal of commitment to Christ and hear him tell the world about it, we are dubious of his state. We feel roughly the same of him as we do the couple who live together without benefit of a wedding day.

This public confession is, in fact, as critical to love for God as weddings are to marriage. It is so critical that God has marked a particular ritual for expressing it. The doorway into a permanent relationship with God is, according to the Bible, baptism.

Baptism

Baptism? We have been discussing deep, personal intimacy with God. Baptism? It is impossible to imagine a less personal aspect of Christianity. What can baptism have to do with developing love for Jesus? Baptism is a Christian ritual of initiation, the way into the church. Nobody questions that it is essential. But it seems essential in the way that an oath of office is essential: we do it, but we don't get excited about it.

The difference, however, is critical. An oath of office is impersonal. Through it we commit ourselves to a job or to a standard of conduct. Baptism is personal. Through it we commit ourselves to a person: Jesus. Oaths of office are dull, but weddings are by their nature enchanting. A baptism is like a wedding.

I hardly ever hear baptism referred to these days except as a sort of technical, churchy requirement. Some Baptist groups do measure their success by their number of baptisms, rather than by numbers of decisions for Christ. But sadly, baptism can be as mechanical a process in Baptist churches as it often is in Presbyterian churches. Once baptized, a new convert may never hear his own baptism referred to again.

This is not the meaning of baptism that I get from the New Testament. There are eighty-nine references to baptism there, the vast majority not to the baptism of the Holy Spirit, which does attract interest today, but to plain water baptism. And these verses rarely address brand-new Christians. They more typically refer old Christians back to their own baptisms, which were not done and forgotten but used as a point of reference in virtually every discussion of life in Christ.

Paul refers to "one Lord, one faith, one baptism, one God and Father of all" (Ephesians 4:5). How many of us would automatically rate baptism on a level with those other three essentials? In the book of Acts, when a person expressed faith in Christ he was immediately baptized. He did not wait to take a class or to see if his faith would jell. New Christians went out and got wet, thousands at a time. Overall, we can encapsulate the New Testament view this way: a Christian is someone who has committed his life to Christ through baptism. Baptism is not an extra thrown in on the Christian life; it is a fundamental point of identity.

In Paul's first conversation with the disciples in Ephesus (Acts 19:1-5), we can almost hear the cogs turn in his brain as he tries to figure them out. He apparently noticed that the Ephesians did not have a dynamic relationship with the living Jesus. So he asked them about their relationship with the Holy Spirit of God. His question proved to be precisely on target; they did not even know of the Spirit's existence. What was Paul's next question? "Then what baptism did you receive?" He found the source of their trouble there, in their baptism. They had received John's, not Jesus' baptism.

Put yourself in Paul's place. What kind of questions would you ask a believer who seemed to lack a good personal relationship with Christ? Thanks particularly to the Pentecostal movement, many Christians would think to ask Paul's first question: "What is your life in the Holy Spirit like?" But how many of us, if we learned that someone had no experience of the Holy Spirit, would ask Paul's second question: "What kind of baptism did you have?"

If someone's faith seemed out of focus, we might ask instead, "Has he ever made a real commitment?" We think of this as the equivalent of baptism; it is an avowal of love and a doorway into deeper relationship. I would make a case, however, that a "decision" is not an adequate substitute for baptism. A "decision" is mainly a mental turn. A person makes up his mind that he has been wrong and cannot, by himself, be right; he expresses this conviction and asks Jesus to come and save him from sin and death. True, he may "go forward" and make a public confession of faith, but that is not the focus of the change. We put the stress on the mental decision. The trouble with decisions is that they are always subject to later review. Their reality seems to depend on whether they were sincere or adequately informed at the time.

I think I can show you what I mean through the analogy of marriage. For many years I have written an advice column for young people on love and sex. Fairly often I hear from couples who want to sleep together but are, for reasons of age or finances or parental consent, unable to marry. But, they ask, since we've made a promise to each other, aren't we essentially married? What difference does a ceremony and a legal certificate really make? Isn't the sincere commitment what makes two people married?

I always have to tell them that they underestimate the powers of law and ceremony, and overestimate the stability of the individual will. As any older person knows perfectly well, as a matter of common sense, these private commitments are as steady as a blade of grass. The public marriage is no guarantee of fidelity, but it comes much closer than those private promises, however sincere. The fact that we have to dress up, get up in front of everybody we know, go through an elaborate religious ceremony, and emerge in everyone's eyes and expectations as a married couple does a great deal to solidify the love we feel. The ceremony has an intrinsic power of its own.

And this is what I think we must mean, at least partly, when we say that baptism is effective. Abuses of this have made many Christians leery of putting weight on baptism at all, lest people think that merely going through the ritual is all that is required for heaven. A baptism without faith is not what God wants, just as a wedding without commitment is not what lovers want. But the baptism has power just as the wedding has power—power that cannot be separated from faith but which is distinct from it. Baptism's power, I think, lies in its demand that our body get into the act of commitment. It will not let our decision be purely mental, subject to later review. "Did I really mean it?" people ask of their mental decisions, whether to lose weight, quit smoking, or follow Christ. That question is irrelevant to our marriage vows or our baptism vows. Whether we meant it or not, we are in it. Later on we may see that we really had a very limited understanding of what we were getting into. But we did it with everybody watching.

Because baptism, like marriage, is physical, it is highly memorable. I can no longer quite bring to mind the mental process through which I grew to love my wife. But I remember clearly—I have pictures to help me—our wedding. I celebrate it annually on our anniversary.

Our churches are plagued by lukewarm Christians who say the right things and believe the right things but are not really changed by them. Nothing makes these Christians think differently from people in the world around them, and when they meet severe temptations—to gossip or to live greedily or to sleep with someone they are not married to—no lever exists to pry them away. They are not intensely in love with Jesus, and no lever presses them toward cultivating their relationship with him. For the New Testament church, the commitment of baptism was one such lever—a primary one. Baptism was not done and forgotten; it was constantly remembered as the great turning point in a believer's love for Jesus. "Don't you know that all of us who were baptized into Christ Jesus were baptized into his death . . . in order that, just as Christ was raised from the dead through the glory of the Father, we too may live a new life?" (Romans 6:3-4).

How do we make baptism significant again? We celebrate and renew our marriages every year. Why not our baptisms? We could annually review our own lives in terms of what baptism has meant. I do not think, however, we can reverse the tide as lonely individuals. I think we can do it only as a church, as a community that together gives baptism the highest honor. Working together we could make it a central focal point, an awesome and joyful ceremony of death and new life that is accorded the greatest importance. I feel sure Paul would be shocked to learn that we have Christians in our churches who have never bothered to be baptized. (This is a greater sign of carelessness in the Christian life than church members who have never bothered to be married to their partners.) I feel sure he would be shocked at the casual way we fit baptisms between the anthem and the announcements and worry primarily that a baptism service will mean getting out of church late. If we carried on weddings in such a casual way, would we not expect marriages to suffer? Just so, our lack of concern for baptism makes love for Jesus suffer.

No matter how much stress we lay on baptism, we will not renew its importance if we continue to view it as an oath of office—a technical requirement. Baptism opens the door for a lifelong love affair with Jesus. It should be a beginning lived and relived, told and retold. If we understand how personal it is, perhaps it will regain such meaning for us.

Infant Baptism

I suspect we have devalued baptism partly because it has created such fierce battles between otherwise loving Christians. In an effort to preserve "one faith" we have left "one baptism" to a secondary emphasis. Since I think the New Testament's emphasis on baptism ought to be renewed, I would like to try to remove this obstacle by talking about infant baptism.

I cannot help talking about infant baptism, for that is where the problem really lies. I am quite aware that even in raising the topic I fall into danger of utterly alienating one side of the issue or the other, or both. Let me begin by saying that I do not intend to persuade Baptists to baptize their babies or to persuade Episcopalians not to. I want merely to have those on both sides stop battling long enough to ask sympathetically whether baptizing babies can be made comprehensible in terms of a "personal relationship with God."

Everyone understands and supports believers' baptism; it is what we see practiced in the New Testament, and it accords well with the twentieth-century emphasis on individual, intellectual decision. It also fits well with the emphasis on "personal relationship," for it parallels the avowals of love we make to friends and lovers. But infant baptism doesn't fit so neatly. In fact, at first glance it does not fit at all. Babies can't make up their minds to love Christ nor can they vow their fidelity to Christ. The fact is, they don't even know what is being done to them, and later on, when they understand what *was* done to them, some want nothing to do with it. This is not a leap of recognition, since no cognition is involved.

Do we enter any committed and loving relationship this way — unconscious? As a matter of fact, we do. The longest love affair — or love quarrel — any of us has is with parents. It begins through a cataclysmic event, perhaps the most awful thing that has ever happened to us: we are born. Our mothers risk their lives to bring us through it. They never forget it, and they don't let us forget it either — we remember our birthday throughout life, even after our parents are gone. The event is remembered *even though we do not remember* it nor had anything to do with it. It matters because it began a new life: our life within our family.

Through childhood, I took my relationship to my parents totally for granted. I was not, so far as I remember, particularly grateful for them. I never "worked at" the relationship. Voluntary relationships to friends and girlfriends occupied my attention. But as an adult I have increasingly realized how much my parents formed me and form me still. I realize now what was true all along: my parents are the most important force in my life. I see others who, having poor relations with their parents, are psychologically in pieces. That relationship we enter into so unconsciously, that we take so for granted, works very powerfully on us.

Did I have any choice in loving my parents? I did, but under all natural conditions the choice was a foregone conclusion. They loved me. They were part of me. Everyone expected me to grow up to love them as an adult, to volunteer consciously to continue (and grow in) the relationship that I entered as an unconscious, squirming infant. It was a choice but not an equal choice.

I hear parents say they want to let their children decide about religion for themselves. The truth is they cannot give such a choice; their children already have it. I could have chosen to reject my parents' faith in just the same way that I could have rejected their love. The choice was mine. I also could have chosen to ruin my life. I could have estranged myself from my parents, though I would not have ceased being their son because of it. I would merely have lost all the benefits of being their son: their care, their nurture, their guidance, their company. So I would also have lost the benefits of Christ if I had chosen not to have them. But why should I?

A baby born in a truly Christian home will have a choice but not an equal choice. He will either embrace all the benefits of Christ, which he lived in from the beginning, or he will choose to leave them. It is a choice, but since Jesus is matchlessly good, we expect a positive decision. If our Christian families deserve the name of Christ, most of our children will grow to love the Lord. "Train a child in the way he should go, and when he is old he will not turn from it" (Proverbs 22:6). And along the way, of course, children will pray to Jesus, he will protect them, and they will participate in the body of Christ. In effect they will be "in Christ," enjoying the benefits of life in him as much as they are able.

This is how I remember my growth in Christ. Of course I experienced crises and dramatic breakthroughs. At the time they seemed the difference between night and day. But looking back, the difference does not seem quite so dramatic. I always knew how to pray. I always knew who Jesus was, and I always saw him as a friend, not an enemy. The breakthroughs were, I think, breakthroughs from a childish, taken-for-granted relationship to a more fully conscious, adult relationship. Underneath was continuity; Jesus always held me, and I never, at least for long, spurned his grasp. Possibly I am unusual, though I do not think so; a great number of Christians whom I know grew up in Christian homes—not perhaps perfect Christian homes or even evangelical Christian homes, but homes where Christ was honored, prayed to, and obeyed.

I believe that Christians who do not baptize babies nonetheless see their children as participating in Christ. They pray with them, they pray for them, they expect them to participate in church. They expect and ask Christ to protect and care for their children. They are optimistic, in faith, that their children will grow to embrace Christ as adults, and they do not hesitate to prepare them for this. Because of their birth into a Christian family, the children have a form of relationship with Christ. The question that divides us is this: When in the spiritual growth of a Christian child ought he or she to be baptized? When should the relationship of love be celebrated? As soon as possible after the relationship begins? Or at the time that conscious and decisive faith shows itself in the individual?

I am not going to try to answer that question. I have my own belief for myself and my family, but as the Bible is not at pains to decide the question, neither am I. (There is no decisive information in the New Testament about whether babies should be baptized; that is, we have no cases where babies are baptized and no cases where babies are excluded. The arguments for or against baptizing babies are inferential, arguments from silence, or based on theological presuppositions.) What I want to do is enable us to learn something from each other.

Those who baptize babies place a dramatic emphasis on God's gracious act in placing a child in a Christian family. They see Christian faith as something we can pass on to our children with substantial confidence. Faithful Christian parents, they say, can rightly hope to raise children who love God, just as they hope to raise children who love their parents. They give them the family name of Christ as confidently as they give them their human family name. Those who baptize babies expect their nurture to be decisive, and they help us remember that Christian education for our children isn't merely a supplement to the secular education they get in school. We are teaching them how to breathe; without this they may choke and die. To vote for infant baptism is to vote in favor of the centrality of family and church life in making a person. This emphasis is needed in our atomistic society.

Those who baptize their children only after they have shown conscious faith emphasize the need to consciously recognize and avow faith. They demand a declaration of love. A love for Jesus that never reaches a dramatic avowal is not a true love, they say. While they recognize the importance of Christian nurture, they stress the breathtaking honor God has given each person, to choose whether to love or reject the one who first loved them. This is the crucial moment, they say, and they want nothing to diminish its significance. Their emphasis is needed in a society that blames everything on a person's environment and little on his personal choice. To choose believer's baptism is to emphasize an individual's personal responsibility for his relationship to God.

In the first centuries of the church, historians say, some Christians baptized babies while others did not; yet it does not seem to have been an issue to quarrel over. Today too we seem to be reaching out to each other from both sides. Baptists have increasingly adopted a ceremony of child dedication, while many denominations that have traditionally practiced infant baptism have now within them strong movements that prefer believer's baptism—even Roman Catholics and Episcopalians. Perhaps the time is ripe to say that either choice may be valid. Perhaps we may recognize "one baptism" again.

My concern, primarily, is that we recognize baptism—period. I don't worry about it as a legal requirement. I do not picture God as so fussy as that. But I do worry that we miss the full joy of a deep personal relationship with God. Our society has had a fling at love without any emphasis on marriage and has found that something is missing. And likewise, our Christian community has had its fling at loving God without any emphasis on baptism, and we too have found something missing.

For those who were baptized as babies and grew up in the embrace of the Christian family, baptism can be celebrated like a birthday—always remembered, though unremembered, because through the crisis of a birthday new life began.

For those who were baptized as adults, knowing (at least in part) what they were doing, it can be remembered and celebrated more like a wedding. Memories will be recalled through photos, through tokens of the day. But whether remembered as a birthday or a wedding, baptism is a doorway into a love relationship that has no natural end. We go in and are never expected to back out. Why would we? Inside, we find love and joy. In Christ, through the Holy Spirit, we live in love.

I have concentrated on the ritual of baptism because that is the outstanding public expression of love in the Bible. It is, however, only one form of a greater phenomenon that punctuates every deep relationship. Marriage partners need to say often, "I love you." They need to recall and celebrate the growth of their love. If we want to grow intimate in God's love, we must also take time to tell him, "I love you." Such simple words! But how easily we forget to say them. And if we do, we suffer. When the love we experienced in the early, euphoric days drains away without our notice, our personal relationship dries up, and we have only a shell of religion left.

A force does not care whether we avow our love and commitment. Persons, however, are intimately known only by those who love them and are not ashamed to say it. God, who is altogether personal, expects and demands that avowal of love. He also gives us vows of his own.

6

CONVERSATION

~⊱

Silently gazing into a friend's eyes may seem purer, and certainly more romantic, than mere talk. But conversation, not silence, builds relationships. Though I will never minimize the effect of beautiful eyes, I expect to talk to the people I care about—and to hear them talk back. We do not build relationships on a sentence or two spoken every few years. Conversation between real friends is a constant stream.

So I have a problem with God. I have never had a conversation with him; I have never heard his audible voice. Though I sometimes feel powerful religious emotions, I am cautious in interpreting my impulses and feelings as messages from God. I do not want to take the Lord's name in vain. I do not want to say, "The Lord told me," when in reality I heard a mental recording of my mother's voice. I have spent any number of hours talking to God, and he has not yet answered back in a voice that was undeniably his.

I know he can speak that way. In Scripture God's voice was heard from heaven a number of times. The Old Testament prophets and priests asked him direct questions and apparently got direct answers. I have no good reason for denying that the same voice may still speak, but it has not spoken to me. And to the best of my knowledge, even those who say God's voice has spoken to them do not claim it as an everyday occurrence.

Yet I do, like all Christians, talk to God. I speak to him out loud or in my thoughts about things he already knows. I do this because I have been told to pray, to make my requests known to God, to offer praise and worship to him. But I have not been told why. If I must praise God, it is not for the same reason I praise my friends; God does not need a lift. If I should thank him, it is not because he needs encouragement or information. He knows whether I am thankful before I say it. And why should I ask him for anything? He knows what I need before I ask. He also cares more than I do about anything worth caring for.

Some people say that we should pray not because God needs it, but because we need it. When we praise him, we remind ourselves of what is fundamentally important. When we thank him, we humbly remember our utter dependence on his care. When we pray for people, we are encouraged to then go out and do something to help them. From this perspective prayer is a self-help exercise.

No doubt prayer does these and other good things for me, but if they are the principle reasons for praying, my "personal relationship" is in trouble. Prayer that is only a useful exercise is not conversation. It is more like writing a diary, which is also good for you, but is entirely private and one-sided. When we address our prayers to God, we expect God to be listening. And if he is listening, he cannot be listening in the way earthly parents listen to their children saying the multiplication tables — with only half their attention, to see that they have them right. If he is listening, he must listen to respond.

How does God respond? I say he "speaks" to me through the Bible, an ancient and unchanging book, or through sermons or hymns, or through experiences. But what sort of conversation is that? It is not really an exchange. The Bible stays the same no matter what I say to God. The words of the hymns don't change according to my needs. And sermons and experiences can "say" something quite different to me than they do to you.

I see no way to pretend that our communication with God is ordinary, interpersonal conversation. It is not just like talking with a friend. But then, who says that relating to God should be ordinary? I may find, if I explore further, that my conversation with God is deeply personal in some less ordinary way.

What am I searching for? What is the fundamental condition for *personal* communication? I would say it should be at the very least some form of communion — something by which words draw two persons together. Is there any communion in a soliloquy of praise and request spoken into thin air? Is there any communion when I sit in my kitchen reading the Bible?

To answer this, we need to go back to basics. We need to think and marvel at how words draw people together.

PERSONAL COMMUNION

Let me begin with the only person (other than God) who knows me from the inside—me. And let me start with a confession: I talk to myself. Through constant effort I am learning not to vocalize the words, but my wife still catches me mumbling to myself now and again. Even when I make no sound, I mentally "speak" a monologue of my most candid thoughts about anything and everything. I do it all day, hardly knowing I am doing it. In fact, virtually the only times I do not talk to myself are when I am talking aloud to someone else or when I am asleep. (Perhaps, though, even my dreams are a vivid form of inner monologue.)

You would see how intensely personal this is if you caught me doing it out loud. When this happens, I am extremely embarrassed. I worry whether you heard something terribly revealing. I have never liked anyone to say to me, "A penny for your thoughts." This pressures me to reveal myself, as though someone said, "Take off your shirt and let me see how fat you are." My internal conversation is intensely private.

When I talk to myself, however, I am not communicating any news. I am reminding myself of things that, at the moment I speak, matter to me. I am rehearsing things I have said. I am imagining things I will do later in the day. Sometimes I am berating myself. Sometimes I am congratulating myself. I am not, however, telling myself something I do not know.

This internal conversation is very important to my relationship with myself. I raise concerns into conscious consideration so that I may reach a sense of unity with myself over them. I "confess" my sins to myself. I express faith in myself: "C'mon, Tim, you can do it." Like prayer, it draws me into communion even though nothing new is said and there is no true "back and forth."

We do not want to carry this comparison too far, however, for

"I" and "myself" are not two people. What happens when two people converse? Early in the relationship a great deal of new information must be shared. Each one must tell the other about his thoughts, his memories, his hopes. When Popie and I were first in love, we spent hour after hour talking. We had so much to learn about each other that we never ran out of important things to discuss. Even now, especially when we are separated for a few days, we need time to share our new experiences and thoughts.

Ordinary conversation is for communicating information. If I ask questions or relay requests, I assume that the person I am talking to does not know that I have these questions or needs. I must *inform* him before he can do anything about them. Similarly, if I compliment or thank someone for his kindness, I assume he does not know that I admire him or that I am grateful to him. I must inform him of these facts. Much conversation, of course, simply revolves around describing our activities and thoughts. This too is informational.

However, another dynamic comes into play. Even when they have nothing new to tell each other, friends still talk. This is a quiet, less urgent form of conversation, more intimate than our informational exchange. Popie and I talk over things we both already know; we raise people we love and situations we care about to mutual consciousness. Our children, for instance. "I'm worried about Katie," my wife may say, and I do not have to ask her why for I am already feeling that same concern. Yet we need, for the sake of our relationship, to share our concerns. Sometimes our conversation may alter the way we act with our daughter; at other times, merely talking together about our concern is enough.

In these relaxed conversations we encourage each other with praise and thanks. I know Popie admires and loves me, but I need to hear it from her. Even in areas where I feel complete self-confidence, I enjoy her praise. It draws us together. At other times I must confess to her that I am sorry for something I did. This is not really news to her. She knows I'm sorry, and I know she will forgive me. Yet the words need to be said because they bring us into communion again.

The more intimate two people become and the more constantly they are together, the less information they have to share. Yet they do not talk less. Conversation continues even though the once-urgent gush of information has slowed. With new friends we rush to tell each other about our pasts. With old friends we talk about our pasts, too, because we find intense pleasure in reliving memories and shared moments—"Remember when. . . ." We exchange our current views not because our old friends will be surprised but precisely because they will not. We draw an intense, familiar enjoyment in hearing opinions from an old crony. "I knew you would say that! You haven't changed a bit," we chuckle.

Old friends are like old dogs lying together in the sun: sharing the same sunlight is all that matters. Except dogs miss out on the full joy; they cannot talk about it. I say to my wife, "Doesn't the sun feel wonderful?" and, "This reminds me of the sun porch we had in Palo Alto." I say nothing new, and she does not really need to respond. It is almost as though I were talking to myself. But the words, and her listening ear, draw us into communion.

Personal communion in conversation does not depend on exchanging information; it does not even depend on hearing a response. Personal communion is a matter of being together and talking about the things that matter most. The deepest and oldest friends commune in this way.

Here, I believe, is the key to understanding what is most personal in prayer. We do not pray to tell God what he does not know, nor to remind him of things he has forgotten. He already cares for the things we pray about; his attention to them has never flagged from the beginning, and his understanding is unfathomable. He has simply been waiting for us to care about them with him. When we pray, we stand by God and look with him toward those people and problems. When we lift our eyes from them toward him, we do so with loving praise, just as we look toward our oldest and dearest friends and tell them how we care for them, though they already know it. We confess to God what we are and what we have done. We express our faith in him. We thank him for what he is and what he has done for us. None of this is news to our heavenly Father. We speak to him as we speak to our most intimate friends—so that we can commune together in love.

PARTICIPATING IN POWER

Prayer begins with communion, but it does not stop there. The New Testament encourages us to think of prayer as an opportunity to ask for help. We are told to request what we need. We are told that "we have not because we ask not." God does not depend on our requests to do the good he intends, nor can prayer make him do what he does not care to do. Yet the biblical teaching is unmistakable. He acts in response to our requests.

Again the question surfaces: Why does he want me to ask, since he already knows what I need? If I pray, like Jesus, "Let your will be done," am I not saying that I want God to do what he planned to do in the first place? Then why bother to ask him? Can it really be possible to change God's will? Does prayer have any power to affect events?

Another human analogy may illuminate this situation. Suppose a friend plans to change jobs. His direction is clear; he is sure it is the right move. He has only to act. So will he discuss it with me? Yes, often he will, though not because he wants my advice. He already knows the choice he should make, and I probably know very little about his profession. He discusses it because he wants my company; he wants my support, my agreement, before he acts.

God has chosen to root his power in our shared concerns, to act in communion with us. He does not *need* our consent to act—he *prefers* it. Put simply, he waits to act until he has talked it over with us. And he rarely takes the initiative. He waits until it matters enough to us to bring it up with him.

Stated that way, prayer is a startling responsibility. It is not just our own personal welfare that depends on it. It is the welfare of the world. Why would God choose to depend on us? Why wait for our fickle attention to focus on the thing that needs doing? We find this difficult to understand because power is our first priority. We are worried about things getting done, people being healed or fed or helped. God is not worried about getting things done. He has no lack of power. He is the highest power in the universe. He makes his power subservient to our fickle attention because he is working toward the reconciliation of the world in love. When at long last we come to him with our concerns, we take the first small step toward what he wants most: communion.

God's decision to wait for our prayers is his second humiliation to the flesh. In the first he stripped off his glory and became a man to destroy the forces keeping man and God apart. Now he holds his power in check and waits for us to come. Reconciliation to us is his first priority. Just as on earth he chose to live within and act from the limitations of human flesh and blood, so now he chooses to do the same from the limitations of our concerns.

Why he cares so much for our company or precisely how our prayers affect his course, we may not understand. But Scripture leaves no doubt that in prayer we have the tremendous privilege of participating in his power. To grow stronger in prayer I need not work myself into a mental state that denies probability, or find a praying technique that produces magical results. Growing stronger in prayer must mean growing stronger in an intimate, loving union with God, for he is the source of all power. My prayers, however polished, however fervent, have no power at all to do anything, unless God gives them that power. He acts, not in response to technique or fervor, but in response to people who love him and put their faith in him.

A WORDY GOD

But what about the other side of the conversation? God must speak to me, not just me to God. Some people say, "Prayer is not just talking. You must listen too." What do they mean when they say "listen" in prayer? To what do they listen?

I think they usually mean meditating on our concerns as we pray, "chewing them over" in company with God's Spirit and his Word. We "listen" as God's Spirit, our link to Christ, teaches us to discern truth from error, to "put things together" and see them from God's perspective. As we lift up our small and changeable concerns into his broader and eternal concerns, his Spirit teaches us how to pray — that is, how to share his perspective.

This shared perspective results in the "inner impressions" that many Christians take to be God's voice. They may express it as: "I feel the Lord is saying. . . ." When we commune with someone on a daily basis, we intuitively understand his point of view. Sometimes this perspective comes to us uncannily while we are thinking about something else entirely. I might, to use a simple example, suddenly wake up knowing just what birthday gift a close friend would like. That information seems to come out of thin air, but really it did not. I have been thinking about his birthday; I have been in regular communion with him. I "listened" to him though I did not depend directly on his words; I "listened" intuitively to his personality.

A Christian who is in constant communion with the Holy Spirit and his Word will wake up to many such insights. These are not infallible instincts. They always need to be checked with other Christians and with the Word of God. But they may spring from God himself— from our personal communion with him.

If we survey the book of Acts, for instance, we find that many decisions were made without verbal instructions from God. Instead, the apostles relied on a mature and thoughtful consideration of priorities. Perhaps the most crucial matter that faced the early Christians was what behavior to require from Gentile believers. This would determine whether they became a truly multicultural church or remained a Jewish sect. The Council of Jerusalem met to decide. No voice spoke from heaven to arbitrate the sharply differing opinions. The issue was decided on the basis of what they had observed God doing (15:8-9), on their own experience (15:10-11), and on the Old Testament Scriptures (15:15-18).

Sometimes God breaks into our consciousness with a more direct message, although this kind of direction is relatively rare, both in the Bible and in modern experience. God rarely says, "Join this committee," or, "Don't go out of the house today," just as he rarely gave Paul messages like, "Come over to Macedonia." But he did occasionally speak that way in the Bible, and I think he may today. If we get this kind of message, we had better obey.

But we should not confuse it with messages from "inner impressions." In the Bible, the word of God broke into whatever people were doing. None of these people said, "I *feel* that the Lord is telling me something." They had no question about whether God really spoke to them; they could only choose whether or not to trust and obey his voice. The angels and visions and dreams and voices that brought God's Word were indisputably foreign to the minds that received them.

But while God does not always, or even often, break directly into our consciousness with angels or visions, he is far from silent. He is, in fact, a wordy God, invariably linked to a verbal message. Our greatest fund of words from our eternal and unchanging God is in written form, in a book that cannot be added to and does not change. We are creatures living in time, and so are our words; they vary like the wind from day to day and moment to moment. God's sureness is reflected in the invariability of his self-revelation. The Bible is the same for us as it was for Calvin, for Francis of Assisi, for Benedict. Augustine wrote that the Bible is a river in which a lamb could safely wade and an elephant swim. But for all it is the same river. God does not change, though we do. He speaks to us primarily through Scripture.

Is the Bible personal? Messages from angels and impressions springing from personal communion are certainly personal. Is an ancient book, written in practically dead languages by an assemblage of writers, however inspired, a voice directed to me? Can I commune with God through it? An honest answer, however little we like it, must admit that people can and do read it as a dead book, a collection of religious writings without personal reference. Only God's Spirit in communion with us can take its words and communicate them personally.

We may say that the Holy Spirit speaks personally to us, but how? Where in ourselves, in our inner processes, may we locate his voice? The question has many answers, for the Spirit of God is not limited to one way of working. The God whose sense of beauty loved the ocean storm as well as the water skeeter on a mud puddle, creates equally varied things in human hearts. Yet there are predictable patterns to his spiritual work, just as there are patterns to his physical creation.

The Bible refers to the Holy Spirit as a teacher, encourager, and inspirer. He gives us vision and faith and shows us how things fit together. Sometimes this revelation is sudden, sometimes gradual, but always inevitable. One mark of conversion, it seems to me, is the insight that enables us to make sense of our own history and put it into line with God's history. A Christian can usually begin to say, "So that is why that happened to me!" or at least, "I can see now that through everything that happened, God was with me." This insight comes to us personally through the Holy Spirit, and it comes as he helps us understand Scripture, the story of God's history with humanity.

The Spirit unites us to Jesus, and in an intimate communion of prayer and worship the objective truth becomes *my* truth, the eternal word *my* word for my time. (Think of it as the difference between reading Ann Landers' column on an ordinary day and reading her column the day she answers your letter.) The Holy Spirit underlines Scripture: "This is meant for you." Such inspiration is what makes or breaks Bible reading. I once heard a Christian scholar complain that he was bored with the Bible. I can only think that the personal voice was not speaking to him. As beautiful as the Bible is, as varied and fascinating, it has its limits as literature. We can know it well enough so that we do not see new things in it. It may become like a series of lectures we have already heard—boring, no matter how brilliant. But when the voice is personal, this dynamic is reversed.

Old friends don't stop talking when they run out of new things to say; they find increasing pleasure in saying the same old things because of the pleasure of sharing them in communion with an intimate companion. I don't say that friends never go through dry periods, but they persist through these and find even deeper communion than before. We can have the same experience with the Bible. We read it, study it in groups, and hear it taught and preached. We may experience dryness, but we persist in listening and discover ever-deepening wisdom. The Bible's comfort grows more comforting, its illumination more brilliant, and its insights more profound even as it conveys less and less new information. The Bible, as paper and ink, does not accomplish this in itself. It is the Spirit of Christ who magnifies the words of the Bible so that we recognize its truth as our truth and hear God's voice speaking personally. Meditating on this voice, even while we pray, we see our purpose for living and are guided in the right direction. In this way, our reading of Scripture becomes communion with God. Such personal communication is not automatic, but it is the normal Christian experience of a personal relationship with God.

SHARED SILENCE

Despite the joy of conversing with God, many Christians find in some periods of their lives that they have no more words. They cannot pray. Yet they feel that God is with them in their silence and that they are communing in a way not possible while struggling to speak.

Some have gone so far as to suggest that silence is the ultimate form of prayer: without thought, without words, with simply a spirit opened lovingly toward God they commune with him. I am, I admit, uncomfortable with taking silence so far, not only because the Bible does not acknowledge such a form of prayer but because I do not think prolonged silence is usually a sign of health in relationships. People who love each other talk; words, more than silence, have the power to join persons.

But silence does have its place in the deepest relationships. It provides an interlude, a chance to reflect on words and the communion they have produced. Silence may also be a reaction against the babble of civilization, an opportunity to slow down and relax in the warm embrace of friendship. It may heal the hurt that words and activity have produced. It may speak of love that we are too inarticulate or emotional to express. To cite a small example, my wife and I find pleasure in reading together on the sofa. Though we do not talk, we find comfort and acceptance in our shared silence.

"I gave last rites to a dying friend this spring," my brother, an Episcopalian priest, writes me. "What meant the most communion between us was when I fed her some ice cream. Sometimes words are unnecessary, even harmful. What do you *say* to a sunrise?"

I once spent time at a monastery where the members lived under the rule of silence. The sisters did not speak to each other or to me, though we worshiped together several times a day and ate all our meals together. At first it seemed awkward and strange. But as I settled into it, I found that warmth developed between us in that silence. More personality was communicated than I would have thought. What particularly struck me, though, was the power of the few words we did speak. They were all spoken in worship, in simple services held three times a day primarily devoted to reading or singing the Psalms antiphonally. I remember how loud those words of the Psalms sounded after so many hours of silence, how their sound lingered in my head long afterward.

Silence allows us to reflect on words and then leads us back to the spoken word again. I may watch the sunrise in silence, but the words of Genesis help me to know its meaning, and I must ultimately reflect its meaning back to God in words of praise.

My grandfather, a Presbyterian missionary, suffered a stroke in his old age and had global aphasia for the last ten years of his life. This strange disease takes away the ability to communicate in words, whether written or spoken. Apparently the stroke scrambles the communication pathways of the brain. My grandfather could still think clearly, but he could not communicate his thoughts. His words came out garbled, as though he were speaking a foreign language. He could rarely understand our words either. He had the stroke while in Pakistan, and after he had recovered enough to travel, he was put on a plane to England, where my mother met him. One of his urgent wishes, which he communicated through gestures, was to go to a good Shakespearean theatre. He believed that if he could hear some-one speak in really clear, stentorian tones he would understand. He was, of course, disappointed.

The letters he wrote were extremely curious. They looked at first glance just like his normal hand. But a closer look revealed that the sentences were garbled. "It will take me a little while to unravel this," I thought. But when I tried, I found that I could not make any sense of it at all. Curiously, an occasional word or phrase would come out undisputably right, but my grandfather never knew whether it was right or wrong. They all sounded right to him when he spoke. He maintained, however, most of his knowledge of the Psalms, and his ability to lead in prayer. These circuits of the brain, I imagine, were so broad from frequent use that they were not destroyed with all the rest.

It was possible to communicate simple information to my grandfather through gestures, facial expressions, and tone of voice. This was tedious but it worked. My grandfather was retired, and his needs were cared for, so he really had little information he needed to communicate. But for all of us who loved him, those ten years were intensely sad. He was well cared for and with people he loved, but he could not speak or be spoken to. He was lonely because his communion with others had been broken abruptly and terribly. Words had been taken away.

He would come to Thanksgiving dinner at my parents' house, his broad Scot face beaming, to hold babies on his knee and enjoy a good meal with a family that adored him. He would try to talk, to crack a good joke as in the old days, or to describe the questions he had about why God was making him suffer. We could understand that he was trying to joke or to make theological conversation about suffering. But only with the greatest effort could we understand him or make ourselves understood. We would try, flounder, fail, smile, and shake our heads apologetically and give up. Eventually my grandfather would find a comfortable chair in the corner and doze. He made it clear that he wanted to die. He was not allowed to for ten long years.

Words are crucial to personal relationships, not just because they communicate information but because they bind people together. Lose them through aphasia or some other means and you will learn what it means to be alone, really alone.

I take this as a terrible and penetrating challenge to speak my words to God as often as I speak my words to myself while "talking to myself." This, I think, is what Paul meant by prayer without ceasing; the constant, verbal reference of every thought and every deed to God. It is also a challenge to read his Word and hear him speaking personally through the voice of the Holy Spirit. When we do this, his words become embedded in our minds so that he can be speaking to us through them as often as we speak to him.

INVITATION AND PRAISE

In the end, when we see Jesus face to face, what kind of words will we use? As human beings, we want to ask questions and get answers, to clear up all the things we have wondered about. But when the Bible lifts the curtain drawn over the age to come, that is not what we see. The book of Revelation gives us a picture of what to expect, and it is far from the graduate-level seminar we want to satisfy our intellectual curiosity. In Revelation we are promised no long chats, no questions answered. The only words mentioned there are songs of praise: "To him who sits on the throne and to the Lamb be praise and honor and glory and power, for ever and ever!" (Revelation 5:13).

What does God say in return? According to the picture Jesus drew of the end of the world in Matthew 25, his words to us will be an invitation: "Come, you who are blessed by my Father; take your inheritance, the kingdom prepared for you since the creation of the world" (25:34). Perhaps, we might speculate by drawing Revelation and Matthew together, this antiphony will go on forever. "Praise and honor and glory and power," we will sing as he says, again and again, "Come! Come in!" Our praise and his invitation suggest an eternal communion of exultation and accomplishment.

But here is an interesting fact: These words—invitation and praise—are what our personal life of prayer and Bible reading are teaching us now. Our prayers begin and end with praise, as Jesus taught us. And God's Word is one extended invitation. Perhaps, then, that final, most personal confrontation with God will seem very familiar — much like the way we have been speaking with him personally all along.

I suspect many surprises await us. The things we wanted throughout life may turn out to be unimportant, while the things we had, which never seemed quite enough, may turn out to be the very substance of our joy — the seed that has grown, to our eternal surprise, into a large and beautiful tree.

CHAPTER

7

A HOME

～

Have you ever awakened in the dark without any sense of where you are? It has happened to me on business trips. I fall into a motel bed, dog tired. In the middle of the night I suddenly awake and cannot get my bearings. I cannot find the light switch, my glasses, the bathroom, anything. I cannot remember where I am. For a moment, in that darkness, I am in a nightmare confusion. No terror seems impossible. My identity is uncertain. Then I find the light, turn it on, and sit on the edge of the bed looking at the familiar objects I bumped into in the dark. I look at my clothes and my papers strewn around the room, and my identity returns to me. I am not lost in a dark hell, only a Holiday Inn.

From this I learn that my sense of self is partly gained from my surroundings. I ordinarily think of myself as bounded by my skin. Everything within this pink membrane is me. I can easily determine where "I" begins and ends. But the boundary is not really so precise. My personality extends beyond my skin. I am always trying to extend myself outward, to brand my environment with it, to make a familiar and personal nest.

Clothes are not simply to keep me warm and dry. They are an extension of my personality. For instance, I could never wear women's clothing or Indian robes or an Arab turban without feeling like a caricature of someone else. I would feel equally stupid going to the grocery store in a ski outfit or anything with sequins. In a sweater and blue jeans I am most myself. Whether they wear three-piece suits or strictly "functional" outfits from the Army-Navy surplus store, all people convey a certain image by the clothing they choose to wear. This isn't just an American or Western preoccupation. The impulse to decorate our bodies and clothing seems to be universal. The most fashion-conscious people I have ever observed are the cattle-herding Masai of Kenya, who can spend hours daubing their hair with red clay and creating elaborate hairdos.

We extend our personalities even further by making homes. When I became a father, I discovered in myself a new and rising desire to own a house and "provide" for my family. I had financial and practical reasons, but my longing for a permanent place that belonged to us—a nest—was just as significant. When Popie and I shopped for homes, we discovered that we had very definite ideas about what a home should look like. We wanted one that would be "us." We also discovered, by looking at the frightful decoration in some homes, how different other people's ideas of home could be.

For a home is more than four walls. Interior decoration, like fashion, is based on a very powerful urge to create a personal space; that is, to push our sense of self out into our environment. I once did political canvassing in a large circular apartment complex. Its design was so uniform that I completely lost track of where I was—what floor I was on and how much of the circle I had traveled. I actually worked back to my starting place without realizing it, until a familiar (and annoyed) face came to the door. Each apartment followed the same floor plan. Yet while I, coming from outside, felt bewildered, the tenants did not. They had decorated their apartments to suit themselves. They would not have confused their own apartment with someone else's for even a moment. Each one was distinct. We make our dwellings "ours," which also means we make them "us."

This sense of place as an extension of personality even reaches into geography, which we cannot change. I have found that I am a Western American. By Western I mean the ability to see long distances. (I don't care whether I ever see another cowboy boot.) The dry, mountainous terrain of the West makes this possible. I feel at home in it. Other parts of the world, such as New England or France, I find beautiful but not alluring. Too many trees block the view; the smaller vistas are too tame. They are not me.

Homesick people have a habit of trying to re-create their home geography when they wander. In *Out of Africa*, Isak Dinesen wrote of the Kikuyu who were uprooted from their homes when her coffee farm was sold.

> It is more than their land that you take away from the people, whose Native land you take. It is their past as well, their roots and their identity. If you take away the things that they have been used to see, and will be expecting to see, you may, in a way, as well take their eyes. This applies to a higher degree to the primitive people than to the civilized, and animals again will wander back a long way, and go through danger and sufferings, to recover their lost identity, in the surroundings that they know.
>
> The Masai when they were moved from their old country [by British colonists who wanted their land] . . . to the present Masai Reserve, took with them the names of their hills, plains and rivers in the new country. It is a bewildering thing to the traveller. The Masai were carrying their cut roots with them as a medicine, and were trying, in exile, to keep their past by a formula.

Is this tendency found only among the "primitive"? Citizens of New York, New Jersey, or any of the New England states (or Paris, Texas) might think twice before saying so.

This attachment to a place, this extension of personality beyond our own skins, is why we must visit people in their homes if we really want to know them well. The oftener we are there, the better. If we can say of someone, "I'm always in his home," we are surely intimate. And to understand someone most completely, we must see the environment that formed him, the place where he grew up. We must visit his high school, meet his family, and eat a meal at the kitchen table where he sat as a child.

A PORTABLE GOD

How, then, can we become personal with a God who, according to orthodox theology, is everywhere? All of him is in every place completely. In fact, because he is everywhere, he is "nowhere" in the sense that we cannot limit him to any location. If you have trouble making sense of this, you are in good company. When we think of something being everywhere, we think of philosophical principles or physical forces. Perhaps we can think of God like gravity — being everywhere. But that presents a problem, for while we can feel gravity and see its results, we cannot talk with it.

Yet people in the Bible did not seem to have this problem. While they knew God was omnipresent, they also knew where to find him.

God originally attached himself to a people rather than a place, and a nomadic people at that. He promised himself to Abraham and his children in Babylon, traveled with them to Palestine, and later to Egypt. The gods the pagans worshiped were all local deities, believed to rule in certain areas. Their personalities were so determined by location that it was difficult to distinguish the two. For example, the fertility of Baal and the fertility of the farmland around his shrine were inextricably intermixed. By custom, when people moved into a new area, they worshiped the local god. The Israelites violated this pattern; they had a portable God. Or more accurately, they belonged to a God whose horizons were unlimited.

God did have his mind set on a place for his family, however. He talked about it so often that it became known over the years as the Promised Land. When his family grew into a nation and finally settled down there, they replaced their portable worship place with a permanent temple. God accepted this building as his house; in fact, he drew the plans for it. To be sure, God was not limited to that place any more than I am limited to my house. His people knew that Yahweh could be prayed to and known in any place. Yet his home was the temple in Jerusalem, decorated according to his wishes. To go into God's temple was, in some sense, like being invited home by a friend. There was a limit to the intimacy, however. They could never enter the holiest place. Trespassing could mean death. Yet in the temple they met God and soaked up the atmosphere of his earthly home. The building and its art were not mere incidentals; their beauty and familiarity were a direct expression of the fair beauty and personal love of the Lord.

To us, a temple sounds austere and impersonal. We would expect the Israelites to speak of it with awe, to approach it with fear. Yet some of the most marvelous psalms exult in the temple as the most wonderful, restful, beautiful place on earth. The Israelites dreamed of it while far away, as travelers dream of home: "One thing I ask of the LORD, this is what I seek: that I may dwell in the house of the LORD all the days of my life, to gaze upon the beauty of the LORD and to seek him in his temple" (Psalm 27:4). "How lovely is your dwelling place, O LORD Almighty! My soul yearns, even faints, for the courts of the LORD; my heart and my flesh cry out for the living God" (Psalm 84:1-2). Unless I misread these and other psalms, the Israelites were not admiring the temple as I admire the cathedral at Chartres. They were not dreaming of art appreciation. They were homesick. They longed for the temple because they longed for the person who lived there. They loved God, and so they loved his home, the place where they met him.

The temple, because it was God's home, was mankind's home as well. At least, the Israelites wanted it to be. They reached the gate of the temple with profound relief. "Even the sparrow has found a home, and the swallow a nest for herself, where she may have her young— a place near your altar, O LORD Almighty, my King and my God. Blessed are those who dwell in your house; they are ever praising you" (Psalm 84:3-4). *We* would probably prefer to be *far* from the altar. When we think of animal sacrifice, we may even be a little disgusted. The meat, the blood, the struggles of the dying animal—it is too rich for us. But in the ancient East those were very attractive, festive details. Slaughtering an animal was their idea of a party, with the priests in their ceremonial garb, dressing up for a celebration. But the temple offered more than just a feast. It was the Lord's feast. He joined them in the festivities. In his house and in his presence they entered the place of real rest, for in the temple was complete protection, security, and love. No one could harm them there; they had no business to transact there. They were there to enjoy the company of God and their friends. What else is a home if not this?

This same sense of love and safety extended to Jerusalem, for that city too was God's home. Thoughts of Jerusalem evoked fierce emotions in the Israelites during their exile: "How can we sing the songs of the LORD while in a foreign land? If I forget you, O Jerusalem, may my right hand forget its skill. May my tongue cling to the roof of my mouth if I do not remember you, if I do not consider Jerusalem my highest joy" (Psalm 137:4-6).

To the people of Israel, God's willingness to embrace them, to take up residence in their city, to invite them to feast there, was unimaginable joy and privilege. But this astonishing fact was topped by something more astounding: God deserted the house and let it be torn down. He let his people go into exile. In a sense he destroyed everything he had built; he reversed the exodus and sent his people back into slavery. He abandoned the land he had taken for his home. The destruction of Jerusalem and its temple dazed them like the early death of a beloved parent.

In their bruised bewilderment it seemed that God had stepped backward. True, a small portion of them were able to return from exile, and they managed to rebuild the temple despite considerable opposition. Later it was desecrated again by invading forces and pagan gods and eventually rebuilt by Herod. Jesus worshiped there; the apostles preached there. Yet it had lost its luster, as had their once-great nation. Israel had no king, and their temple was more a fortress or a monument to Herod than God's home. Israel wanted a leader to put the promises back into the Promised Land. They expected someone who would glorify the temple, who would make it what it once had been, and more.

When the Messiah came, he did not do what they wanted. He did not oppose the temple worship, but he did not renew or reform it either; he treated it with the deferential and unconcerned respect one shows for a noble but fading institution. He predicted that the temple would not last, and within a few decades of his death the temple was destroyed, never to be rebuilt. By that time, however, for the followers of Jesus the temple had been superseded by something far better. "For Christ did not enter a man-made sanctuary that was only a copy of the true one; he entered heaven itself, now to appear for us in God's presence" (Hebrews 9:24). Now all could enter the Most Holy Place by the blood of Jesus. "You have come to Mount Zion, to the heavenly Jerusalem, the city of the living God. You have come to thousands upon thousands of angels in joyful assembly, to the church of the firstborn, whose names are written in heaven" (Hebrews 12:22-23).

WE ARE GOD'S HOUSE

At first glance the replacement of the earthly temple with a heavenly one appears to be a total loss insofar as a personal relationship is concerned. God is once again everywhere; we cannot get a fix on him. The ancient Israelites seem to have been better off than we, having a building where God really lived, where the decoration and architecture became as familiar as home, a building that even smelled, with the sacrifice, like home cooking. The wealth and reverence that Christians through the ages have poured into their cathedrals and churches show that we wish for something similar. We naturally attach personality with place, and the heavenly Jerusalem seems too vague to be anywhere.

But take a closer look. Those who wrote of heaven did not foresee a mental state for disembodied spirits; they saw a city—a "city with foundations, whose architect and builder is God" (Hebrews 11:10). This city will be more real, not less, than our earthly cities.

We do not know much about heaven, but we know enough to grasp why the temple had to disappear. As real as it was, it was not real enough. The temple could raise hopes but not fulfill them. Its repeated sacrifices only foreshadowed the coming reality: one sacrifice with eternal effect. In the temple there was always a barrier between God and his people because the people's sin meant that they would be destroyed by the sight of God. You could visit the temple, but you could not enter the holiest place where God was. It was like visiting the home of a friend and having to stand on the front porch and talk to your friend through a closed door. You came away with a bittersweet longing for complete access to his home. This is what heaven is: God's real and eternal home, with the door to every room thrown open. Because Jesus' sacrifice dealt effectively with sin, we can go in at will.

I can think of a few famous people whom I deeply admire and would like to know personally. I stand in awe, for instance, of the great poet W. H. Auden. Imagine that, at a party, I met him. Suppose that he not only shook my hand but took a sudden, unaccountable interest in me. Suppose we fell into deep conversation and this famous figure glanced at his watch and said to me, "It's getting late. Why don't you come home with me so we can continue this conversation?" I cannot imagine anything more likely to convince me that Auden was seriously interested in my friendship. I cannot imagine anything more likely to make me glow with pride.

Such an invitation has been extended to me by someone I want to know far more than Auden: Jesus himself. "I am going [to my Father's house] to prepare a place for you. . . . I will come back and take you to be with me" (John 14:2-3). The Father's house is a real place, and the Jesus who will meet me there is the real ever-living Lord. His invitation proves that he wants the most intimate kind of personal relationship with me. But the invitation also comes with a command: "Wait."

We can know Jesus, here and now, in many of the ways we know other people—by conversation for instance. But here we draw a blank. We have no temple, and the better temple is beyond our reach. We long to visit Jesus' home, and we are invited there—but not yet.

However we dress up our churches, with awesome stained glass or soaring roof line, they cannot begin to approach what we long for. Creating an atmosphere conducive to worship is quite different from the feeling the Israelites had for their temple. We ask God to be with us in church, whereas it was God who invited the Israelites to the temple. And when we see heaven, it will be because *he* has issued the invitation.

There is one sense, however, in which we can see, here and now, God's home. Hebrews 3:6 says, "We are [God's] house," and 1 Peter 2:5 proclaims, "You . . . like living stones, are being built into a spiritual house to be a holy priesthood, offering spiritual sacrifices acceptable to God through Jesus Christ."

"House" has, in Hebrew, a double meaning. It can refer to the building a family lives in or to the family itself. The "house of Jesse" may be the building Jesse calls home or it may be Jesse's family. The coupling of the two meanings is not accidental, of course. People—family members—make a home. I remember returning, many years later, to the house I grew up in. It was the same physical structure; even my name was still printed in charcoal in the garage. But its impact on me was sad. It was no longer home because my family no longer lived there. The old place held happy memories but no life. A house without its family is an empty shell.

What we see in the church, I think, is the family that will inhabit the Father's house. Like Abraham and his descendants, we are a people of God looking for our place. Just as he did in Abraham's day, God has attached himself first to the family, and eventually he will lead us to a place of his choosing. Already, however, the atmosphere of his place exists where the family gathers. Already we can experience the air of our destination: the joy, the family feeling. And God is with us, though we still cannot see him.

The subject of God's home reminds us that God is fully personal. It reminds us of the intimacy with God that still lies beyond our sight. To know God fully we will have to enter our permanent home. But on this earth we can know the character of that home by the family that will live in it.

CHAPTER
8
FAMILY

～

In the nineteenth century on the east coast of Africa, Arab traders were still pursuing the slave trade. They bought captured Africans far inland, then marched them hundreds or even thousands of miles to the coast. There they had the British to contend with. Having abandoned slavery themselves, the British were determined to force others to stop it as well. When they apprehended an Arab slave ship, they would free the slaves.

The problem then facing the British was what to do with the freed slaves. Many were in bad physical condition. They had walked across miles of desert and hostile territory. Physically they were unable to return to their own people, even if they knew the route, which they did not. They had never before traveled far from their villages and had no concept of geography. They had never seen a map. Nor did their British saviors know enough about this land to help them locate their villages. Inland Africa was then practically uncharted, its geography a compilation of a few facts and many rumors. Some of the bravest and most famous men of the century wandered for years through its territory, hoping to stumble on the source of the Nile. In our modern world it is hard to imagine such a situation. It would be something like trying to find a small town somewhere in the U.S. if no maps or signs existed, if none of its citizens had ever traveled beyond their own homes, and if each county spoke a different language. You could only meander from one town to the next, hoping to stumble on the right one. Africa, four times the size of the continental United States, had these difficulties and more. It was an extremely dangerous place to travel.

The freed slaves were thoroughly "lost." They did not know where they were or where they had come from, and they had no hope of ever finding out. They were free to go home but had no idea where home was. Out of necessity they stayed on the coast near the Indian Ocean and established a new life there. Missionaries taught them agriculture and Christian faith. But these newly established villages were fraught with problems, the most serious being the discouraged state of the freed slaves. Disoriented and passive, they often retreated into an interior world and lost the will to live. Many of them died, for no obvious reason other than discouragement.

The African slave trade was so awful that descriptions of the slaves' physical suffering overshadow their mental suffering. Although physical abuse had ended for the freed slaves in East Africa, mental suffering continued. Their experience shows how deeply family ties matter. Such ties make it possible for us to live.

I would not automatically think of families as quite that crucial. In the ordinary course of events, we can easily take our families for granted. In fact, most people spend the first ten to twenty years of their adult lives trying to define how they are different from their families. We don't want to be known just as so-and-so's son or daughter; we want to be known as individuals. To do so we escape; we leave home for college or work, we marry and establish our own homes. Only after that do we begin—sometimes—to appreciate what we owe to our families.

But our very individuality is formed in a family. School teaches us mathematics, but our families teach us how to love, how to hate, what to admire and what to shun, what is funny and what is shameful. From my parents I learned such paradoxical quirks as to love books and music and to loathe spending money on them. They taught me nearly all the things that are basic to me; their personalities are embedded in mine. But they are inlaid into me so subtly and beautifully that I cannot tell what is uniquely mine and what I inherited from them.

"MEETING THE FAMILY"

Some years ago I got a terrible shock when I looked at a return address I had scribbled on an envelope. It was my father's handwriting. I had written exactly as he would. It was as though I was possessed, as though someone else, my father, lived in me. I had looked in the mirror and seen my father's reflection.

Becoming a parent has brought similarly eerie revelations. I hear myself talking to my children in precisely the voice and the words I heard, and sometimes hated, as a child. I hear my parents' voices coming out of my mouth.

We are something like an old painting an artist has painted over. When the canvas is exposed to X-ray photography, hidden faces are revealed under the top layer of paint. That is why, when we try to get to know someone well, we want to meet his family. Here the hidden faces come into the full light. A person's family is not just his background, his context; it is an integral part of who he is. Seen only in the office or at school, he is unrooted. At home with his family we can capture the full flavor of his personality.

A reporter working on a profile of a famous person invariably tries to interview family members. Through their eyes, he hopes to see how the famous person became what he is, to get beyond the public mask and into the inner personality.

It is a great compliment to be asked to meet someone's family. Usually it is a sign that you are considered a permanent rather than a temporary friend. You are being invited to meet the very foundations of the person's life, perhaps to be accepted by them as an unofficial member.

For couples thinking of marriage, this first visit to "meet the family" can be an ordeal. The woman being introduced to her future in-laws worries about getting a nod of approval, while her husband-to-be is nervous because traits that he has covered over with a thin wash of paint will be exposed. If his dad sits wordlessly in front of the television set all evening, it may make his strong, silent behavior seem less mysterious. "So this is what I am marrying," his fiancée will think. She may even see him transformed before her eyes into a different person. People change when they go home; they act like the children they once were.

Couples who are thinking about marriage do well to pay close attention when they "meet the family." We do, in many ways, marry our mate's family. It's not simply that we are forced to relate to them on Christmas and Thanksgiving. We meet them every day in our partner's personality. It can be unnerving and annoying to find your wife reacting to you the way she reacts to her father. How on earth could she confuse you with him? But we cannot avoid it: When we marry someone, we become a character in their family history.

Likewise, a personal relationship with God must come in the context of his family. In fact, none of us would even know that Jesus exists if we had not been told by members of his family.

A person's family is the context he has come from: the father and mother who bore him, his brothers and sisters, aunts and uncles, and cousins. With Jesus, though, this is reversed: he is the context out of which his family must spring. When Jesus' mother and brothers came to see him, he spoke clearly of his real family: "Pointing to his disciples, he said, 'Here are my mother and my brothers. For whoever does the will of my Father in heaven is my brother and sister and mother'" (Matthew 12:49-50). Paul, following this example, called Christians the adopted children of God. He also called the church the "body of Christ." In the church we find the down-to-earth focus of Jesus' personality. Jesus is invisible to us, but through his family he makes himself known.

The practical implication is that one place to look for a knowledge of Jesus is church, where Christians gather. And that is precisely where most people do look. If someone on my street gets a religious urge, he is likely to express it and explore it by going to church. There he will learn the plain facts about Jesus. But will he meet Jesus personally? Is the church the place to go if you want not just to know about him, but to know him directly?

Annie Dillard writes that the most striking aspect of church services is that no one breaks out laughing. She has a strong sense of God's transcendent splendor, and the shuffling mechanics of church services seem drastically beneath splendor. I sometimes feel the same discrepancy. Where, in the swirl of Sunday clothes, outmoded music, a program somewhere between Rotary and TV talk, a ritual involving symbolic portions of bread and wine, and conversation in the Fireside Room over coffee—where do we find Jesus? If this is his family, how am I to see him in them? How exactly am I to see him in the crumpled face of an old lady who cannot get over her shock that the church has hung banners? How do I hear him in the voice of a teenage kid who keeps whispering to his girlfriend while the pastor speaks? The family of Jesus is very earthy and ordinary, and I want to know a heavenly Jesus who is truly extraordinary. Practically speaking, how is it possible?

I suspect many people feel this question. They come to church not because they have a particular taste for organ music, but because they are looking for the reality of Jesus. Where will they find him? Underneath the coffeepot? Hidden in an Easter lily? In the sermon? Will someone's mouth open during fellowship hour and Jesus' voice pour out?

To answer honestly and helpfully, we need to think about how Jesus' true identity is tied up in his family.

THE FAMILY OF CHRIST

Jesus has a family, and if we want to know him, we must know the people he has chosen to be with, the people he has formed and still is forming. If we want to love him, we must love them. They are his children, and if we want to be his, we must become one of them. In them we will not only see the kind of work that Jesus does, but sometimes, fleetingly, we will see Jesus himself.

The body of Christ, like most families, has many faults. It is far from what it ought to be. It remains, however, the only human offspring of Jesus' personality. Many influences shape Jesus' family, but they never eradicate its origin. Blood does tell.

When someone "commits his life to Jesus," he often knows far more about Jesus' family than he knows about Jesus himself. If you ask him to describe Jesus he probably can only say something very general like "loving" or "compassionate." If you ask him to describe the particular group of Christians he is joining, however, he can say much more. A new Christian will not, typically, proceed immediately to an intensive study of the Gospels or to long hours of prayer and meditation to know Jesus better. Most of us are attracted to something far more earthly: a particular church, a para-church group like Campus Life or InterVarsity, a Bible study group, a loose association of people, or even a single person whom we admire. We solidify our commitment to Jesus through a commitment to Jesus' family, as we find it locally. These people help determine the style of our new life in Jesus; we generally buy the same Bible translation, adopt the same religious phrases, make the same ethical choices, even learn to punctuate our prayers with the same phrases. We associate Jesus with that group and that style. We learn about Jesus indirectly as well as directly, through participating in his family. Only later, if at all, do we begin to distinguish the group we were converted in from Jesus himself. Only then does Jesus become a distinctive character in our lives, someone we can "take with us" when we move to a new place. For some, however, the group's spirit and the Holy Spirit always remain indistinguishable.

I used to think that this cultural entrapment showed a highly disreputable side of Christianity. I suppose my ideal Christian was one big brain, detached from anything likely to make him lose his objectivity. This person would decide to become a Christian without being influenced by others; he would choose Jesus because of his study of the great world religions and philosophies. His style would spring straight from the New Testament.

I have changed my mind, not just because few such philosopher-Christians exist, but because I have seen that lonely, brainy Christians are not the most faithful to Jesus. They are often as adrift and disoriented as the freed slaves I described: They have nowhere to call home. They tend to stay unhappy and unproductive, always learning but never knowing. By contrast those who quickly become participants in Jesus' family grow in faith. We can forgive a great deal of cultural entrapment when we see active, fruitful lives. The reason for this vitality is obvious, if we think about faith as a personal relationship to Jesus. His flesh and blood carry more of his personality than a set of bloodless ideas. If we know Jesus' family, we are not far from knowing Jesus as a person rather than an idea.

Not all who pray a prayer of commitment continue in faith. Those who do are usually, studies show, the ones who already have Christian friends or who very quickly make them. The others, whom we never see again, are not necessarily insincere; they just have no focal point for their prayers or decisions. Jesus is an abstraction and continues to be one because they do not know his visible family. This is why pioneer missionaries put as much of their energy into founding churches as they do into preaching the gospel. They know from hard experience that thousands of people may accept the good news, but if they never form a family the good news will slowly dry up in their lives. Individual, atomistic Christians have no strength to endure. They almost never pass their faith on to others, even their own children. They need the nurturing of a Christian family.

So when a new Christian slavishly adopts the opinions and styles of the group of Christians he was converted in, we may have more cause for rejoicing than alarm. He will inevitably absorb cultural trappings that have very little to do with Jesus, but with them he will absorb the fundamental point of origin for the group: the life and love of Jesus.

THE VINE AND THE BRANCHES

Throughout this book we have been asking where in our own lives we can locate a personal relationship with Jesus. Yet Jesus has already touched us very personally through the Christians who brought us into his family. We have absorbed their style, their priorities, their personality — and through them, we have absorbed some of him. This does not end in our first year of new life; it goes on. He is the living source of our church family life and of our life. He shines through us, if darkly, and thus we become his instruments of love toward each other.

Practically, what does this require of us? First, a deepening knowledge of Jesus involves a stubborn appreciation of the particular part of his family we were born into.

For example, I will always be a twentieth-century evangelical protestant from a mainline denomination in America. Even if I react against that, it forms my reference point for understanding Jesus. Recognizing, even rebelling against, the limitations of our own spiritual background is a natural part of growing up. But real maturity comes when we accept those limitations and see beyond them to the fundamental character of Jesus. We must determine to see more than tired institutions in our native church; we must look for Jesus. A person who has never forgiven his parents for their failings can never be fully at peace with himself. Similarly, a Christian can never be entirely happy in his relationship to Jesus until he has come to peaceful, grateful terms with his spiritual family and can see in them part of the nature of Jesus. This perspective does not come cheaply; it may cost great conflict and inner turmoil.

Second, a deepening knowledge of Jesus involves learning to know his family scattered in many strange places.

I was born into a specific family. I will always owe them my life and feel my closest attachment to them. But my more distant relatives—cousins, uncles, and aunts—help me see my family in clearer perspective, to have a broader view of where I came from. Likewise, when we see God's nature expressed in many different people, in different cultures and traditions, we see more of him. We also more easily separate the real Jesus, who is transcultural, from the peculiarities of our background. For instance, my background made me think of Jesus as someone who appreciated worship in thought and attitude. My physical body had nothing to do with it, I felt. Nor, certainly, did the building I was in. A church building was, to me, walls and roof. Jesus did not care two cents about it. But when I lived in France and worshiped in a Gothic cathedral each week I developed a different perspective on Jesus. As that incredible beauty became familiar to me and seemed to merge with my prayers, I began to glimpse the reason why so much wealth and work had gone into churches. I began to think of Jesus as one who appreciates worship in stone and glass as well as thought and attitude, and this led me to a subtly different but wider appreciation of his nature.

In Africa, in Asia, in Latin America we may also meet our Lord's family. Many western Christians see missions as their opportunity to bless the world. We less easily recognize that the world will bless us with a bigger view of Jesus.

This widening consciousness of Jesus' family means becoming a world Christian, not bound by national or cultural borders. It also means becoming a historic Christian, recognizing that Jesus' family is not composed simply of those who happen to be walking around. We have the good fortune to follow on the experience of two thousand years of Christianity, twenty centuries of people expressing Jesus' nature in their various mental and physical circumstances. Not all the great men and women of God lived in the Bible period. Recognizing and appreciating the believers of the past is not merely an interesting piece of historic study; it is a way to see Jesus more clearly.

His family is composed of all those who love and follow him, present and past. They are not dead! They live and love Jesus today. We are going to meet them and share a city with them.

Actually, we know them better than we realize. In our religious traditions, whether they are ancient ones like the Catholic mass or more recent ones like the altar call, we embody wisdom from our forefathers. Every Christian has a tradition; every local congregation does things the way they do not simply because the Bible says so, but because their tradition has taught them that Jesus honors such procedures.

"We've always done it that way" need not be a curse. We do not have to accept tradition wholesale, but we ought not to scorn it wholesale either. Why, otherwise, have church buildings, choirs, Bible studies on Wednesday evenings? Why dress up for church? Why close our eyes and bow our heads to pray? Why have a missions committee? Why a Sunday school? Why a cross in the church? If we are determined to do without tradition—that is, to do without the witness of Christians who lived before us—we will have to rethink everything. In the end, of course, we will only create a new set of human traditions.

Tradition is a link to the family of Jesus who lived before us. In it, we may find the imprint of Jesus.

Still the original question persists: Where in this conglomerate of Christians can we locate Jesus personally? We may stick with the church of our birth, expand our view to the worldwide church, study history and tradition to absorb the thinking of previous generations. But how, practically, does this vast and varied church through the centuries reveal a personality?

To answer this question, I find our basic family analogy quite helpful. The way I love and understand Jesus in his family must have similarities to the way I know and understand people in their families. I think of my wife particularly, since I know her better than anyone else, and since in marrying her I found myself grafted into a family I would not otherwise have known.

Popie's family is different from mine. They live in the deep South; I grew up in the North. Her father is a successful surgeon; mine a pastor. Our families' values differ. More fundamentally, our families differ in the way that all families differ: in the mix of personalities and styles. To understand these differences is to begin to understand what makes Popie who she is. She is quite distinct from her family, but her life comes from them, and they are part of her life.

My differences from them sometimes made early visits to her home wary and tense. I was in love with Popie, not with them. Initially, I did not visit her home because I liked to. But I never had a moment's doubt about it—blood is thicker than water, and I *would* visit them. I would do my best to please them. Very gradually, almost beyond my awareness, this persistence with her family enriched my relationship with Popie. I began to love her family, to love the South, to understand her reactions and her sense of humor better. Sometimes I saw her sister do something or say something that was purely Popie, and because I saw it I knew Popie better. She seemed deeper and richer because I knew her, roots and all. It began with a willed decision. It grew into a joy.

So it is with Jesus' family. They may be a thorny bunch—certainly less lovely than Jesus. We do not see him in them at once, even if we look very hard. We are more likely to notice how *different* they are from him. Only when we decide to stick it out in the family and serve them do we begin to draw any benefits.

Increasingly, as our churches have grown more sophisticated and our society more mobile, Christians have regarded churches with the eyes of consumers. They ask, "Where will I be fed?" and think nothing of driving thirty minutes to find the answer. They jump from one church to the next, searching for personal satisfaction ("blessings").

But we do not relate to our families this way. Good or bad, they are our people. We show up at family gatherings whether we feel like it or not. We do not come to a family Thanksgiving dinner merely looking to be fed. We bring our share of the food. Many of us know how to be loyal to our human family, but not to our Christian family.

Are we loyal to our church family regardless of how its members act? Are we determined to love them whether it is pleasant or not? If so, then silently, secretly, we will meet Jesus in them and understand him in deeper ways. He is the vine, his family are the branches. They have a different appearance, but the life of one flows in the other. In glimpses we will see him, in passing moments. Someone will say something or do something that truly reflects Jesus, perhaps in a way we had never seen before. We will feel, in that moment, more than the influence of Jesus on his family. We will feel his influence on *us*.

We will feel his life flowing to us through his own body. It may not last, but that does not mean it is not there.

Facts are facts. When Jesus adopted his disciples as family, he either spoke pious fiction or he spoke the truth. If he spoke the truth, then we had better take it personally.

CHAPTER

9

MEALS

～

For the five years between my college graduation and my wedding day, I shared various apartments with other single men. Those were rich days, robust, full of good conversation and laughter. Some of the best times were mealtimes.

I knew some single people, sharing living arrangements similar to mine, who never ate together. Each person had his own shelf in the refrigerator, and he cooked — if he cooked — and ate alone, usually in a rush before he hurried off somewhere else. I regarded such an arrangement, for all its convenience, as no better than living alone. These apartment mates were living like passing strangers, like people who meet occasionally in the hallway of an apartment complex.

I wanted more than shared expenses. I wanted a home and I wanted fellowship. Otherwise, singleness would be a long wait in a bus station with a shifting crowd of strangers. Life together, I discovered, meant sharing grocery bills and a table. It meant sitting down regularly at common meals.

What is it about meals? When I think back to my childhood, the family times I remember most clearly are those around the kitchen table. We gathered daily for only one purpose — to eat; yet those good memories are not particularly of food. They were spontaneous times of fellowship and laughter and even heated discussion.

Going out for a meal together has become for many Americans a reflex of friendship. This is a modern adaptation of our ancestors' tradition of welcoming friends and strangers home for Sunday dinner. The institution has changed, but the fact that we eat together has not. Food is an inevitable part of hospitality. If someone comes as a guest to my home, I feel I must offer something to eat or drink. This sign of hospitality is not just American; it is as transcultural as any practice could be. In many parts of the world, you would insult someone quite seriously if you offered no food or drink when he visited, and the visitor would likewise insult his host if he declined to eat or drink it. Whether you like or need the food is not the issue. A host says, by offering food, "Welcome—and share our life."

When I lived in Kenya, we would go visit a family in a rural village and frequently find only the wife at home. She would disappear into the kitchen, start a wood fire between her three stones, boil water, and make tea. For a long time we were left in her sitting room with no one to talk to, not even anything to read. If we were short of time, we sometimes had to drink our tea and leave almost immediately. This made us uneasy, but it did not seem to bother our hosts. It did not seem to matter that we had hardly exchanged ten words. What mattered was that we had come, been received, and drunk tea together.

Through sharing food we show a humble willingness to share in another family's life. We enter their home and in a sense put ourselves at their mercy; we will eat their food whatever it is. Their life, represented by their food, will become our life. We share a common source. The same material that goes into my stomach and becomes me might as easily go into your stomach and become you. Our very stuff, down to the molecules, is the same. We are literally of one substance.

Wherever people meet to socialize, they eat and drink. Whether the occasion is as simple as visiting someone's home or as elaborate as a state banquet, food and drink are essential. The issue is not hunger, but friendship. I cannot think of a single friend with whom I have never shared food or drink. As soon as a purely business relationship moves toward friendship, someone is sure to say, "Why don't we go get a cup of coffee?"

If, then, a personal relationship with God is anything like our other personal friendships, it ought to involve eating together.

The mind does not instantly leap to think, "Of course, we share a meal with Jesus at the Lord's Supper!" Communion, or the Lord's Supper, or the Eucharist, as it is variously known, has become an austere, gravely hushed ceremony, especially good for meditating on sins. Its chief and most obvious characteristic—that the bread and wine are food—has been buried in centuries of solemnity and religious observance. Yet Jesus inaugurated the Lord's Supper as part of a meal, and it seems clear from some of Paul's instructions that the early church treated it as part of a meal, for some were reveling in the meal in a most irreligious manner (1 Corinthians 11:17-34).

The Lord's Supper is a great deal more than just a meal, however. Matthew's account makes clear that Jesus first offered it as a meal within a meal: "*While they were eating*, Jesus took bread, gave thanks and broke it. . . . 'Take and eat; this is my body'" (Matthew 26:26, emphasis added). The language Jesus used was calculated to provoke thought, to mystify and open windows into the dark. He identified the cup with his blood, the bread with his body, and he told his disciples to eat and drink them. He spoke of the wine as the blood of the covenant, poured out for the forgiveness of sins. He referred to a fast he would undergo, not drinking wine again until he drank it with his disciples in his Father's kingdom. The Lord's Supper carries tremendous freight. Through its simple light, as through a stained-glass window, we see scenes of the Passover, of the Old Testament sacrifice, of Jesus' last meal with his most intimate disciples, of his death and resurrection, and of our participation in Christ, now and at the wedding feast in the age to come. I cannot think of any aspect of Christianity that the Lord's Supper does not touch.

But for all the levels of meaning, the Lord's Supper is fundamentally a simple meal—simple food, simple procedure. It is like a strong foundation to a high building: its very simplicity makes it able to support story after story. That you eat only a token amount does not matter. The significance of sharing food is not dependent on how much you eat: if someone in Africa offers you food, you need only taste it; if someone proposes a toast in America you need only have a sip. The point is that you share in the same source of life.

A MEAL IN GOD'S HOUSE

Jesus, in instituting this special meal, was hardly launching a new trend. Abraham and his descendants had made sacrifices of food. As a proof of their devotion to God, the patriarchs sent the fragrant smell of meat to the heavens. When the Law was given to Moses, it was ratified with a meal on Mount Sinai: "Moses and Aaron, Nadab and Abihu, and the seventy elders of Israel went up and . . . saw God, and they ate and drank" (Exodus 24:9-11).

At that time God ordained several kinds of sacrifice, including the burnt offering in which the entire animal was consumed by fire, and the sin offering, in which the meat was burned up or eaten by the priest alone. In some respects these were preliminaries. The climax came in the peace offering, when the offerer and his family ate his sacrifice in the sanctuary. It was a meal of communion with God—a meal in God's house. The popular idea that the Old Testament sacrificial system was strictly a way to remove guilt is mistaken. It did that, but it did not end with that. Built into the system was the goal of personal communion with God in a meal.

That meal was a public affair. Everyone was aware of who was offering sacrifices, for the Tent of Meeting was at the very center of the camp. People had a personal experience with God through their sacrifices, but they also made a public announcement—much as a diplomatic banquet makes a political statement that the two sides can eat together, while allowing them actual camaraderie in the meal. The statement of the peace offering was: "God and I have had fellowship. I am cleansed of sin; I can eat with him."

The Jews also had an important private meal: the Passover. Here the sanctuary was not in view, nor were the priests. It was a family affair, meant to remind successive generations of God's deliverance of his people in the exodus from Egypt. That escape from Egypt had been the great turning point for Israel, converting them from a slave nation to a people of God, bound for the Promised Land. As they reenacted the escape each year, they shared communion based on the memory of salvation.

Jesus grew up observing this Passover meal. It had the weight for his time and place that Christmas has for ours. The Last Supper itself began as a Passover meal.

Jesus wanted to mark his death with a new kind of meal, an ongoing meal in which no lamb needed to die (for the Lamb would give his life, once for all) but a meal nonetheless—a feast with God.

First, it is an offering of Jesus' hospitality. He offers us simple, homely fare. "Take, eat. . . ." We are his guests, however unworthy; he who had no place to lay his head on earth now welcomes us into his heavenly home and offers us the food of the household. When we accept his hospitality and eat his food, we are saying with our bodies, "Lord, I will take and eat what food you give me. I want its nourishment, but even more I want to be a guest in your home. I am not the master here; I do not even deserve the crumbs from your table. I gratefully eat the food you put before me—your food."

Second, it is an acknowledgment of our common source of life. Communion is a social act; we do it as a church. We come to the table together; we eat the same food, joined together around the table in much the same way as we are joined together over a meal at home. The Lord's food goes into our stomachs, from there into our blood, and it becomes us. We are one people because we draw from the same source of life. The person next to me in the pew may be a busybody, a manipulator, or any number of unlovely things. (So may I.) But when we share the Lord's Table, we are on the same level, and we draw our life from the same substance. Eating at the Lord's Table is thus an act of Christian unity. This is why the apostle Paul would not even call the Corinthians' meal the Lord's Supper; he castigated them for not waiting for each other, not sharing their food, not having a family meal but merely eating food in the same location as if by coincidence (1 Corinthians 11:20-21). We cannot experience the fullness of communion as private people. It is something we must do with other Christians: "For anyone who eats and drinks without recognizing the body of the Lord eats and drinks judgment on himself" (11:29).

This unification extends beyond my local congregation, for the same meal of bread and wine has been offered by the Lord for twenty centuries all over the world. Because our food is the Lord's food, these are not many little meals but one continuous meal. Even as I eat, thousands of other believers around the world enjoy the same food. Paul, Silas, Peter, Priscilla, Irenaeus, Gregory of Nyssa, Jerome, Augustine, Bernard of Clairvaux, Theresa of Avila, Thomas Aquinas, Martin Luther, John Calvin, Martin Bucer, John Owen, Cotton Mather, William Wilberforce, Billy Sunday, Billy Graham, Desmond Tutu, Mother Theresa—they all ate this same food, offered by Jesus. I am part of them, and they part of me, because we eat this meal in common. Superficially we may be extraordinarily different. But bread gets inside you. It becomes part of you. When we eat the Lord's meal, we are anticipating in our separate places the single banquet when we shall all sit down together for a meal. "Many will come from the east and the west, and will take their places at the feast with Abraham, Isaac and Jacob in the kingdom of heaven" (Matthew 8:11). That feast has begun, by fits and starts, when we walk to the Lord's Table and "take and eat."

Finally, the Lord's Supper offers us an extraordinary menu: Jesus himself. In offering the bread and wine, Jesus said, "This is my body. . . . This is my blood."

God must have known that his people would expend considerable energy fighting over how literally these words should be taken. There was no precedent for them in the Old Testament. In a sacrificial meal an ox never became anything other than an ox. The sacrificial meals were certainly not considered divine flesh. They were mere dead animals augmented by cereal or oil. Nor is there a precedent in our own experience. No host has ever asked me if I would like to nibble on him. How, then, can we understand what Jesus meant?

It was not entirely unjust that the early Christians were accused of cannibalism. Any religion that has a meal for its sacramental centerpiece and that speaks of eating the flesh and blood of its God is asking for misunderstanding.

Cannibals, humans who eat other human flesh, believe that when they eat someone, they absorb something of that person's personal power. Interestingly, the language describing the Lord's Supper suggests that when we eat the bread and wine, he himself comes to us and gets inside us. We can argue about how this happens, whether symbolically or "really." The end result of Communion, however, is unarguably more than hospitality, more than sharing a meal together. It is not just another church potluck. For while Jesus is present at a potluck, somehow in eating the Lord's Supper we participate in Jesus himself, in his life and his power. "This is my body. . . . This is my blood," he said in introducing his disciples to the Lord's Supper. For all its strangeness, this is the most intimate image conceivable. It enriches Paul's words, "Christ in us."

THE LORD'S SUPPER

What is the connection between Jesus and a thimbleful of wine and a small chunk of bread? How does Jesus "get inside us" through them? I must admit that I am quite vague about the various doctrines of transubstantiation and consubstantiation. I think I understand while I am listening, but as soon as I have to explain them to someone else my brain refuses to cooperate.

I don't intend to try unraveling those views. I prefer to concentrate on something more basic: how the Lord's Supper offers us Jesus' presence through symbols that help us remember. Those who stress the real presence of the Lord in the Lord's Supper say that the bread and wine do more than help us remember Jesus' death and resurrection, that they actually, even physically, bring Jesus to us. Others say that the bread and wine are just symbols. But despite their differing doctrinal views of this sacrament, all agree that the elements are *at the very least* symbols that help us remember. I want to concentrate on this common ground because I have the impression many people do not realize what a powerful thing they say when they comment that something is "just a symbol."

We may speak of two kinds of symbols. The first kind have nothing whatsoever to do with what they symbolize. I may say to you, "Whenever I write 'A' I mean 'Washington.'" This is a type of shorthand. It is arbitrary. I could have chosen "Z" just as well. Some people seem to see this kind of symbolism in the bread and wine, in which case "bread and wine" might be written on the blackboard as meaning, "Meditate on the death and resurrection of Jesus." The symbols of those written letters made of chalk would have just as much to do with Jesus as do the bread and wine.

But another kind of symbol, a much more important kind, embodies the very thing that it represents. We may say, for instance, that John F. Kennedy symbolized the optimistic spirit of the early sixties. Or we may say that Vietnam came to symbolize the lost confidence in American policy. In these cases, the symbol is part of what it symbolizes, the preeminent part. It is not arbitrary. You could not switch some other president, say Johnson, for Kennedy, or some other war, say Korea, for Vietnam. This kind of symbol reverberates off the greater whole for which it stands and of which it is part.

Jesus' meal of bread and wine, I think, forms this kind of symbol. It is not "merely" a symbol, as "A" may "merely" mean "Washington." The meal is part—a preeminent part—of God's grace and reverberates off the larger whole. It calls to mind the thousands of other meals, outside the church, that God has provided. It calls to mind the many gatherings over food that have enriched us and joined us to other people. It calls to mind the sacrificial meals of the Old Testament. It calls to mind the nourishment our Lord constantly provides, even in himself, filling us with his Holy Spirit. It calls to mind his death and resurrection. The Lord's Supper does not merely stand for these things; it is itself part of the sweep of God's grace. God invites us to a meal—the best meal available to us, the ultimate meal that God has yet given to us.

A symbol in its best sense is the kernel of reality, the irreducible core of meaning. Jesus' supper offers us the grace of Jesus: a meal in fellowship with the Lord. He comes to us as other people come to us: over a meal, through his family members who share the meal with us, in his personal (though invisible) presence at the meal, in his words of invitation. Without all these factors, the bread and wine are not consecrated; they are just food, not part of a meal as Jesus meant them to be. But in the full context of the Christian sacrament, they are transformed. They do not merely remind us of God's grace; they *are* God's grace, the means by which Jesus becomes part of us.

God offers us a meal, not just symbolically, but *real*-ly. The food is real, the table is real, and the invitation is real. Those who say that the bread and wine are symbols of Christ, and those who say they are the real substance of Christ, are not, I think, as far apart as they sometimes think. At least we can all say this: The bread and wine are symbols—maybe more, but not less than that. As symbols they call attention not merely to things apart from themselves, but to themselves. For in themselves they are Jesus' gracious offering to us.

LIVING REALITY

All agree that the Lord's Supper is a memorial meal, that we do it in memory of Jesus. What is memory?

Some people think memory is a dusty library of facts stored in a remote corner of the brain. We need a memory, they think, but not acutely. Of course it would be inconvenient to forget dates and people's names, but the actual business of living, which goes on in the present, would not be greatly changed. Some people even say, "Don't live in the past, live in the present!"

Augustine described a famous mental experiment that routed this view. He simply attempted to define life in the present. Is it living "one day at a time?" No, because right now the morning is in the past and the evening is in the future. Is the present perhaps a very short time? A minute, for instance? No, for a minute breaks into seconds, and half the seconds are past and half yet to come. The harder you try to define the present, the narrower the present becomes. It is like a sharply honed blade on the front edge of memory, cutting through the future and turning it to past. The present has such a fleeting existence that no meaning can survive in it. Even a single word has no meaning. By the time we pronounce the second syllable, the first syllable is in the past, in our memory. Thus if we could only listen in the present, we would never understand a word. We would only be bombarded with fragments of sound.

The same is true of meeting a person. If we live in the present alone, he is a constant stranger to us. We cannot understand his words; we cannot make sense of his face; his character does not exist. Without memory, a "personality" does not exist, and a "person" does not exist—only a leering face, making noise. To live in the present is not to live at all. Certainly it is not to live as a human being in relationship with other people.

So when in communion we remember the death and resurrection of Jesus, we are doing just what we must do to experience Jesus as a person today. We are creating a whole picture of his personality by which his present presence may be apprehended. Without memory, even if he appeared visibly before us in unspeakable glory, he would be merely a bright light, another strange face. Memory enables his presence to have personality.

The Passover meal was a time for remembering when God saved the Israelites from Egypt. That event happened once; there was no question of making it happen again at each Passover. But it was not a memory disconnected from the present. It was like the Fourth of July for Americans: we remember the events that led to our nation's independence, but more importantly we celebrate the living nation those events gave us. The Jews at Passover celebrated the Lord's deliverance as a people still delivered and constantly redelivered by that same present Lord. And we at the Lord's Supper celebrate the Lord's death not only as a past event, but as living reality. He is not just a historical figure, dead and gone. He is alive. In Christ we die to sin and live to fellowship with him at his table. Because we remember him, we can encounter him there as a real person. He invites us, still, to share a meal with him and his family.

10
WORK

~~

In my work as a writer I have had to develop a thick skin. To write well you must get rid of everything extra—the phrases that sound superb to you but overwrought to others, the side trip that enables you to sound off on a favorite topic but loses your reader. Striking these out is known in some circles as "murdering your darlings." It feels like it. Rarely does a writer learn to murder his darlings without some stern, steel-skinned editor making him do it. After some years I have learned almost to smile when an editor points out one of my typical mistakes. Mine is the grim smile of recognition: "Yes, that's rabies all right. Take the dog out and destroy it."

You would think that after years of criticism I would not take it so personally. Indeed, I do not take it *so* personally. But I certainly do take it personally. I can think objectively about my work, but I cannot feel objective about it. When someone criticizes my writing, I feel a small, stubborn, hurt boy rising to the surface of my personality. My critics don't hurt my work; they hurt me. They mean well, and I know from experience that I need their criticisms. I even ask for them. Nonetheless, I do not like them.

I said earlier that personality extends beyond skin into clothing, family, and home. It also extends into the things that we do, particularly our work. I don't care too much whether you admire my skill as a gardener, but my self-esteem is really at stake in my writing. I cannot detach myself from it. Someone may say, "Oh, but your real

self is not at stake. If you lost your career as a writer, you would survive to do other things." That is so; writing is not central to my existence. Neither is my right leg. I could lose both and survive, but if I
lost them, I would need to make a new definition of "me."

By "work" I do not necessarily mean "job." Many people make
a living from jobs they don't care two cents about. But I believe every
healthy person does something he cares for and "works" at. It may
be a hobby or a beautifully decorated home or a close family. He
cares about it, works creatively at it, and if you criticize it, you cut not
just the work, but him.

People who lack pride in any accomplishment, on the other hand,
become deeply confused about their own identity. If you have ever
tried to help someone who because of his negative self-esteem cannot hold a job, has broken relationships, and seems deliberately
unkempt, you know what I mean. You can tell him until you are
hoarse that he is wonderful in God's sight. But when he leaves you
and encounters a world that does not want or need him, his self-
esteem plunges again. It may be true that self-hatred is the disease
and low achievement merely the symptom, but unless you find a way
to improve the symptoms, you will find it difficult to cure the disease. Healthy people need to achieve, to create, to work. They find
themselves partly through extending themselves into the world around
them, by doing and creating. When they see what they have done,
they see in tangible form the greatness God has created in them.

It is certainly not true, as some pop theology suggests, that God
is interested only in what we are, not in what we do. The Bible portrays the two as seamlessly knit together. What you are is reflected in
your thoughts, in your actions, in your relationships. That is why, to
the everlasting distress of Protestants, the Bible so often seems to
portray God's judgment based on our works. Jesus, for instance, predicts a final judgment in which sheep are separated from goats on the
basis of the prisoners they have visited, the naked they have dressed,
the hungry they have fed. He does not mention the question of faith.
We are saved by faith, lest any man should boast. But faith without
works is not faith at all. Both reflect, together, a single personality
that God alone sees clearly.

If I want to know my friends, then, I must not merely seek some
internal, immaterial essence. I must look at what they do. If I want

to know a woman whose heart is in raising her family, I must try to see her at work with her family. If I want to know a woman whose heart is in her career as an astrophysicist, I must try to catch some glimpse of how her heart finds its place there. This is one major reason why "shared interests" are so vital to friendship. They do more than give you something to make conversation about. They give the basis for understanding each other's heart.

Understanding a person's work often requires understanding the group endeavor of which he is a part. Modern mythology has it that those who collaborate in a corporation sacrifice personal definition to "the machine." The accomplishments of an employee at IBM, for instance, are swallowed up by the vastness of the company. Therefore you could not "know" him by knowing his work. But this is a false and antihuman way of defining our individuality. Human beings normally work together, and very few things of worth were made by only one person.

Today, we glorify the artist who works completely alone. But before the Renaissance no artist even signed his work. Art was not individual expression; it served a corporate purpose, such as worship. Yet the unsigned artists were great artists, with an obvious love for their work, who created (for instance) the great cathedrals of Europe. To be a cog in a machine is not necessarily depersonalizing. It depends on whether you love your place in the machine, and whether you love the work the machine does. Thus, an IBM employee may be known not so much through his personal contribution to IBM as through an understanding of IBM and his place in it. He is part of something bigger than himself, and it is part of him.

I love choral singing for the very reason that my individual effort is deliberately immersed and lost in a vast sea of sound. When I was in college I had the opportunity to sing with the chorus in several concerts with the San Francisco Symphony. I have only an ordinary amateur voice, but I love good music. Those concerts made the greatest musical expression I ever hope to attain. Not because of my efforts—I do not even know whether I sang well or badly. But I was part of beautiful music made by a first-rate orchestra. I was a part so small as to be unidentifiable, but nonetheless an active part. My "work" was an enterprise I cared for, but which surpassed and surrounded me. If you want to understand my musical soul, don't listen to me, listen to the *Missa Solemnis*.

This is why, I believe, our activity in heaven is described as choral singing in praise to God. Praise is our eternal work, and the joy of it lies not in our individual contribution but in our participation in a vast, beautiful, collective praise. If you want to understand a believer's ultimate meaning, listen to that praise.

"WHAT DO YOU DO?"

The first question we ask someone after learning his name is, "What do you do?" In getting to know God, then, we must ask that question. He may hide his face, but he has not hidden his work.

What does God do? He makes flowers and mountains and starry nights, the severity of the desert and the lushness of the forest meadow. In these he reveals himself as an artist of incomparable imagination. I have sometimes wondered: What if we had never seen a tree until, one day, someone presented one in the Museum of Modern Art? Would it not be a work of sculpture so splendid that all the other sculptors would put down their tools and come to stare? But that is only the beginning of the exhibition; next comes a whale, and after that a stone, and after that a star, and after that a seed, and after that. . . .

But God's work is more than nature. He barely began there. People generally concede that you can know something about God through the universe he has made: "The heavens are telling the glory of God." But to know someone through his work you ought to concentrate on the work he loves best. God does not love stars as he loves me. The heavens, for all their splendor, will outlive their usefulness; they will be rolled up and taken away. So will the world we live in, for all its sensual glory and intricate ecology. They are like the scaffolding that Michelangelo designed for painting the Sistine Chapel—marvelous in its own right, but dismantled at the proper time so that the great work could be more clearly seen. When God had created everything else, he went on to man and woman, creatures who sat up and talked to each other, who talked to him. He has been working to complete these creatures ever since. He even became one. His people are God's great work, to be displayed in an entirely new setting—a new heaven and a new earth.

To marvel at yourself is not far from marveling at God. This is the logic of the familiar Psalm 139: "You knit me together in my mother's womb. I praise you because I am fearfully and wonderfully made; your works are wonderful" (verses 13-14). And then, three verses later, the psalmist lightly leaps to this: "How precious to me are your thoughts, O God! How vast is the sum of them!" From my own wonderful nature as a human being to the wonderful nature of God's thoughts—it is not a great leap, for the latter made the former. In this way, at least, a Christian is obliged to be a humanist. We are made in the image of God. As we observe ourselves, individually and socially, talking and singing, admiring babies and playing baseball, we strengthen our personal knowledge of God. This is not an abstract study. It is personal. It is personal because he made me and is working on me still. His hands are on me; I see the prints.

But God is not just a biological or sociological genius. The splendor of humanity, which biology and psychology and sociology spell out, is not God's greatest work. It is strictly preparatory. Preeminently, he works at that which would put our ambassadors and United Nations representatives to shame: he works to bring all people together into one family under his name.

Paul was one of those who put down his tools to stare at this marvel. "Surely you have heard about the administration of God's grace that was given to me for you, that is, the mystery made known to me by revelation, as I have already written briefly. . . . The mystery of Christ . . . was not made known to men in other generations as it has now been revealed. . . . This mystery is that through the gospel the Gentiles are heirs together with Israel, members together of one body, and sharers together in the promise in Christ Jesus" (Ephesians 3:2-6). You cannot read Paul's writing without feeling his tremendous excitement in this information. He had no personal stake in seeing the Gentiles join Israel. His natural interest would have opposed any integration with "Gentile dogs." What excited Paul was his chance to grasp, after centuries of obscurity, what God was doing. Through knowing and participating in God's work, Paul could know God.

A man who graduated from MIT in the early forties told me that his senior year all graduating students were called in to hear a presentation from a possible employer. They only half listened to this recruiter, for most of them had already made plans to join other firms. The recruiter's conclusion, however, caught their attention: "I hope you are attracted to the opportunities I have presented, because I can personally guarantee that every one of you will join my company." He represented the Manhattan Project, which through the military draft took the entire senior class to help make the atom bomb.

Not everyone who worked for the Manhattan Project knew what it was about. Most people knew only the narrow work of their own division. Security was so tight that even spouses could not be told anything. The man who told me this story said that throughout the war his wife had no idea what he did. Then one morning before going to work, he told her, "Be sure to listen to the news on the radio today. I think you'll find out what I've been doing for all these years." It was the day the atomic bomb was dropped on Hiroshima.

That day revealed his work and thus helped his wife understand him; but it ultimately revealed far more about his nature as a member of the human race. More than any other event of our century, Hiroshima revealed humanity's true and frightening nature as evidenced by the work of our best and brightest minds. Jesus revealed something entirely different. He revealed God's work and, thus, God's character—and it was entirely happy news. God is a lover and a peacemaker, and his work shows it.

SHARING GOD'S WORK

His most creative and painstaking work is the church, the body of Christ. Only by knowing the church and its direction in history can I understand his most beloved concerns. It is a permanent corporation, one that (unlike IBM) will go right through the judgment and on into eternity. It will certainly be judged, and it will certainly be changed, but it will never be done away with. Why will it survive when so much else will dissolve? Only because God loves it—it is his beloved project. He has signed his name on it. Thus, the church and its future make up an intensely personal study for me as a Christian, for I am an integral part of it.

But God did not just found the church and leave it to function on its own or under someone else's direction. He is the founding figure, but also its continuing head. I do not merely study the artist through his art. I join him in making it. We can have the shared understanding that coworkers achieve.

If I lose track of what God's work is or if the church I belong to loses a sense of God's purpose for it, then I lose a major source of contact with God. This is why true mystical knowledge of God comes in the context of a church that knows its business. We cannot put "renewal" ahead of "mission," or say that a church must learn to worship before it does its work in the world. The two are bound together. The real God has work to do, and we know him personally as we join the work.

What is this work? Essentially it is to transform men and women through love—to have a part in shaping beautiful creatures who will reign with Christ. All of us are becoming either those who can stand before the Son of Man without flinching—which implies that we will be far better and more glorious than we are now—or those who will be, in the light of Jesus' glory, a horrible travesty of human nature. Every day in a hundred secret ways the shaping goes on. Every day in a hundred ways we participate in the work. When I get up in the night to give my daughter a drink, I have been summoned by the cries of a creature more beautiful than the gods and goddesses of Greek imagination. I rarely see that beauty; I only see a little girl. But God sees that beauty and wants to draw it out.

Most of life is so humdrum that I can almost believe we are merely intelligent animals and not supernatural creatures. But sometimes I catch a glimpse of God's transforming work in a friend. Right before my eyes, I see someone changed. Only yesterday he was rigid, uptight, fearful. Today, out of nowhere, a new grace has appeared. Where did it come from? How did it happen?

My part in the process is mainly mundane, physical, mechanical. Being most closely involved with my children and their salvation, I see my responsibilities most clearly with them. I care for their needs: food, clothing, shelter, health, education. I try to see that they are treated with justice both at home and in the world outside. I try haltingly to answer their questions about God. I take them to church. I pray for them, inviting God's power to heal and transform their lives. I try to teach them how to love and help them tame their tendency to imperialism. But what makes them become capable of eternity? I do simple, earthly stuff necessary to the transformation but insufficient in itself. What creates in them the beauty of God? It is God working by my side. As I do my work, I sometimes see his part in the transformation. I see, or partly see, something appear in my children that did not come from me. I come closest to touching him when I touch the work he is also touching.

Here and now I share God's work in only a handful of lives. As part of his church, I participate in the faltering spread of good news, the reconciliation of the world. Sometimes supernatural power may be evident in what I do; more often not. Even my secular tasks may be included in his work; I do my daily work with all the love I can muster, even when I cannot see its purpose in the eternal scheme. At the very least I am maintaining the world, keeping it running, until my Master comes. My children are not the only ones who need food and water and clothing while they go through the transformation. But all that I do in God's work and all that I see of his work comes to very little. In the end, even Mother Teresa and Billy Graham transform only corners of the world. I may pray with power, proclaim the gospel with power, do powerfully merciful acts, work powerfully for justice, but my corner is small. Still, it is not at all insignificant. Like an employee at IBM, my individual contribution is swallowed up in a vast movement. My own meaning and my intimacy with God come from my participation in something much bigger than myself: a corporate achievement that I love. I love it because it belongs to God.

God's broader strokes, his great universal movements that are preparing the day when all the universe will be overturned, when earthly powers will vanish and one vast audience will be judged and separated, when a chorus of praise will erupt from the throat of the redeemed—this work I hear of, but I hardly feel I work on it personally. I feel too small for that. Yet Scripture more than hints that even on that day God intends to make me a coworker. In all Jesus' parables, when the king comes home he appoints his faithful servants to rule the land with him. Paul wrote, "Do you not know that we will judge angels? How much more the things of this life!" (1 Corinthians 6:2-3). Perhaps I will then "see him as he is" partly as I participate in this vast and unimaginable work.

It is a serious business, if you can believe it: shaping the future of the universe. It is an opportunity to know Christ as we discern his hidden, magnificent work and work with him at it. If we could really understand all that it is leading to, if we could realize what we do and who we do it with, would it not make us tremble? But we are usually too dull to see.

Work is often dull. People whom I allow to criticize my writing deal with me on most personal terms, but they may not always be aware of it as they plow through dull manuscript pages. The fact remains, however, that they can hardly get more personally involved with me, for I am trusting to their hands work that I love, work that is close to my heart, work that expresses my deepest self. If they keep at it, they will know me better. The same is true of God as he trusts us to care for the work of reconciliation of people he loves.

CHAPTER

11

TOUCH

W hen I am on a business trip, I long for my wife's arms. Her touch has very deep comfort. So does the touch of my children, of my old friends, of my mother and father.

Why is it so? Why do we squeeze the widow's hand or sympathetically pat the shoulder of the defeated athlete? Why do we bear-hug a long-lost friend? What is it about the touch of one skin against another? As with so many other aspects of knowing people, I cannot say why. I only know that if you want to know someone you must touch—at least shake hands. We are what Lewis Smedes calls "body-persons." Our bodies reach out to contact each other.

We normally think of touching friends and lovers. But it applies even to ourselves. From the time we are infants, we explore our bodies. We want to know and feel this substance we are in. Every parent has seen his child make the glorious discovery that he has hands to clap and feet to kick. He is enjoying the pleasure of learning about himself, getting to know himself. I think of it as the tactile counterpart of looking at yourself in the mirror, which we do not outgrow either.

Within a few more years children begin exploring their bodies athletically, independent of their parents. They become intoxicated with the power to run, jump, climb trees, and kick balls. Convincing them to quit these activities at the end of the day can be as difficult as taking an addict off heroin.

As if that were not enough intoxication, they soon encounter their sexual powers. Most children discover masturbation by accident as they are quite innocently exploring themselves. The result frightens them. It is as though their bodies were occupied by foreign powers, powers they find both delicious and horrible. Equally fearsome are the feelings they gain toward members of the opposite sex. Adolescents often withdraw and spend hours slumped down doing nothing. They develop a powerful sense of privacy; they put signs on their bedroom doors demanding that others keep out. They are thinking, privately, about potentialities they cannot imagine in their own parents, powers that will take them to who knows what end. These new powers begin with a changing body that develops hair and protrusions quite unthinkable to a child. Adolescents keep private; so did Dr. Jekyll. Like him they are frightened but also fascinated. They would halfway like to stop growing but cannot.

I am not trying to recapitulate modern psychology. I am simply reminding you of some discoveries we all made. They were intensely physical, but they certainly went beyond that. We discover our bodies at the same time that we begin to define our own personality as distinct from our parents. We form an idea of who we are partly through touch—our own.

To a much diminished extent we carry this exploration on through life. At least, we make all kinds of movements that stimulate our bodies for no obvious reason. We tap our fingers, jingle our keys, rub our hands. We scratch. We enjoy nothing more than a shower. Watch a group of people in a meeting some day and see how often they touch themselves—their faces, hair, hands. The more nervous they feel, the more they do it—which suggests we gain some reassurance from it, some deeper sense of our secured identity. The motions of our hands suggest that we need to keep in touch with ourselves as body-persons.

And then with our hands we explore other people. When strangers meet they shake hands or even embrace and kiss. In the handshake I see two strangers reaching out toward each other, feeling for a clue as to what sort of body-person this might be. For old acquaintances, on the other hand, a handshake is a reassuring "How have you been?" A hug says, "I'm so glad to see you again," or, "I'll miss you." Why do we have this impulse to touch people when we meet them? Why do we feel uneasy if we meet someone and do not shake hands? Why is a refusal to shake hands a grave insult? Because even on the slightest acquaintance, touch is a needed part of knowing others. In East Africa, touch between men and women is forbidden; even a husband and wife do not hold hands in public. But as though to make up for this loss of touch, everyone shakes hands on every possible occasion; when you enter a room with twenty strangers you circulate and shake hands with everyone, without even exchanging names.

Touch goes beyond greeting. Touch allows our hands to be instruments of healing. When you visit the sick or the elderly, they often clutch at your hands more than your words. They may be too sick to understand or too gabby to listen, but they want your hand. In the convalescent homes I have visited, a handshake is rarely a moment's affair; old people do not want to let go. Even crusty old men sometimes like holding hands for a few moments. Touch conveys acceptance, particularly to those who feel alienated from their own bodies. You say, when you touch, "I am not afraid of your body, though it is sick; I love it." Jesus occasionally healed at a distance, and perhaps his power seemed more impressive when he did. Most often, though, he healed by touching, even though it meant contact with people who were by Jewish law "unclean."

The healing touch is not only for sick people. Through touch we convey health to our children. Babies who are not held become sickly and die. They need the warmth of human touch for life itself. Later on they need it, if not for survival, then for wholeness. When my daughter is sad, she says, "Hold me, Daddy." I cannot think of better words. I comfort her through touch and she comforts me.

I suspect we barely tap the healing power of touch. We touch children and old people freely because we have no worry about sexual involvement. But with people between twelve and seventy the tensions of sex nearly always make us hesitate to touch too freely. If we touch, we do it self-consciously.

An experience I had in Kenya hinted to me of the degree to which I am bound by this tension. There is little or no observable homosexuality in Kenya, and consequently men feel free to hold hands without fear of sexual involvement or misunderstanding. When I made close friends with Kenyan men, they reached out to hold my hand as we walked along together. It would have been very rude to snatch back my hand, yet I must admit I felt intensely uncomfortable. I could not think of anything else so long as we were holding hands. I mention this because it pointed out to me the self-restraint I normally use. I know touch is a source of warmth, but I have never been able to use it unreservedly with another man. I have never been able to use it unreservedly with women friends either. I am not suggesting that we abandon our taboos, for I suspect they serve a necessary purpose. They keep some of us out of trouble and force sexual energy into the right channels. But they also keep us from mutual knowledge and healing love. We live in a world that is under a curse, and I think our guardedness in touching is part of that curse. Only in rare relationships of very deep intimacy is this curse lifted. Then the importance of touch becomes extremely plain.

We experience it most in marriage. Here we feel no fear of stepping over boundaries, and so touch may heal without restriction. Touch is, for my wife and me, a constant wordless conversation. She has, through this, done more to help me accept myself than anyone or anything else.

Of many forms of touch, each with its own unique significance and comfort, sexual intercourse alone has the potential to go "all the way." It is utterly vulnerable and intimate. Interestingly, the Bible speaks of this touch as "knowing" each other. With sexual intercourse the whole personality must be engaged. Paul made this point with some heat to the Corinthians, who thought they could sleep with prostitutes without being affected personally. "Do you know that he who unites himself with a prostitute is one with her in body? . . . Flee from sexual immorality. All other sins a man commits are outside his body" (1 Corinthians 6:16,18). Paul was not talking about "body" as we do, as a collection of molecules that we happen to inhabit. He meant something more fundamental: our very nature as physical creatures. He was telling the Corinthians, "Sex is touch that gets to you. It affects you in the most basic possible way, bodily. It is not external to you. It changes you."

Yet intercourse is only one kind of touching. Touch is crucial from the first meeting of casual acquaintances to the deepest and most intimate encounter between marriage partners. We are body-persons and need to communicate bodily. The deepest and most healing human relationships always involve touch.

JESUS' TOUCH

This fact, however, introduces some sadness into our relationship with God, for we do not touch him. The popular chorus "He Touched Me" is religious hyperbole. It reveals a longing for God's touch, but nobody has actually felt God's hand.

Our longing is unfulfilled, but it was perhaps not always so. In Eden, it seems, God's hands were on Adam and Eve as he formed them. The words of Genesis are elliptical, leaving the precise means of creation to our imagination, but the creation story has an atmosphere of physical freedom that makes God's touch entirely plausible. God breathed into Adam; he took a rib from his side and closed up the place with flesh; he walked in the garden in the cool of the day. The suggestion that Adam and God could have held hands as they walked does not violate the atmosphere of Eden. Whether the anthropomorphic picture this brings to mind is accurate I don't know. I have no idea exactly how Adam and God related. But I do know that Genesis' picture of a perfect world is very different from its picture of the world after sin came in.

Then the atmosphere changed radically. Moses talked to God as a man talks to his friend, but there is no mention of touch in this most intimate relationship, nor can we imagine it. The God who descends on Mount Sinai with smoke and fire, the God whom no one can see and live—touch him? It is unthinkable. The only exception is the strange unearthly scene in which Jacob wrestled with God—and there God's touch did permanent damage to Jacob's hip.

When God wanted to *heal* through touch he did it by his heavenly messengers. When Elijah ran for his life from Jezebel, an angel came twice to touch him and urge him to his feet (1 Kings 19:1-9). Isaiah cried out, "Woe is me!" when he saw the Lord, but Yahweh did not move to help. Isaiah's lips were purified through the touch of a coal from the altar, administered by one of the seraphim (Isaiah 6:5-7). Daniel, knocked flat by his vision, was raised by the touch of Gabriel and by the touch of the shining messenger (Daniel 8–10).

The restoring touch from heaven is well known in the Old Testament. But it did not come from God's hand. The psalmists ask freely for many benefits, but they never ask God, "Touch me." The "hand of God" is a frequently used phrase but never in contact with a man or woman; it is a term for power, not friendship. The Old Testament is not the record of a cold, distant, angry God; his passionate love for his people is unmistakable. But he is certainly not a God who touches anyone.

Nor, ordinarily, did his human representatives. If you look up "touch" in a concordance, you will find that in the Pentateuch it is used primarily in the context of "do not touch": Do not touch the holy things, do not touch dead bodies, do not touch the leper. Touch contaminated. When the Israelites brought a sacrifice to the tabernacle, they put their hands on it to identify themselves with it. But they had no human contact. The priest did not lay hands on them. Nor did the prophets, usually. Healing was in their words, not their hands.

Against this Old Testament background, Jesus was absolutely revolutionary. He ignored the "do not touch" regulations. His touch healed, and crowds pushed forward simply to touch him. He touched lepers and women who were ceremonially unclean. For the first time in biblical history an unclean person touched a clean one and the result was not contamination but restoration: "All who touched him were healed" (Mark 6:56).

Jesus also touched little children to bless them. And after he died and came alive again, he invited his disciples to touch him, to feel with their hands that he was no less than the Jesus they knew. "It is I myself! Touch me and see" (Luke 24:39). Thomas, who doubted the Resurrection, was invited to thrust his hands into the scars from Jesus' wounds. So John wrote, "That which was from the beginning, which we have heard, which we have seen with our eyes, which we have looked at and *our hands have touched*—this we proclaim concerning the Word of life" (1 John 1:1, emphasis added). Jesus offered the fullness of an intimate relationship with God, and touch was an integral part of that. He healed and blessed and reassured through touch.

But Jesus' physical body is gone. We cannot see him nor can we touch him. Or can we?

If the church is really the "body of Christ," he has assigned us the role of touching for him. And if he said of the bread we take at Communion, "This is my body," then perhaps we can touch him in some way through that service. The church and the Lord's Supper have a healing impact, and through their touch we experience God in a down-to-earth, physically real way. This is an important aspect of our authority as Christ's body: to touch and to heal. The simple handshake or the loving hug may minister as deeply and spiritually as any words. We may touch as well as speak on Jesus' behalf.

But will we never touch Jesus directly? John's Revelation contains an intriguing hint. John saw a shattering vision much like those that the Old Testament prophets saw, and it knocked him to the ground just as it had them. But there is a subtle and important new ingredient in John's account: it was not an angel's touch that lifted him up. "Among the lampstands was someone 'like a son of man,' . . . his eyes were like blazing fire. His . . . voice was like the sound of rushing waters. In his right hand he held seven stars. . . . His face was like the sun shining in all its brilliance.

"When I saw him, I fell at his feet as though dead. *Then he placed his right hand on me* and said: 'Do not be afraid. I am the First and the Last. I am the Living One; I was dead, and behold I am alive for ever and ever!'" (Revelation 1:13-18, emphasis added).

Jesus, the majestic glorified Jesus with eyes like fire, touched John and raised him to his feet. He gave the healing touch, not through an angelic messenger, but in person.

There are other New Testament hints that we may someday experience the same. They are even less frequent and less explicit than the references to seeing God's face, but they are enough to make us hope that the physical freedom of Eden will be restored in the age to come.

In the story of Lazarus and the rich man, Jesus referred to Lazarus after death reclining on "Abraham's bosom." The figure of speech is drawn from the way people sat at a Palestinian banquet, with each guest able to lean back on another's chest. John leaned on Jesus in this way at the Last Supper. It is a physical freedom that we find almost unimaginable—reminiscent, to me, of my experience holding hands in Kenya, because I cannot imagine leaning so freely on anyone but my wife. In Palestine it was a great honor to lean in this way on the principle guest, and so when Jesus describes Lazarus as leaning on Abraham's bosom, he is suggesting a feast at which Lazarus has the highest honor—an honor that involves physical contact. We may legitimately imagine heaven as a place, it seems, where God's people from all centuries will be physically comfortable together and where our touch will heal continuously.

But that is only intimacy with each other. What about intimacy with God?

We know this much for a start: that Jesus lives bodily. He did not dissolve into space when he left the disciples (though earlier he had vanished from a room); he led them out to an open place where they could witness his bodily departure. Apparently he did not want them to think of him as a purely spiritual entity, as they might have had he merely disappeared into thin air. He wanted them to believe that he continued to have life in the body, even though they experienced him only in the Spirit. What exactly "life in the body" means for the risen Jesus, we do not know. It is hard to think of him as living in a specific location, such as behind the moon. It is difficult to imagine his glorified body—shining, brilliant, with eyes of fire. But he has not dissolved. John, in a vision, saw him and felt his healing touch. And he will come to our planet again in a way that will be universally seen and acknowledged. He will come on the clouds, with power and great glory. We will see him face to face. Perhaps we will also touch him.

Revelation portrays the heavenly kingdom as a place of healing, as a place where every tear will be wiped away, as a place of complete and absolute comfort. Perhaps the healing and comfort will come from God as they usually come on earth: in a loving embrace.

JUDGMENT OF FIRE

Perhaps, however, our view of the healing touch of God is inadequate. Perhaps we have sung too glibly, "Precious Lord, take my hand." For we must consider another part of God's physical image, one that is probably the least attractive in all the Bible: fire.

The Judgment Day will be revealed as a burning fire. The Bible says: "The heavens will disappear with a roar; the elements will be destroyed by fire, and the earth and everything in it will be laid bare" (2 Peter 3:10). How earlier readers pictured this firestorm I do not know, but any reader today can only think of nuclear conflagration. For most of history a vivid imagination was needed to believe this prediction. Today it seems like almost a natural ending.

But the fire at the end of this world will not be the unplanned result of some horrible nuclear accident, some catastrophic Three Mile Island. It will be the result of a deliberate, divine, personal judgment. John the Baptist predicted it with dreadful zeal: "I baptize you with water. But one more powerful than I will come, the thongs of whose sandals I am not worthy to untie. He will baptize you with the Holy Spirit and with fire. His winnowing fork is in his hand . . . he will burn up the chaff with unquenchable fire" (Luke 3:16-17). Jesus confirmed that this was his mission: "I have come to bring fire on the earth, and how I wish it were already kindled!" (Luke 12:49).

The fire is not reserved for the damned alone: "Everyone will be salted with fire," Jesus said (Mark 9:49). For fire is a purifying agent, as well as an agent of judgment and destruction. "Fire will test the quality of each man's work," Paul said, speaking of this judgment fire (1 Corinthians 3:13). It will touch everyone and fiercely destroy all that is made of "wood, hay, and straw."

But fire is not only an agent of judgment. It is also a description of God himself. The biblical descriptions of God inevitably make comparisons to the brilliance of fire or molten metal. The Old Testament visions are very like the New Testament descriptions of the glorified Jesus: "His eyes were like blazing fire. His feet were like bronze glowing in a furnace. . . . His face was like the sun shining in all its brilliance" (Revelation 1:14-16). Jesus shone like this on the Mount of Transfiguration: "The appearance of his face changed, and his clothes became as bright as a flash of lightning" (Luke 9:29). Hebrews 12:29 makes the image of fire fit not only God's appearance, but his activity: "Our God is a consuming fire." Jesus will be "revealed from heaven in blazing fire" (2 Thessalonians 1:7). He has always been, in his glory, too brilliant to look at and certainly too fiery to touch. His nature purifies, illumines, judges like fire.

If this is true, do we really want the healing touch of God? His hands must burn with the painful fire of pure love, a fierce and purifying love. In contact with such love we can imagine our impurities exploding into smoke and flame until, when the fire dies for lack of fuel, what is left glows like molten gold to match the glow of the one who touches us.

Flannery O'Connor's story "Revelation" tells of something like this. It starts out, as do most of her stories, with bizarre small-town Southern characters painted in her unmistakable neon. In a doctor's waiting room an assortment of people make restless chitchat. One is a woman named Mrs. Turpin, plump, self-satisfied, religious, sensible. Mrs. Turpin likes to talk. Her antagonist is a silent, plain, book-ish college girl who is overweight, extremely unpleasant in person-ality and clearly a trial to her mother. The girl grows so angry at Mrs. Turpin's inane, self-satisfied small talk that she throws her book and hits Mrs. Turpin in the eye. Then she leaps on Mrs. Turpin and tries to strangle her. She calls her a wart hog, a blow that seems to hurt Mrs. Turpin more than the book.

The girl is pulled off and sedated, and Mrs. Turpin is sent home. She stews on the insult all day. Something about the girl's malice will not dissipate. Mrs. Turpin has always looked on the bright side of life and been pleasant to everybody. Everybody thinks she is a nice lady. How can she be called a wart hog? But at the end of the day (and the end of the story) while hosing down her pigs, she stands staring at a long purple streak in the sunset and sees a vision. It is a revelation of her heavenly destiny, and it shows that the girl's judg-ment was not completely wrong.

> She saw the streak as a vast swinging bridge extending
> upward from the earth through a field of living fire. Upon it
> a vast horde of souls were rumbling toward heaven. There
> were whole companies of white-trash, clean for the first time
> in their lives, and bands of black niggers in white robes, and
> battalions of freaks and lunatics shouting and clapping and
> leaping like frogs. And bringing up the end of the procession
> was a tribe of people whom she recognized at once as those
> who, like herself and Claud, had always had a little of every-
> thing and the God-given wit to use it right. She leaned for-
> ward to observe them closer. They were marching behind the
> others with great dignity, accountable as they had always
> been for good order and common sense and respectable
> behavior. They alone were on key. Yet she could see by their
> shocked and altered faces that even their virtues were being
> burned away.

Nobody, least of all me, fully wants to be purified. I want the comforting, warm embrace of Jesus; I do not want to be burned. I suggest, however, that we cannot avoid it. And I suggest that it is nei-ther impersonal nor malicious. It is the touch of a God too bright and too fiery for our impure eyes to see or our impure bodies to touch. Yet I believe he will touch, for touch is part of love. And his love is a love that converts and heals its objects. His touch will hurt, but only for a time. Then we will glow with the brilliant fire of his divine love.

Perhaps it is so. Or perhaps this is only an image pointing toward something else. For all the good graces of his personality that God gives us here, we still see him through a glass darkly. To know him as he knows us, we must be transformed. Our sins must be burned away, and the good news is that they will be. They will burn but our lives will not. We will emerge from the fire free and full of praise, sure that the fire was a deeply loving embrace. Expectation of such an incredible destiny should make us worship God for all he is worth: "Since we are receiving a kingdom that cannot be shaken, let us be thankful, and so worship God acceptably with reverence and awe, for our 'God is a consuming fire'" (Hebrews 12:28-29).

12
STORIES

I know quite a lot about C. S. Lewis. I have read nearly all his books, three collections of his letters, and several books about him. I admire him both as a writer and a man, and sometimes he seems quite real to me. But if I started telling people that I knew him, rather than just about him, they would refer me to the psychiatric authorities. Knowing about a person is not the same as knowing him. Facts do not fully convey personality.

Applied to God, this distinction suggests that I can become expert in theology and biblical knowledge, yet not know God personally at all. We have probably all known people who seem to fit this description. Able to speak at great length and in great detail about the Bible or theology, they show no signs of the love, joy, and peace that come from personal contact with God.

We hunger to know God directly, not just to know the facts about him. In reality we need to know God this way. It is our salvation.

Conversely, however, knowing God does not allow us to dispense with knowing *about* God. Some Christian mystics have pointed, in highly metaphorical language, to a contemplation of God that leaves behind doctrine and Scripture, and bathes in his unmediated love. It is hard to pin down precisely what these mystics meant, for they did not write doctrinally, nor did they claim their words adequately described what they experienced. But the ordinary experience of knowing people makes me wary of pursuing their path.

Facts are essential to knowing any person. People who love each other may have moments when words and facts seem irrelevant and bothersome. Sometimes love does seem to soar above words, but it always returns. One moment I gaze lovingly at a friend's face, and the next moment we are talking about a movie we have both seen. The two ways of relating are not at odds with each other; they reinforce each other. If I were doing premarital counseling and I met a couple who loved each other so rapturously that they never felt the need to talk, I would suspect their "love" to be a flimsy infatuation. Love requires knowing *about*.

Since this is true, how do we go about "getting the facts"? I suggest that we do it primarily as storytellers.

When we think of our friends, we rarely hold in our minds a personality inventory or a résumé. What we have, I think, are stories that make up a larger story: snatches of narrative, anecdotes, conversations, and description. We see a picture of how our friend looked when we first met. We vividly remember a rained-out camping trip. We picture some late-night philosophical discussions at the Laundromat. Out of these and many other such fragments we patch a sort of movie documentary with our friend as the hero. From it we can fabricate lists of facts or analytical reports about the person. But that analysis is never the image we carry around in our heads. We do not know our friend through a list of propositions about him. We know him through the story of his life, especially as it has touched ours.

If I am right, this has something to say to theologians. Their characteristic approach to God, regardless of their theological point of view, is to make lists. Evangelical scholars in particular have insisted that God can be understood not merely "existentially" but in terms of propositions about his nature. I think they are right: I cannot imagine any person about whom propositions could not be made. My sister is humorous, earthy, conscientious, intelligent, and so on. God is omnipotent, omnipresent, omniscient, loving, pure, holy, and so on. But such propositions ought not to be elevated too high, for they are not the primary means for knowing persons. We know physical phenomena largely through such methods; we quantify gravity or the pressure of a gas. We cannot tell stories of these. But of people and of God we can.

I think it is no coincidence, but a direct reflection of this, that the

Bible is above all a storybook, a collection of stories by different authors writing in widely different styles that together tell a comprehensive and consistent story about God. Since God has chosen to communicate himself through stories, we ought to try to understand him through stories. It is not a brainless thing to understand and savor the full meaning of stories. Some of our greatest minds—the Shakespeares, Tolstoys, Faulkners—have given their lives to it.

BIBLE STORIES

My mother is a tireless storyteller. All my growing years I heard her tell true stories about the members of our family. Some stories extended back to long dead relatives, even to brothers who fought each other in the Civil War. But primarily her stories described people I knew. She told how my grandfather ran away from Scotland to the Wild West because God wanted him to be a minister; he thought (the story goes) that if he managed to escape university education God would have to leave him alone. (When he got to the West and became a ranch foreman, God still pursued him until he went to seminary and then to India as a missionary.) She told how my father's mother taught him manners by making him help her on and off the San Francisco cable cars. She told of her own arrival in America from India all alone at the age of sixteen, during the war, with $400 tucked in her brassiere to pay for college. (My father had stories of his own too: how my mother had "trapped" him by going out to buy a tight red sweater. My mother would adopt a shocked tone: "Chase! It wasn't a bit tight.") Looking back, I can see that some of these stories contained morals, but the morals were seldom articulated. For these were stories about people we knew and loved, and the principal reason for telling and retelling them was to explain and enjoy the personality central to the story.

I always felt that I knew all the facts of my family history—until I tried to use them as the basis of a novel. Then I found out how little, factually, I knew. What I had, really, were snatches—snatches repeated and elaborated so many times that they seemed more extensive than they really were. Oddly enough, realizing that I lacked many facts did not make me feel that I lacked knowledge of my family members. I still felt that I knew the essential stories of their lives and that while it would be extremely interesting to know more, additional facts would only reinforce what I knew.

I realize that not everyone has this secure feeling toward his or her family. I had, and have, a deep sense of my parents' reliability and trustworthiness. I believed, and believe, that there were no secrets kept from me that could be essential secrets; they would not reveal that my father was in fact an ogre or that our much-talked-about concern for our relatives would turn out to be, on adult examination, pious nonsense. I did not get all the family history, but I felt that through my mother's stories I got what really mattered. The stories helped me to know all about my family and ultimately to know myself as one who sprang from those roots.

My mother also told baby stories — stories about me and my siblings. These stories, to this day, form a mirror for me of my own personality, so much so that I wonder whether they captured the essence of my personality even while I was a baby or whether by hearing the stories frequently repeated, I came to think of myself as the child of those stories. For instance, my mother always told of how cheerful a child I was. She would take me to a neighbor's house and leave me, and I would sit in the neighbor's high chair perfectly content as long as a constant supply of iced cookies was kept in front of me. I still see myself as that child: chubby, agreeable, good-natured, practical. Was I really always fated to be that? Or have the stories made me think of myself that way? I suspect it is a little of both. Parents ought to pay careful attention to the stories they tell on their children.

My mother is not unusual in her role of storyteller. Most families develop snatches of story that they repeat over and over. And as people grow up, they develop a small library of such stories about themselves. As a child I used to love to think over the story of my life as a sort of *Boy's Life* drama: I saw myself, as a natural consequence of the sort of boy I was, rescuing Suzanne, the blond girl every boy in my school was in love with. I saw myself defeating Monty in the annual track meet. (I would never have told anyone else these stories — they were too personal.) I still think of myself, though less dramatically, as the protagonist of a story — a story that extends through my boyhood, into college, through my first job, into marriage, and, like an old fashioned Saturday-matinee serial, "to be continued" into my future. Sometimes it is still a heroic Boy Scout story. Other times it is a modern dreary existential novel. In either form, I tell parts of my story when people want to know all about me, and I expect the same from others. When I say to a new acquaintance, "Tell me about yourself," I expect not statistics or a résumé, but a story about where he grew up, the kind of family he had, what he has done, and what forces or choices have brought him to the present.

We do not mistake these stories for objective history. While they are true, they are also impressionistic. They are factual, yet not a recitation of facts. They are *stories*. And stories, as any beginning fiction writer can tell you, depend on presenting the right detail, not all the details. Stories leave a great deal out. They try to present character and setting and a sense of movement.

The Bible is most certainly a book of stories, and a story. The story ranges from the Days of Creation to the Day of Judgment, a sprawling epic of God and man. The individual stories, of Adam and Eve, of Cain and Abel, of Abraham and Isaac, of Moses and Pharaoh, of Ruth and Naomi, of David and Solomon, of Isaiah and the Suffering Servant, of Hosea and Gomer, of Jesus and Pilate — these stories, and many, many more, form some of the most vivid narratives ever written. Even more remarkably, these stories are not a mere collection; together they tell a single comprehensible story, so that each of the stories, while it stands by itself, echoes and is echoed throughout the whole vast structure. With what literature can we compare this verbal cathedral?

James Michener's novels, I think, are structured something like the Bible; they typically follow families through big swatches of history. Or to make a loftier comparison, William Faulkner's chronicle of Yoknapatawpha County offers the multiform, jumbled consistency that the Bible does. But as soon as you make these comparisons you see how puny any purely human literature stands in comparison with the Bible. There may be poetry more glorious than the Psalms (though not much), and there may be better narrative than Ruth, and perhaps you can find a piece of writing that captures the horrifying perversity of life better than the crucifixion scene in Luke's gospel. But we do not have another document that combines these — and census reports and legal charters and personal correspondence and much, much more — and yet never loses the thread of a single story. Nothing in literature is nearly so grand as the story of the Bible.

STORIES WITHIN A STORY

While people who study the Bible acknowledge that it is a storybook, many do not enjoy it as that. Ours is a factual and analytical age, and that is how most people read the Bible. They read the stories and historical detail as a code to break. What they seek are lists: lists of God's attributes, lists of his gifts, lists of his expectations. "The Bible as Literature" is to many evangelicals a dubious approach, perhaps because nonbelievers sometimes use it to keep from having to take the book seriously. "The Bible as Literature" means to the secularist "The Bible as Tall Tale." Unfortunately, Christians do not approach the Bible as literature much differently. Our first question in Bible study is "What does this story teach us about . . . ?" We seek to analyze it, not appreciate it. A "serious discussion," theological or otherwise, is for us one in which all the stories have been squeezed out: no anecdotes, no humorous or ironic asides, no personalities, no drama, no poetry.

But is that a serious way to talk about God? The Bible suggests that stories are the most important way to talk about God. The Bible tells the story of a religion that elevates storytelling to a sacred position.

In the Old Testament the exodus from Egypt became a central story for expressing faith. The Jews told it again and again, so that it was not merely dead history to them, but a current that still flowed, a current on which they rode and rejoiced. Several psalms, for instance, rehearse this theme from the history of Israel.

Israel put up a memorial stone near the Jordan River to provoke questions that would lead to storytelling (Joshua 4:20-24). They celebrated the Passover for the precise purpose of recalling and reliving their rescue from Egypt (Exodus 13:8-10). When the Jews spoke of themselves as "sons of Abraham," the term summoned up stories of faith and sin: of Abraham with his knife to his only son's throat, of Abraham lying to the powerful Egyptians about his wife Sarai. The Jews were children of these stories. They were living another chapter in the story that Genesis began.

Jesus' storytelling is also famous. He did nearly all his teaching in parables. To talk about justice, he told the story of a particular unjust judge; to talk about obedience, he used the story of a particular servant. When the Gospels comment on his use of parables, they refer back to the tradition of historical storytelling. Matthew 13, reporting that he taught entirely through stories, cites it as fulfillment of Psalm 78: "I will open my mouth in parables, I will utter hidden things, things from of old" (verse 2). That psalm goes on to tell the familiar historical story of the exodus. That was more than history; it was a parable, a proverb (the two words are the same in Hebrew) to be pondered and savored. Thus, Jesus' parables were seen as part of the traditional storytelling of Israel.

Jesus' parables, of course, are stories within a story. The Gospels are among the most memorable stories ever told. They are not mere biographies, for they leave out many facts. But these missing facts do not leave us in the dark. The stories of the Gospels reveal the character of Jesus. We believe that more facts, were they available, would merely reinforce our knowledge of his personality.

The New Testament epistles are more theological and analytical than the rest of the Bible, but the fact that they are letters, not philosophical treatises, reminds us that storytelling is never far away. Real characters wrote these letters—personalities whose relationships show through in every chapter. Just as you can read theology behind the stories Jesus told, so you can read stories behind the theology Paul wrote.

Living in Africa helped me learn the importance of storytelling. The indigenous church in Africa is growing at a tremendous pace through Africans spreading the Word to Africans. The Old Testament has greatly facilitated this. When translating the Scriptures into Luo and Kamba and the hundreds of other languages, missionaries gave priority to the New Testament. Probably some translators had difficulty seeing the urgency of translating Leviticus, for example. But when the Old Testament finally began to appear in the various languages, it nearly always provoked deep excitement among the people it reached.

No doubt this was partly because African culture is similar in many respects to biblical culture; the Africans could identify with the settings of Old Testament stories. Still, there is a tremendous difference between Palestine in 2,500 B.C. and Uganda today. Why did Africans find the Old Testament so exciting despite these differences? Because, I believe, the gospel as a story going back to the foundations of the world made perfect sense to them. It made sense because the God of the Bible is a personal and intimate God, and so they—

especially those without the benefit of classes in philosophy and science—knew that to know him they had to know his story.

Can we relearn this in our scientific age? I think we can. After all, everyone loves a story. Movies are stories; television shows are stories; best-selling novels are stories; even news events are stories. We simply need to realize that this kind of enjoyment is not a trivial way to pursue the knowledge of God; stories are not to be left behind in our children's Bible storybooks. To enjoy the Bible as an epic is to enjoy it *as it was written*, and this takes full adult intelligence.

My theme, though, is not literature appreciation, but the appreciation of God through a personal relationship. Just as families tell stories of those they love, just as we trade personal stories when we first meet, just as we identify ourselves as the hero of the story of our own lives, God tells personal, intimate stories on himself.

To hear such stories is a privilege given in a personal relationship. Good friends know the stories of each other's lives in a way that mere business associates do not. When someone tells us all about his past, his family background, his disappointments, his marriage, his choice of career, his plans for the future, it means that he wants to get personal with us. And God, the God who made us, has made that gesture of friendship. He has told us all about himself.

But that is not all. A really lively story reaches out of the book and involves you in its world. You begin to think you are Sherlock Holmes or James Bond. Animated cartoons carry this power even further: someone may jump out of a television set and drag a "real" character into the cartoon with him. The border between reality and story may even get uncomfortably confused at times. Some of this is inevitably part of the Bible's story too. The characters—particularly God's character—will not stay tucked in the pages. We would like simply to watch them and hear them speak to each other, but they will not let us do that. Suddenly they are speaking to us and beckoning us to join them in the story.

God's voice speaks out of his story. He even asks us to speak back to him and promises to answer if we do. At the moment we are reading his Word, he is a character outside our door, knocking to come in.

There is no other story like his story, through which, in truth, the chief character comes alive.

13

PRAISE

W alter Trobisch writes poignantly of a girl whose self-hatred had brought her near to suicide:

She was a beautiful Scandinavian girl. Long blond hair fell over her shoulders. Gracefully she sat down in the armchair offered her and looked at us with deep and vivid blue eyes. . . .

As we discussed her problem, we came back again and again to one basic issue which seemed to be the root of all the others. It was the problem which we had least expected when she entered the room: She could not love herself. . . .

To point out to her the apparent gifts she had—her success as a student, the favorable impression she had made upon us by her outward appearance—seemed to be of no avail. She refused to acknowledge anything good about herself. . . . She had grown up in a tight-laced religious family and had learned that self-depreciation was Christian and self-rejection the only way to find acceptance by God.

We asked her to stand up and take a look in the mirror. She turned her head away. With gentle force I held her head so that she had to look into her own eyes. She cringed as if she was experiencing physical pain.

It took a long time before she was able to whisper, though unconvinced, the sentence I asked her to repeat, "I am a beautiful girl."

We tend to think of praise primarily as a religious activity, so its importance in personal relationships doesn't come quickly to mind. But lack of praise is a very real barrier to good personal relations. This becomes evident when we think of those who have bad relations with themselves, who are afflicted with a negative self-image. To help someone like this, like the girl who rejected herself, we need to offer more than encouragement. Trobisch tried pointing out the girl's good points. He could even have taken a poll to prove to her that most people believed her beautiful. But she would have rejected that too. No doubt many people had told her she was beautiful and capable. She needed more than information about herself; she needed to respond correctly to the information, and thus to herself. Trobisch's therapy was to try to break into her inner self-cursing with a positive, truthful word—not a word from him, but a word from herself to herself. If she could learn to praise herself, it would be her first step toward relating to herself normally and healthfully. She would begin to know herself for who she really was. Trobisch's therapy was not self-flattery, nor the power of positively thinking dubious propositions. He only wanted her to acknowledge the truth and say it out loud in a word of praise. That is a fair definition of praise: telling the truth out loud.

The girl's feelings were extreme, of course. For most people, self-doubts and bad days merely punctuate an overwhelming current of self-regard. Self-love is so ordinary that Jesus used it as a reference point: "Love your neighbor as you love yourself." When I was in elementary school, the teacher sometimes solved the first problem on a sheet of homework to show us how the others were solved. Jesus used our love for ourselves in the same way. "Notice how you love yourself," he said, "and love your neighbor in the same way."

We naturally, unthinkingly, care for ourselves. We wash and groom ourselves every day without fail. *Our* problems invariably make us feel low, not other people's. Most of us translate this self-regard into a constant stream of compliments; we notice when we do things right. In playing softball I may be unsure how many hits someone else made, but I am sure to know how many *I* made. And I do not forget to compliment myself on the achievement.

Proof that you love yourself is simple: In a group photo, whose face do you find first? If you think it is a bad photo of yourself, can you still call the photo a beauty? My belief is that virtually everyone—even the Scandinavian girl—looks first to find himself or herself and judges the photo mainly by that. If by chance we like our picture, it makes our day.

Walter Trobisch's beautiful Scandinavian did not lack self-concern. She was, in fact, so preoccupied with self that she was trapped. She could not relate well to others because she was mired in confused and contradicting thoughts about herself. She cared for herself but had twisted that concern through a false piety into expressions of self-hatred. If she could begin to praise herself, she would return to a natural God-given mode: giving gladness and thanks for what we are, and moving from there to caring for the needs of others.

Praise for yourself is so common that a psychologically healthy person is probably not even aware that he does it. Self-praise is the very natural and constant reference, conscious and unconscious, of everything to our own value, or "worth-ship." I know what is good in myself, and I "say it out loud" not merely in words to myself and others, but in my posture, in my dress, in my body language.

So should be our praise to God. We should be always looking to see him in the picture. If a constant, loving current of regard toward God pervades our lives, it will open the way to a warm, responsive relationship. To "know God," just as to "know ourselves," depends on this fundamental attitude of praise.

POWER TO CHANGE LIVES

When I turn from praising myself to praising others, however, I find a great difference. Praise for other people does not come naturally. We do not automatically praise each other any more than we naturally love each other. We have to be taught.

Most of us know perfectly well how to praise ourselves; even if self-cursing has smothered it, the potential for self-praise is already there. We do not really learn it so much as relearn it, like riding a bicycle after many years without one.

Yet many people really have no idea how to praise others. Even those they love deeply never feel their warm, joyful regard. If we urge such people to begin to praise others, they find it irritatingly awkward and unnatural to do so. They have to learn from scratch. I know I did.

When I think of praise, my mother comes quickly to mind. She had a dogged persistence in it. I wish I had an ounce of gold for every time she told me—me, the slump-shouldered, scowling, pimpled teenager—"You look so nice when you smile." Of course she disciplined and corrected me and my siblings, but her admiring comments far outweighed her rebukes. She thought we were wonderful; I never doubted that. Because she loved us, she praised us.

My father's praise was not so verbal, but his attitude convinced me that he was proud of me and would be intensely proud of me whatever I did. At my high school graduation I gave a valedictory speech that began, "The students at Bullard High School live under the iron hand of oppression." It was somewhat radical for its time, and afterward no other adults knew quite what to say to me. But my father said, as soon as he saw me, "You have an excellent grasp of the English language." He meant it. He was always proud of his kids.

While my parents' praise contributed to a healthy and secure relationship between us, it was one-sided. Though I loved them, it was an unconscious love. I was not aware of them and their feelings. It never occurred to me to praise them as they praised me. I was not, anyway, a very warm adolescent. I had deep feelings for people but did not know how to voice them. It was not until my late twenties that I began to learn the power of praise between people and thus began to praise my parents. Only then did our relationship become mutually free. Only then did I see into my parents' personalities. There has been, in my experience, a clear relationship between praising people and knowing them.

I learned about praise from the woman who became my wife and from a circle of friends whom she had influenced. They blew the cover off my guarded words with their free praise. When they saw something they liked in someone, they just said it. They showed it too by telling other people about it, by hugging you or smiling at you. They were so free with their appreciation that some people didn't know how to take it. But everyone who came into the light of their circle was warmed.

I could almost see stiffness and cynicism falling off others as they fumbled, delightedly, to gruffly acknowledge some florid, though sincere, compliment. It occurred to me after some time that praise was more than simply a social grace—it was a power to change lives.

I saw the warmth changing and shaping people, and I felt it shaping me.

I felt it opening up doors that had long ago stuck shut. They creaked and balked at opening, then let blue sky and warm fresh air into long-darkened rooms. And almost without my realizing it, a response was awakened: I began to praise back—not only Popie and her circle, but others whom I had known for years. One friend told me he was quite startled at the affirmations, hugs, and pats coming from me.

Even the smallest amount of praise, if it is truthful and sincere, builds to greater praise. It reverberates within the relationship.

It is the same in our relationship with God. It may seem odd to talk about praise as a means of knowing God, for praise depends on what we already know about him. We "tell of his excellent greatness" when we praise, mirroring his glory back to him. We cannot tell of what we do not know.

Knowing someone, however, goes beyond gathering information. In the Bible, "to know" often carries the sense of being in warm, responsive relationship. In fact, "knowing" is used as a term for sexual intercourse. A more mundane sense may be found in Proverbs 12:10: "A righteous man cares for [literally, *knows*] the needs of his animal." Here, "to know" means to respond with proper care. Similarly, to know God (or any person) is to respond properly to him. That requires praise.

Praise is more than words. For example, Psalm 150 suggests that we praise God with a crashing cymbal. We cannot pray with a cymbal. Praise finds its optimal expression in song. Revelation pictures all of creation circling God's throne and *singing* his praise. Singing involves the body, mind, and emotions; it fuses them together. We put our breath into it; we shape our mouth to the lyrics, the tune, and the rhythm. Good singing—good praise—involves all of us, body, mind, and spirit.

VULNERABLE PRAISE

Praise of God is fundamental to my relationship with him. It opens a channel of loving regard. When I bring my requests to God, I stand by him looking toward mutual concerns, but when I praise him my eyes are lifted in intimacy and warmth toward him. I look to his face.

But I find it difficult to express myself to God, even in private, this way. I fear looking silly—even to myself. Like a boy told to kiss his aunt, I become suddenly shy and uncomfortable. Praise makes me vulnerable. When I praise, I take off the mask of the hardened critic and expose myself as an ardent fan and lover.

David knew about those fears. His wife Michal sneered at his reckless dancing in worship: "How the king of Israel has distinguished himself today, disrobing in the sight of the slave girls of his servants as any vulgar fellow would!" He answered her as well as it is possible to do: "It was before the LORD, who chose me. . . . I will celebrate before the LORD. I will become even more undignified than this, and I will be humiliated in my own eyes" (2 Samuel 6:20-22). He was quite prepared to be humiliated, on one condition: that he did it before the Lord.

We get no credit for acting like a fool; the art of praise is not to out-emote others, to raise our hands higher, to dance with more reckless abandon, to roll our eyes or clap our hands. The art is to get our eyes off ourselves and onto God so that we do not know or care how we look. This makes us vulnerable in a way that making a religious spectacle of ourselves cannot. We can be extremely aware of our performance in trying to praise. We can be, in effect, praising God for the sake of our neighbor, to make an impression on him. David did not do that. He did not argue with Michal over whether his dance was appropriate. He simply answered, "It was before the LORD." If we learn to focus on him, we can respond to God—without shyness, and without showing off.

What we know of God, what he has done for us, his character, his love, everything contained in the phrase "hallowed be thy name"—these are the basis for praise. We focus on these and begin to respond to them by acknowledging them aloud. And as we respond, our vision of God grows clearer.

I may find this easier to do under certain circumstances. A beautiful and familiar worship service may help me put aside other thoughts and concentrate on God's beauty. My posture—kneeling or closing my eyes or opening them to look at a cross or raising my hands—may help me. A piece of music, especially a well-loved familiar one, may help. We may legitimately experiment with worship to see what helps us best. What helps one person will not help another. But whenever the means draw attention to themselves or even to the experience they engender, however warm, praise has not reached its goal. Ultimately we must not only say or sing certain "praise" words or adopt a certain "praise" posture or feel certain "praise" feelings; we must focus on God and do it before him.

Why? Because the goal of praise is not an experience; it is a relationship. The best aids to worship are those that because of their simplicity or familiarity become clear as glass. We do not see them at all; we see through them to the Lord.

PRAISE THE LORD!

"Flattery will get you nowhere," can be truly said in regard to our relationship with the Father. Flattery is false praise.

Flatterers begin their career, I believe, with a correct observation: It is a good thing to praise people. But they continue it for the wrong reasons. They notice that praise makes people feel good, that it warms their relationships. *You can't have too much of a good thing*, they figure, and do it without thinking at all. They gush compliments.

At first, flatterers impress us with their remarkable discernment. But soon we realize that they don't mean a thing they say. They would adore our clothes if we wore a sack. Flatterers think they are very nice people, but they really, with their false currency, drive out genuine praise and thus weaken relationships. In a society of flatterers, we cannot tell what people actually think, and fairly often, I suspect, flatterers do not themselves know what they really think. They just prattle.

Some people praise God the same way. They praise him for the good feelings it gives them; they praise him because they think it makes everyone else feel good; they praise him because they think that is simply what every good Christian should do. They do not focus their minds on God. The result is that their false praise drives out the true. Praise becomes mere pleasant-feeling babble.

Of course, we can hardly say nice things about God that are not true. In a sense, whatever praise we give him is necessarily realistic, for God is all good things and true. But we can give hollow praise— thoughtless and insincere. Some Christian groups encourage us to praise God on automatic pilot, as though by the sheer number of our cries or the sincerity of our tone or the size of the emotional cloud that covers our brain, we will be heard. Inevitably such thoughtless praise leads to confusion and insincerity in our relationship to God. I have seen it too many times: young Christians who are overwhelmed by the joy of such praise until one day they wake up and realize they have become phony. Praise has become a purely human religious ritual, lifting the emotions but having nothing really to do with God at all.

For praise to lead to greater knowledge of God, it must involve the mind as well as the body and spirit. He is, after all, no fool. He knows very well the difference between saying, "Lord, Lord," and meaning it.

I don't mean that every bit of praise should be scrutinized for its theological content. Nor do I mean that we should become cautious about praising God, examining our motives constantly to see that we are sincere. I just mean that we need to speak directly to God, not to ourselves or our neighbors. As we look at him, we will naturally praise him for real qualities we see. Our awkwardness will fade into the background as our attention is less and less on ourselves and more and more on him.

But how can we learn to focus? We feel awkward, and that makes us think of ourselves no matter how we praise. How can we get over our awkwardness so that praise is a natural habit? I think the answer lies in our human relationships. Just as we learn to praise in them, so we learn to praise in relationship to God.

As in human relationships, praise must be made a daily, not a sporadic, event. Praise between friends is rarely an orgy of emotion. Sometimes it does become quite emotional, but usually only when that intense emotion is built on a foundation of calm, daily praise. I do not necessarily stop everything else to praise my wife. I do it constantly as I talk to her. She is a reference point for whatever I do and say, and I let her know that: "Would you like me to go to the store?" "What do you think of our new neighbors?" "I'd like to get to know the Brewsters, but what do you think?" And the motivation for this constant reference is also clearly stated: "I love you," "I admire you," "You handled that situation beautifully," "What you said made perfect sense." This goes on all the time, consciously and unconsciously, verbally and nonverbally, though sometimes it does concentrate in a single time of sheer praise.

I heard an old man, who seemed to overflow with joy and thanksgiving, say that his life had taken a turn when he committed himself to witness every day. By "witness" he did not mean an evangelistic appeal; he meant praising the Lord, "telling of his excellent greatness." He would not let a day go by without telling *someone*—Christian or nonChristian—of God's goodness. Such daily praise opens up a deeper perception of God, and thus leads to more praise. For praise leads to praise. It may feel awkward at first, but you get the hang of it.

We learn best, I believe, in the company of others. Many (like me) who find it awkward to praise God publicly, find great freedom in congregational singing. There, individual contribution is entirely submerged. We make an effort to blend with other voices and to sing together as a single voice. We want to sing as well as we can, but not to draw attention to ourselves. We want to draw attention—especially our own—to the beauty of the song and thus to its object, our Father. Perhaps this is why biblical worship, from the Psalms clear through Paul's "psalms and hymns and spiritual songs," is very musical. Choral singing is one activity in which many people can overcome their stiffness and lose themselves in praise.

But music is not by any means the only way we learn to praise from a group experience. A church worship service is a planned experiment in group praise, in which individuals learn how to praise by being part of a group that does it naturally and harmoniously. The experiment need not stop when we leave the church. I learned how to praise other people by being part of Popie's circle. They infected me with their spontaneous environment of praise. The people of God, wherever I meet them, ought to infect me with that same kind of environment, with praise directed not merely toward each other but toward God.

We often miss this crucial link. As a group we praise in church—at least we sing hymns and recite words meant to express praise. As individuals we praise in private. But in between those two experiences we are often too shy to say anything in praise of God, whether at work, in the hardware store, at the movie, or over dinner. Our praise clusters in church and in personal devotions; it does not spread throughout our lives. Thus, not surprisingly, our sense of Jesus' presence tends to be restricted to church and devotions, rather than spreading through all of our life.

I am not suggesting that we become people who spout "Praise the Lord" at every opportunity. Such praise may be, like flattery, thoughtless or contrived—not really praise at all, just religious words meant to reassure ourselves. Rather, I wish we could form covenants together, whether as friends or members of churches and Bible studies, to learn to praise God thoughtfully at every opportunity. Such praise would be highly varied, as we are varied people. It need not, I think, be contrived or embarrassing to others. Most importantly, this continuance of praise could help make our lives into one whole piece: instruments of praise saying aloud what is surely the Truth above all truths. Great is the Lord, and greatly to be praised.

In heaven we will praise God "face to face." The current of song will pour straight from us to him. But we need not wait until then. We can start the singing early. As we do, I believe we will also anticipate, in small measure, that "face to face" knowledge of his glory. Something straightens out in our relationships when we begin to sing others' praises: we see and hear their goodness more clearly. Praise opens our eyes and ears; it alerts us to each other. Knowledge is converted from a static body of information to a dynamic interchange.

We will do well to obey the psalmist's summons: "Let all breath praise the Lord." That means not only, "Let all who live and breathe praise the Lord," but also, "Let every last ounce of air go into it: Praise the Lord!"

14

FORGIVENESS AND SACRIFICE

~←~

According to common sense, a bird in the hand is worth two in the bush. Every single day, despite tantrums and tears and by manipulated rewards ("If you pick up your toys now I'll read you a story!"), my wife and I work strenuously to convince our small children to ignore this rule of common sense. We are trying to teach them to do just the opposite, which makes no sense to them: to sacrifice pleasure now to get more pleasure later.

Being creatures of common sense, they cannot see the point in quitting play now and going to bed (which they do not enjoy) so they can enjoy play more, fully rested, tomorrow. They cannot see the point in eating vegetables now when they know there is ice cream (which they much prefer) in the freezer. Our children are naturally suspicious of grand promises about the future, and we must work hard to allay their suspicions.

If we succeed, they will become like us—people who make such sacrifices reflexively. To put off pleasure, we do intricate mental surgery. We cut ourselves up into separate personalities, one receiving carefully calculated benefits at the other's expense. We eat dessert at the end of the meal, saving the best for last. The "me" at the beginning of the meal gives up dessert so the "me" at the end of the meal can enjoy it. Similarly, we study to pass an exam tomorrow. We work out to get in shape, expecting to enjoy a trimmer waistline at some future date. We drag ourselves out of bed to go to work, expecting to be rewarded by a paycheck. What makes us do these tiresome, thankless tasks? Why does anyone get out of bed in the morning when it is so much more pleasant to lie drowsily under the warm covers? The force that gets me out of bed is hope. Today's "me" sacrifices for tomorrow's. Mature human beings know how to do this almost as second nature. We didn't get it from nature, though. Our parents and teachers drilled it into us just as we must drill it into our children.

We use grand language to talk about this—altruistic, almost religious language. We "give up" smoking, "sacrifice" desserts, even though we do all these grand deeds for ourselves.

This quality of sacrifice—deferred gratification is its more ugly name—is the basis for civilization. Nobody would build anything, plant anything, learn anything if they did not live by sacrifice. A society built on instant pleasure would soon be back in the caves. That is why we lavish such admiration on those who demonstrate "disciplined" lives. What they do is not altruistic; they do it for their own benefit. Yet they are perhaps the closest to saints our secularized society has: "heroic" dieters, "spirited" or even "driven" workers, "uncompromising" coaches. Even if we have no wish to imitate them (few people wish to be saints of any kind), we admire their qualities, for we know we need their willingness to sacrifice for the future, and we usually wish we—and our children—had more of it.

There is another reason, though, why we so insistently teach sacrifice to our children, and it is not the future of civilization. It is because we care about their happiness. Even if they stood to inherit millions and would never need to work, we would want our children to learn to sacrifice because self-sacrifice is fundamental to knowing and being in a healthy relationship to ourselves.

Demoralized people cannot sacrifice—cannot diet, cannot study, cannot exercise. They become alienated from themselves, even self-disgusted. They have tried to change, they say, but they lack whatever it takes. Consequently, they enter a cycle of self-loathing, with failure reinforcing failure. In such a state they cannot "know" themselves. The ability to sacrifice implies the presence of self-forgiveness. Perhaps we have dieted unsuccessfully in the past. But we lovingly forgive ourselves for that when we forego a second helping. We believe in ourselves through the eyes of faith; we will diet today and be thin tomorrow.

Sometimes, it is true, people diet to the point of death or study to the point of mental and physical exhaustion. I knew a girl in college who felt so desperately insecure about her academic capabilities that she studied day and night. By her fanatical devotion to study, she made herself miserable and practically incapable of relationships with other people. This may look like sacrifice but it is not. Sacrifice is *for* something good, something that outweighs the pain. It is hopeful of the future, not fearful. It makes us stronger, not weaker. It maintains a natural balance because it weighs the present sacrifice against real expected benefits. When we are motivated by fear, we cannot maintain a balance; there is no limit to the possible terrors our minds can conceive.

"Sacrifice" sounds extraordinary, and of course it may be. But it is not always a grand, fateful gesture; it is also ordinary, daily behavior, hopeful in its outlook. It is the natural path for faith, hope, and love toward ourselves. Without it we could hardly live. Certainly we could not live as healthy, mature people on good terms with ourselves.

NATURAL SACRIFICE

The term "sacrifice," however, usually refers to what one person gives up for another—not what we give up for ourselves. When we turn to inter-personal sacrifice, the subject at first seems very different. A mother may deliberately die to save her child, or a pilot may stay with his damaged plane to keep it from crashing into a housing development. These sacrifices make headlines. This is grand, "real sacrifice."

But for every one of these, hundreds of sacrifices go hardly noticed. A mother sacrifices twenty times each day for her small children—sometimes she virtually sacrifices her sanity—but no one thinks she is extraordinary for doing it. People talk about a mother who will *not* sacrifice for her children—a mother who neglects them because they interfere with her pleasure.

Sacrifice is normal when people deeply love each other. Extraordinary sacrifices usually come when someone extends love toward people he does not know—toward a drowning stranger, for instance. It is extraordinary to extend love to a stranger.

But where love is natural, so is sacrifice. Lovers even look for opportunities to sacrifice. Sometimes this is overdramatized: "I'd climb the highest mountains for you or swim the wildest sea," the infatuated lover is supposed to say. Silly as it may be, this hyperbole reflects an impulse that lovers really feel. They sense correctly that sacrifice can bind them together, for it is the most tangible proof we have of human solidarity. One person gives up and the other gains, but there is a conservation of blessings; we do not lose by sacrificing, because what is good for the person we love is also good for us. In a sense it is just as "selfish" as sacrificing for ourselves. If we love people deeply enough, their benefits are ours.

These benefits extend far beyond externals. O. Henry's famous story "The Gift of the Magi" tells of a poor couple who sacrifice everything for each other and end up losing the external things they love most. But they gain something better — a deeper love.

She has long beautiful hair. He has his pocket watch. With Christmas coming, and no money, they both desperately want to give something to each other for Christmas. To afford gifts, they each make secret sacrifices. He sells his watch to buy combs for her hair; she sells her hair to a wigmaker to buy him a watch fob. When they present their gifts to each other, they discover that they have sacrificed in vain.

But have they? The story ends this way: "Here I have lamely related to you the uneventful chronicle of two foolish children in a flat who most unwisely sacrificed for each other the greatest treasures of their house. But in a last word to the wise of these days let it be said that of all who give gifts these two were the wisest. Of all who give and receive gifts, such as they are wisest. Everywhere they are wisest. They are the magi."

Wise, when they lost their two most treasured possessions? O. Henry means that they lost things but gained each other. Even though the plans went astray and the sacrifices proved to be a bad bargain, the most fundamental joy — the relationship itself — grew stronger and was more enviable than any watch or any hair. Sacrifice may be based on a hopeful calculation of costs and benefits. Yet it provides a greater benefit merely by speaking the depth of its love.

The more deeply we are bound to a person, the less likely we are to think of sacrifice as a sacrifice. Sacrifice for a loved one is no more melodramatic than putting off dessert to the end of the meal. It is just natural to give up one thing to get another. I remember a conversation with an African in which we talked about the difference between our ideas on extended family. He grasped as a novel idea that if my brother were unemployed he would not necessarily feel free to move his family in with mine. The idea practically knocked the wind out of him. I remember still his sad, bewildered face as he shook his head in disbelief: "But if your brother could not afford a nice house, and you could, why . . . ?" The sacrifice he might make by sharing space with his brother's family did not strike him; it was the lack of such a sacrifice that seemed unbelievable.

Like many people, I wish Western society were less fragmented, had closer bonds of extended family. Such a wish, I realized then, cannot be divorced from the sacrifices involved. Any increasing bond involves giving something up.

SELF-SACRIFICE

Sacrifices large and small are the natural, daily material of close relationships; they show that the people involved see each other's benefit as their own. It is not surprising, then, that Christianity is rooted in sacrifice—primarily Jesus' sacrifice for us but also our sacrifice for him. Like all bonds of love, our relationship to God involves sacrifice. I find some obstacles, however, to making the connection.

Since childhood I have known and believed that I can have a relationship with God only because of and through Jesus' sacrifice of himself on the cross. I have heard innumerable preachers say that Jesus has given his life for me and that, in fact, he loves me so much he would have died to save me even if I had been the only human on the earth. Yet this sacrifice has often seemed to me, for all its importance and all its love, a distant and oddly impersonal fact.

For one thing, loving sacrifice is normally reciprocal. One person sacrifices for another; the other sacrifices in return. They don't keep track. But they do presume a kind of equality. If, for instance, only one of O. Henry's lovers had sacrificed for the other—if the woman had given her hair, but the man had thought of giving his watch and decided against it—we would not find their love so unusual.

Sometimes one lover would like to sacrifice but cannot. A woman may suffer a stroke, for example, and be paralyzed so that her husband must care for her. People rarely find this dependency easy. They would more readily be bonded together if they were co-victims, sharing a hospital room.

But with God we are thrust permanently into the dependent position. He has no needs; what can we give to him?

I grant that sometimes we seem to sacrifice for him. We give up things that we love because we love Jesus more. And Jesus asks us to do this: "If anyone comes to me and does not hate his father and mother, his wife and children, his brothers and sisters — yes, even his own life — he cannot be my disciple. And anyone who does not carry his cross and follow me cannot be my disciple" (Luke 14:26-27). But the sacrifice is apparently for our benefit, not his. Jesus quite frankly promised his disciples — and his frankness has appalled many idealists — good return on their investment. "'I tell you the truth,' Jesus said to them, 'no one who has left home or wife or brothers or parents or children for the sake of the kingdom of God will fail to receive many times as much in this age and, in the age to come, eternal life'" (Luke 18:29-30). His parables of the treasure in the field and the pearl of great price make the same point in a more general way: The kingdom of God is so rich and so beautiful that anyone who finds it will gladly give up everything he owns to get it — and the trade will be a bargain. Our sacrifice for Christ is *self*-sacrifice. It is for our good.

Paul described his own life in these terms: "Whatever was to my profit I now consider loss for the sake of Christ. What is more, I consider everything a loss compared to the surpassing greatness of knowing Christ Jesus my Lord, for whose sake I have lost all things. I consider them rubbish, that I may gain Christ and be found in him" (Philippians 3:7-9). Though he had apparently traded a secure, admired position for the leadership of an outlawed splinter group, Paul considered the exchange a steal.

Whenever you hear people making a great deal of their sacrifices for Christ, you may suspect that they do not yet grasp their position in Jesus. Our sacrifices do not ever make God our debtor even to the slightest degree.

We hate this dependency. It is nice to be saved — once. When we face our lostness and are saved from it, we burst into song: "Amazing grace, how sweet the sound, That saved a wretch like me." But it is not easy to live as a dependent daily. We don't like to be pulled from the water, gasping and choking, day after day after day. That is why legalism — an attempt to save yourself by some kind of religious activity—surfaces repeatedly in different forms. People try to deny that they are dependent, to block out the helplessness of their position.

How can we make this one-sided dependence a real source of intimacy, rather than an irritant? I think we may learn something about it by examining a dependent relationship in which we all live at some point: that of a child to his or her parents.

Now that I have small children of my own, I am beginning to realize the magnitude of my parents' sacrifice for me. They poured out their lives, with no reward except seeing me grow. They had seemingly unlimited faith, hope, and love; they could forgive anything. They derived their pleasure from my pleasure because I was their child.

But note: This one-sided grace does not create, of itself, a fully intimate relationship. It does not make the child a friend to his parents. He remains self-centered.

We do not expect small children to appreciate what we do for them. We only hope that someday they will appreciate what we have done and, more importantly, that they will appreciate *us*. We sacrifice for our children not hoping that they will pay us back with sacrifices of their own, but hoping that they will love us.

When children are grown, their parents' sacrifices are either fulfilled in an adult intimacy or disappointed by a lack of it. Many grown children continue to be indifferent to what their parents did, and a melancholy aridity, a disappointed silence sets in.

Other children do become aware and begin to say thank you. They begin to do small favors for their parents, not to repay them for their sacrifices—for they cannot—but merely to please them. Parents find their most wonderful reward in children who want to see them and talk to them. Any sacrifice that leads to such love is worth it all. But the sacrifice itself could not achieve the relationship. Somehow the children must themselves come to the point of being grateful. They must love their parents as they have been loved, and therefore know their parents as they are already known.

We are in such a position with Jesus. Like a parent, he sacrificed his life for us. We cannot sacrifice for him in any equal measure. But the New Testament does call us to sacrifice. Paul, for instance, asks the Romans to make their bodies a living sacrifice to God (Romans 12:1). Hebrews speaks of a "sacrifice of praise."

God does not need my offerings, but he wants them because they reveal my love for him. My sacrifices do not repay him, but thank him. How can we live in a relationship of one-sided dependence? Not by trying to repay him, to make things even. Only by thanking him, again and again.

That is precisely what the Old Testament sacrifices did. There is no doubt that God found them pleasing as long as they represented a faithful attitude on the part of the worshipers. He liked, the Old Testament says, the smell of the roasting meat. He did not eat it—he did not need it—but he was glad to know that it was given. It represented his people's love for him, their awareness of what he had given them, their willingness to sacrifice what he had given them if he required it. If these sacrifices covered over sin, however, it was on the basis of the sacrifice still to come—the one that Jesus made. They were reflections, drawing their true form from the original.

The original casts reflections both forward and backward in time. Our sacrifices please God too. They please him because they represent our hearts. They offer symbolically the one thing he wants from his one great sacrifice: us.

FINDING COMMON GROUND

We do have, then, a kind of reciprocity in our relationship to Jesus, though it remains an entirely dependent response. This leads us, however, to a second difficulty: we are grateful for what we understand. So long as I was a child, I did not appreciate what my parents had done. Only when I could put myself into their place and particularly when I actually was in their place as a parent, could I respond to their sacrifices with real thanks.

The second difficulty with Jesus' sacrifice, then, is its cosmic significance. I have no experience with which to compare a sacrifice for the sins of the world; I have nothing to relate it to. I can respect and profit from what he did, but I cannot easily relate to Jesus *personally* through it.

A comparison may help explain what I mean. World War II was fought at two hideously frightening levels. On one level, foot soldiers, pilots, and tank drivers slaughtered each other by the thousands, mauling the European and Asian continents. On the other level, in precision laboratories far from the battlefields, the top-secret Manhattan Project worked on the atomic bomb. The best physicists in the world applied themselves to this grim project. No blood was shed, but those physicists never doubted that they were part of the battle. They were fighting to defeat the Axis powers, just like the most frightened private on the front line.

As it turned out, their achievement had a far wider effect than those of the foot soldier. When World War II ended, the soldiers went home. Families mourned their dead and, for the most part, went on with their lives. The war became a memory. The atom bomb, however, did not disappear into memory. It is still with us; its potential for carnage hangs over the world more oppressively than ever. It affects not just the generation that invented it but every unborn generation to come. Those physicists unleashed a gigantic evil power, and its effect has spread everywhere. The foot soldiers were engaged in evil localized in time and place. (I don't mean they were individually to blame, just that war is always evil, no matter how necessary.) The physicists were engaged in evil without earthly boundaries.

Soldiers who fight side by side often experience tremendous camaraderie. Even to this day, men from that war gather for nostalgic reunions. Despite the horror they lived through — or perhaps because of it — they are drawn together. But would this camaraderie extend to those who fought the same war through physics? Suppose that, during the Normandy invasion, one of the Allied foot soldiers had been introduced to Robert Oppenheimer, the genius behind the bomb. Suppose someone had explained what Oppenheimer was doing, explained that his work might ultimately win the war the foot soldier was fighting. Would the foot soldier have felt a personal bond with Oppenheimer? He would not, I feel sure. He would probably have peered at Oppenheimer as though the physicist were some creature from outer space. To him the splitting of the atom would have remained an impressive but impersonal achievement. Oppenheimer's endeavor was in a different league from his, though both were working for the same goal.

In a similar way, Jesus' monumental sacrifice is in a different league from anything we have experienced. The comparison is odious, for Jesus' accomplishment is wholly good, while Oppenheimer's cursed even the unborn. As a handful of physicists unleashed far more evil power than millions of blood-soaked soldiers, so one man has unleashed more good than billions who have strived to do good.

Jesus' victory opened the way to himself. We may experience the power of the atomic bomb without experiencing Oppenheimer, but anyone who experiences the power of Jesus' sacrifice must experience Jesus. He is more than a historical first cause; he is a living God who joins himself to men and women because of and through that historical event.

How can we understand it? How can we experience camaraderie with the one who made it? We cannot go through any sacrifice remotely like Jesus'. We can only experience it vicariously.

When John Kennedy became president of the United States, millions of people identified themselves with his boyish, handsome face. He was their president in a very personal way. His achievements became their achievements, not only because he was their official representative, but because they gave themselves to him. They lived *vicariously* through him, and when he died they cried as though a close friend had died. Kennedy's legislative achievements were far less significant than this sense of relationship which many people felt with him—even people in other countries who were not legally tied to him at all.

In the 1984 Olympics I held my breath while Mary Lou Retton did her gymnastic routines. I am sure millions of others did the same. We wanted her to win, to do well for us. We gave ourselves to her. We felt anxiety, despair, rapture as she competed. When she won the gold, it was our victory. We celebrated it with her although, technically speaking, it had nothing to do with us. But our vicarious involvement went even further: *We felt that Mary Lou Retton was a friend.*

What made this vicarious relationship possible? First of all, we felt that somehow, in some small way, we were in her position. I have never in my life done a flip, but from my own low-level competition at basketball or tennis I have some idea what must go through my hero's mind as she stands ready to compete.

And then there is "charisma." Not just anyone can inspire vicarious relationships. Some personal quality must invite people in.

If anyone ever had this quality, it was Jesus. He had a peculiar authority whenever he spoke or acted. Had he wanted to be a popular political leader, he could have been an immensely successful one. He had an effect on people purely by the force of his personality, as he still does. The record of those whose lives have been changed radically just by reading the Gospels is astonishing; it spans many cultures and strata of society. What shines from the New Testament is not the skill of the writers, who did not possess classical eloquence, but the personality of Jesus. Even in print he has the charisma to inspire a vicarious relationship.

Still, there is the problem of common ground. We cannot understand what it means to sacrifice for the sins of the world, so how can we identify with Jesus' struggle even vicariously? We cannot, except partly. We cannot sacrifice in the way that Jesus did; we can, however, sacrifice.

This will put us at a level where we can understand, a little, what he did for us. The redemptive value of sacrifice is not commonsensical; it must be experienced. It must be taught to us, as we teach it to our children. This is one reason why the church has put value on charity and even poverty — so that we may better understand what Jesus did. We may never really grasp how his death two thousand years ago set us free from sin, but through our own sacrifices, however small, we may experience a tiny portion of what Jesus did. And as we understand, a little, what he did, we can give ourselves to him vicariously in his death. His victory becomes our victory. He becomes, in a far deeper sense than Mary Lou Retton does, our friend.

THE SACRIFICE OF FORGIVENESS

Let us try to go deeper. Jesus' sacrifice leads to our forgiveness. How?

As we have seen, there is a natural link between sacrifice and forgiveness. To sacrifice for ourselves, we must forgive ourselves. We must, in fact, forgive ourselves again and again; we must surround ourselves with grace. It is also true that to sacrifice for others we must first forgive them. No one ever fully deserves what we give them; we can find plenty of reasons for holding back. Real friends see faults but forgive them.

Not only does forgiveness come before sacrifice; it is itself a kind of sacrifice. Anger and unfaithfulness will bounce back and forth between two friends, gaining momentum with each rebound. Feuds grow this way, as two parties feed their anger with more and more reasons why they are right. The only way to stop it is to sacrifice — to take the anger and absorb its energy, to suffer its hurts in faith that something better can rise from the wounds.

Our relationship with God requires sacrifice and forgiveness, but it is not our sacrifice. We could not and would not give up a thing for God. Sin goes far too deep in us. It has twisted us all out of shape, making us hardly recognizable to the one who made us. We push God away, hiding behind excuses of being too busy to find time for him or of not being inspired by our church or of not having an answer to some question about the meaning of suffering or—you name it; the variations are limitless. Behind these excuses we hide our hostility toward God. We hide it even from ourselves. We are constitutionally incapable of sacrificing ourselves for the real God; our nature will not let us forgive him. We can forgive others, conditionally, because they are weak like us. We cannot so easily forgive God for being perfect, for knowing everything, for being above us, for being our maker. We cannot easily accept absolute, eternal dependence. It is the ultimate insult to our pride.

Consequently, our "sacrifices" for God easily become manifestations of our sin, not our love for him. We use them as a bargaining weapon: "If I do this for you, God, will you do this for me?" We try to use these sacrifices to control his behavior and bring him down to our level. But this will never lead us to deeper intimacy with God. If we are to know him, we must know him as he is: our perfect, all-knowing God who sacrificed himself for us when we were helpless. He gave up, not just his glory to become a man, but his own life— the just for the unjust, the deserving for the undeserving. His initiative broke the barrier. Ours not only could not, it would not.

In the act of giving his life for us, God forgave us. He looked at us through the eyes of faith; he saw us in love.

To forgive someone you must absorb his sin rather than reflect it back. You must accept the blow that falls on you from your friend, rather than striking back. Jesus absorbed the full pain of our sins, which in their fullness led to death. Our sins killed him for the same reason they were killing us: they reject God; they twist us away from him; and without that intimacy with God we die. "My God, my God, why have you forsaken me?" was Jesus' death rattle. God placed on Jesus the sin of the world: our rejection of God. The angry move was ours—and Jesus suffered for it. In his death our alienation reached its full extension. He carried it to the limit. It did all it was capable of doing. He absorbed our full rejection, sacrificing his life to it. When the anger was absorbed, it lost its power. Then we could begin anew, forgiven by him. We could begin anew in relationship to Jesus.

～

Having said all this, I admit that I still have only glimmers of the mechanism whereby my sins were carried by Jesus so many years ago. Mostly it is lost on me; it might as well be nuclear physics. What particularly helps me, however, is the deepened realization that Jesus, looking toward death, could see his sacrifice as a basis for relating to me. We know it was difficult for him—that he sweat blood. But why did he go through it? "For the joy set before him [he] endured the cross, scorning its shame" (Hebrews 12:2). But what joy? A part of the joy was, I think, the same kind of joy I look for when I sacrifice for my children or my friends: I want to be one with them. Surely one meaning of the phrase, "Jesus died for me," is that he sacrificed himself to be my friend, my brother. It was a cosmic achievement, but it was also deeply personal.

How can I know God personally? I can know him through the Cross, where he died for me. The impact of his sacrifice is still felt wherever his people are found. Living in its power, I can step forward into the presence of God at will. In fact, I am ordered to do so: "Since we have confidence to enter the Most Holy Place by the blood of Jesus, by a new and living way opened for us through . . . his body . . . *let us draw near to God*" (Hebrews 10:19-22, emphasis added).

CHAPTER
15
SUFFERING

~⤙

Sometime in your life you will probably suffer. Some great pain will flood your heart with sorrow and agony. You will not understand why, and though you look for a good reason, you will not find one.

That is the essence of suffering as I define it. It is different from sacrifice. Sacrifice is a bargain we choose to make, giving up one good to get another. A mother, for instance, may give up her own life to save her child's. That choice is sacrifice. If that same mother helplessly watches her child die, she and the child suffer. No redemptive result gleams out of the dark. Neither she nor the child understand why they are in such pain. It comes without warning, exacts its terrible cost, and then, without explanations, it leaves.

None of us would choose to suffer, yet we are strangely drawn to consider it. We who are as comfortable as any people in history—who have, for instance, practically no experience of a prolonged toothache or the death of a mother in childbirth—find intense and paradoxical fascination in studying others' sufferings, as though we might find in those sufferings a key to the meaning of life. We love to read about disasters and catastrophes, about cancer victims and those who suffered under tyrannical regimes, about child abuse and divorce and murder. Books on the theological problem of suffering—*The Problem of Pain, When Bad Things Happen to Good People, Where Is God When It Hurts?*—find a ready market. It seems almost as though we feel deprived in our relative comfort and reach toward others' suffering, as though we long to fill some lack in our own experience.

Doubters use suffering to force Christians against the wall: "Explain why your God of love let babies die at Dachau," they demand, "or we will not believe in him." We have not been able to explain, at least not in a way that convinces many people. We float a few guesses as to the general purpose of pain in the universe, but when it comes down to the particulars — why must this child suffer in this particular way? — we are as blind as anyone. We do not know where the blows come from or why. We can only hope and believe, through faith in God, that they have a point. Yet believers and non-believers still scrutinize suffering as though some lesson lies there, yet to be drawn out.

Many who have suffered in hospitals or concentration camps have written of it. None of them, to my knowledge, has offered a convincing and comprehensive reason for suffering. Yet strangely there is no more uplifting, positive, hopeful reading in any bookstore than the literature of suffering, written by those who have suffered.

This literature does not justify suffering or make it worthwhile; it merely describes what suffering is like. I want to focus on one aspect of what they describe: the profound effect suffering has on relationships. Suffering affects people's relationships with themselves, with others, and with God.

LONELY SUFFERING

Suffering is lonely, and its most obvious effect is to bring the sufferer into a new relationship with himself. Suffering does not teach from a textbook; it works with the material already in a woman or man. It purifies this human material, cutting away layer after soft layer until only firmer stuff remains. All the dross goes: the ambitions, love of money, vanity about appearance, everything that sets us above others in our own mind. Suffering purges everything that is not central to life.

At first we cannot believe that we must suffer. Surely there is a mistake. Protests should be lodged with the authorities; experts should be summoned. The problem must be solved! But days pass and the realization grows that we may never leave the prison alive, that we may never make any semblance of fidelity out of this horrible marriage. The mind and the body cry against this outrage. Hair falls out, flesh wilts, courage fails. Past achievements mean nothing. In the present we are useless; our future does not exist. So much for all our plans. We must bid them goodbye if we are to stay sane and learn to live with this new unyielding companion. We cannot afford to live in regret too long.

Solzhenitsyn speaks plainly of this need to embrace what is real. After detailing the fifty-two means of torture his captors took to break prisoners, he asks the ultimate question:

> So what is the answer? How can you stand your ground when you are weak and sensitive to pain, when people you love are still alive, when you are unprepared?
>
> What do you need to make you stronger than the interrogator and the whole trap?
>
> From the moment you go to prison you must put your cozy past behind you. At the very threshold, you must say to yourself: "My life is over, a little early to be sure, but there's nothing to be done about it. I shall never return to freedom. I am condemned to die — now or a little later. But later on, in truth, it will be even harder, and so the sooner the better. I no longer have any property whatsoever. For me those I love have died, and for them I have died. From today on, my body is useless and alien to me. Only my spirit and my conscience remain precious and important to me."
>
> Confronted by such a prisoner, the interrogator will tremble.
>
> Only the man who has renounced everything can win that victory.

Solzhenitsyn might have added: Only a man who has renounced everything knows fully how precious is his spirit and his conscience. A second, and stranger, effect of suffering is the loss of innocence, a loss of that proud sense of deserving something better than pain. Not all who suffer learn humility, but many do. Suffering strips off the self-congratulating veneer. A woman who has always been considerate of others finds herself constantly angry at her family and loved ones who surround her hospital bed. A cultured man finds himself envying another prisoner his share of a ration of food and plotting how to get it from him. We see that we are not as pretty as we imagined. And beyond this, suffering often engenders self-examination. We can't help asking, "Why me?" Solzhenitsyn quotes his fellow prisoner Boris Kornfeld to this effect: "On the whole, you know, I have become convinced that there is no punishment that comes to us in this life on earth which is undeserved. Superficially, it can have nothing to do with what we are guilty of in actual fact, but if you go over your life with a fine-toothed comb and ponder it deeply, you will always be able to hunt down that transgression of yours for which you have now received this blow."

Finally, suffering teaches us the absolute limit to our abilities. Sufferers cling to the illusion that they are responsible for removing their own suffering: the sick by mustering "prayers of faith" that will wrestle healing power from God; the prisoner by searching for techniques by which to manipulate prison guards; and others through desperate searches for medical or psychological or political expertise that will change everything. I am not saying that such attempts are useless. At the very least, they are symptoms of being alive, for while there is life there is hope. But the vast number of sufferers simply suffer and can do nothing to help themselves. The issues that count—pain, death, torture—they cannot control one iota. Bruno Bettelheim, a famous child psychiatrist and survivor of the Nazi camps, denounced the supposition that prisoners willing to sell their souls had the best chance of surviving: "The harsh and unpleasant fact of the concentration camp is that survival has little to do with what the prisoner does or does not do. For the overwhelming majority of victims, survival depends on being set free either by the powers who rule the camps or—what is much more reliable and desirable—by outside forces that destroy the concentration camp world by defeating it."

Bettelheim points out that while no one could himself defeat suffering—What victim has the power to match his oppressor? What blind man can fight back against the blows?—some people do cope better than others: "It is a well-known fact of the concentration camps that those who had strong religious and moral convictions managed life there much better than the rest. Their beliefs, including belief in an afterlife, gave them a strength to endure which was far above that of most others. Deeply religious persons often helped others, and some voluntarily sacrificed themselves—many more of them than of the average prisoners."

SHARED MISERY

In losing ambitions, innocence, and competence to save themselves, sufferers may come to know their own inner core far more realistically than do we who have not suffered. They may also know others better—others who share in their suffering, particularly. While suffering is lonely, it is, paradoxically, also the fountain of deep friendships. It is remarkable how many relationships can be traced back to shared misery. We have, to name a few examples, married couples who cheerfully remember their first poverty-stricken years together; we have war buddies wounded by the same shell; we have cancer victims who shared the same hospital room. Even friendships made in school often form around the shared loneliness and frustration of growing up.

When they had nothing else, they had each other. They can meet years after and feel this bond of comfort: "Here at last is someone who knows what it was like." People who have suffered are often peculiarly receptive to others' experiences; they hear the nuances of pain that others miss. Such a person may not talk of his suffering at all, but somehow other sufferers detect him. They are drawn to him because they sense he cannot be shocked by the violence of their pain, and because, as one who has survived suffering, he embodies real hope. People who have suffered understand each other in a way that others who have not suffered cannot.

I do not want to make too much of these positive aspects. Suffering is at all times an uninvited and unwelcome guest. But along with its bewildering pain come good revelations: a purified and clearer knowledge of self, and deeper ties of shared comfort with other sufferers. We would not choose to suffer to gain these benefits—it looks like no bargain. They are, nonetheless, very personal benefits.

THE VOCATION OF SUFFERING

When we turn to the New Testament to study suffering, we find ourselves in a totally different atmosphere. Our eyes blink in the astonishing light. Here, it seems, suffering was not an agonizing problem.

It was as natural to the first Christians as the air they breathed. Jesus had predicted that his followers would suffer the same troubles he did, and never was a prediction more thoroughly fulfilled. The early years of the church were played out against a background of official and unofficial harassment, of arrest, imprisonment, torture, and death. Every Christian lived and breathed this atmosphere, so much so that Louis Bouyer writes, "The importance of martyrdom in the spirituality of the early Church would be difficult to exaggerate. . . . After the elements of the New Testament, certainly no other factor has had more influence in constituting Christian spirituality."

Against our age's belief that suffering is a monstrous affront, the New Testament assumes that suffering is a Christian vocation entirely natural and even grimly desirable. Paul wrote the Philippians, as though announcing a sweepstakes winner, "It has been granted to you on behalf of Christ not only to believe on him, but also to suffer for him" (1:29). He told Timothy, "Everyone who wants to live a godly life in Christ Jesus will be persecuted" (2 Timothy 3:12). The early Christians saw themselves as part of a continuous chain of suffering witnesses to God's truth, dating from the murder of Abel by Cain.

They believed the world was in rebellion against God, and therefore God's people must often be hostilely received. To do God's work involved at the very least mockery, and more probably actual persecution. Such suffering proved you were in the battle against evil. The book of Acts says that the apostles, after being flogged by the Sanhedrin, went off rejoicing "because they had been counted worthy of suffering disgrace for the Name" (Acts 5:41).

Not only was suffering necessary to God's work, it was also good for those who suffered. Suffering produced perseverance, which in turn produced character (Romans 5:3-4). If Jesus learned obedience through suffering (Hebrews 5:8), so could his followers. Someone who has "suffered in his body is done with sin," Peter wrote, and "as a result, he does not live the rest of his earthly life for evil human desires, but rather for the will of God" (1 Peter 4:1-2).

No one in the New Testament addressed our fundamental question: Why suffering? Why *did* God allow the first believers to be disowned by their families, to be called heretics by the most respected religious leaders, and eventually to be killed as a public entertainment? Jesus was coming to triumph over all this evil; why couldn't he come a little sooner? He had healed people of diseases; why didn't he protect his followers from persecution? These questions were not even raised in the New Testament.

MEETING GOD IN SUFFERING

If we want to find people who struggled with the meaning of suffering somewhat as we do today, we should not look in the New Testament. Instead, turn to the Old Testament. Its atmosphere is comparatively modern. Nobody in the Old Testament treated suffering with gratitude. They treated it more as we would—as an ugly fact to be searched for meaning.

What meaning did they find? Most often they concluded their suffering was punishment for sins. Sometimes, especially in the later prophets, suffering was also a purifying agent, separating the remnant of Israel from the disobedient masses. The book of Isaiah even contains the idea of vicarious suffering—that the Servant may suffer for others' sake so that "by his stripes we are healed."

But these conclusions are not reached easily. All come in an atmosphere of somber and prayerful reflection, and as answers to a terrible question: "Why have you deserted us, O God?" Job embodied the ultimate case of suffering: a man caught in terrible pain not because he was bad but because he was good. Job scorched heaven with his demand for an explanation. He was not patient but persevering; he would not shrug his shoulders and give up his quest for understanding of God's justice. He kept on demanding an answer from God. At the very end of the book his answer came, not in an explanation but in an appearance of God himself, who answered Job's questions with more questions—withering questions. "Where were you when I laid the earth's foundation?" Yahweh roared. "Tell me, if you understand. Who marked off its dimensions? Surely you know!" (Job 38:4-5).

The argument is very like that in Isaiah, which Paul echoes in Romans 9: "How can a pot ask questions about the potter's method?" This argument suggests that it is almost impossible to think *up* in the order of creation—to go from the position of the created to the creator. Think *down* to your own created works, such as pots, the Bible says, and you may have some idea how crude your questions sound to God. The problem is not that man is so low but that God is so high—as high above us as we are above pots. The creator cannot be a peer called in question by his creation.

God gives Job, in a poetically grand manner, one instruction: Take the first three chapters of Genesis seriously. Yet this message has two sides. In content, God tells Job to shut up. In form, he rewards his noise. For God delivers the answer personally. He cares enough not to send a message but to come personally before Job's eyes. He will not—or cannot—answer Job's questions the way Job wants them answered, but he will answer. Job got what every righteous man longed for: the actual presence of God.

Thus, rather than carrying Job's questions forward, the New Testament writers carry God's answer: We will meet God if we persevere in our sufferings. "Be patient, then, brothers, until the Lord's coming. See how the farmer waits for the land to yield its valuable crop and how patient he is for the autumn and spring rains. You too, be patient and stand firm, because the Lord's coming is near" (James 5:7-8). The New Testament writers could grasp God's answer to Job's question because the answer was not hypothetical to them. God *had* appeared in Jesus; he had met their longings. He promised to return. Rather than crying, "Why, Lord?" the early Christians cried, "Come, Lord Jesus."

THE JOY OF SUFFERING

The early Christians suffered just as unjustly as Job did. But the New Testament asks no agonizing and searching questions about it. Its writers write and act as though the point of suffering were well known. Perhaps, to them, it was. They lived in a different world from Job's. They lived in a world in which God had suffered.

We think of Jesus' death as a sacrifice to save the world, but before it was sacrifice, it was suffering. Jesus' death and resurrection were not a mechanical exercise. He sweat blood over the thought of death. He asked to get out of it. He understood the horror of losing life better than anyone else. On the cross his death cry was one of incomprehension, echoing Psalm 22: "My God, my God, why have you forsaken me?"

The early Christians gladly accepted suffering because they longed, like all people of God, to see God face to face. They also longed for any foretaste of that full and personal intimacy. In suffering, they came into fellowship with Jesus in a deeply personal way. Job had found fellowship with God only at the end of his suffering. The first Christians found fellowship with God all through their sufferings. For Jesus was a fellow-sufferer who lived in fellowship with them as they suffered. They wanted to be as near him and as like him as possible, to experience the "fellowship of sharing in his sufferings" (Philippians 3:10).

Stephen's death—the only martyrdom described in the New Testament—had this note of dramatic and personal fellowship with Jesus: "They were furious and gnashed their teeth at him. But Stephen, full of the Holy Spirit, looked up to heaven and saw the glory of God, and Jesus standing at the right hand of God. 'Look,' he said, 'I see heaven open and the Son of Man standing at the right hand of God'" (Acts 7:54-56). He suffered, and as he suffered he saw Jesus.

This became typical of the martyrs of the first Christian centuries. They left a remarkable and slightly chilling record of their preparation for martyrdom. They saw it as a doorway into the fellowship of Jesus. Bouyer writes, "The Christian writers were quite convinced that Christ revealed himself, conqueror of death in them as in himself, at the moment when they consummated their martyrdom. The martyr himself, naturally, was the immediate beneficiary of this revelation, but something of it might be communicated to those present. For this reason, martyrdom appeared as the greatest charismatic experience in the ancient Church."

He cites the experience of Felicitas, who while in prison delivered a child through painful labor. "If you wail like that," one of the jailers said to her, "what will you do when you are exposed to the beasts?"

"Now," she answered, "it is I who suffer; then, there will be Another in me who will suffer for me, because it is for Him that I will be suffering then."

How very far we have descended from that attitude! We have many authentic martyrs in our century, but they are something of a curiosity to us rather than "the greatest charismatic experience" of our church. Just try to find a book on contemporary martyrs at your local Christian bookstore.

This lack of interest may indicate that our talk about a "personal relationship with Jesus" is not so deep after all. If we were strongly infected with the expectation that we will personally meet the wounded healer, wouldn't we be more interested in the experience of those who walk "in his steps" now? As it is, the phrase "in his steps" has been transmuted from its original context of suffering to a rather abstract ideal of imitating Jesus' virtues. The actual joy of suffering, so clear in the atmosphere of the New Testament, has disappeared.

The joy of suffering? To us, that sounds like a religious plaque: sentiment, but not sense. We do not want to suffer joyfully. We are even somewhat proud of our Job-like questions, under the guise of being "totally honest." If we must suffer, let the pain come in a splendorous, existential agony. Let it really hurt. Otherwise, keep it far from us. Use drugs to mute screaming nerves, blow up the unjust government, divorce the painful partner, abort the unwanted child — anything can be justified to prevent undeserved pain.

SUFFERING IN JESUS' STEPS

There is quite a distance between a martyr and a cancer victim. People who encounter the New Testament's positive attitude toward suffering sometimes ask, "What does this have to do with me? Those people were persecuted for their faith. I've never seen anything I could call persecution. What possible relevance can these verses have to my own pointless, nonsacred suffering?"

Ours is superficially a tolerant age; it kills faith with indifference rather than wild animals. It is a rare American who can point to real persecution. We go searching for it among a few snubs and a little public scorn, but we seldom find an impressive example. In America, leading Christians make their appearances on talk shows, not in the arena.

Failing persecution, we turn to the pain of cancer or joblessness or dishonorable children. The trouble is that these forms of suffering also afflict nonChristians. Nothing marks them as sacred. They are not inflicted on us because we claim the name of Jesus. They can, however, lead us to fellowship with Jesus when they are understood as part of Jesus' calling.

How can cancer have anything to do with Christ's work in the world? That question seems difficult until we remember what suffering is to those who experience it: it is incomprehensible pain. The same question we ask of cancer pertains to all suffering: What is the point? A few martyrs have died seeing clearly that their deaths would strengthen God's work. But many more lie in unmarked graves. In the chaos of persecution they were slain without publicity and seemingly without purpose. When the gun points at your head, I do not imagine you think of the terrific story that will be told about your death. More immediate to the situation must be fear, pain, worry about loved ones left behind. To suffer for Christ is to obediently face the sufferings that come our way and to believe that through them we trace his steps—through pain and death to life and immortality and fellowship with him. The cancer victim or the person trapped in a painful marriage may do this as well as the martyr.

Peter's first letter, which deals extensively with suffering, actually speaks of suffering "in his steps" while addressing slaves under oppressive masters. Their suffering had nothing, apparently, to do with their faith. They were being beaten, as slaves have been beaten in every place where slavery has been allowed. Peter wanted them to make sure they did nothing to deserve punishment, and then said simply, "It is commendable if a man bears up under the pain of unjust suffering because he is conscious of God. . . . To this you were called, because Christ suffered for you, leaving you an example, that you should follow in his steps" (1 Peter 2:19,21). The key distinction, making their sufferings a commendable calling "in his steps," was their consciousness of God.

Those who embrace suffering as part of their calling in Christ remain blind to its purpose. They may not see how their battle affects the larger battle. They can see, nonetheless, that bravery and obedience are called for, just as for a soldier in battle. As those on Jesus' side, suffering as his servants, they may gain a glimpse of him walking ahead, fighting for them.

SELECTIVE SUFFERING

For the majority of us who live in comfort, there now arises another question: How may we participate in the fellowship of Christ's sufferings? Must we become masochists looking for pain?

To this two things may be said. The first is that rarely in history, if ever, have *all* Christians suffered persecution. Even in the Roman Empire, according to most historical accounts, persecution was sporadic and mostly unofficial. But all Christians shared in the atmosphere of suffering, perhaps because they regarded suffering for Christ as such an honor and a way into his presence and fellowship. They honored their martyrs and treasured the martyrs' testimonies.

We too have our martyrs, but they are practically unknown. After several years in Kenya my wife and I began to learn about persecution and death that had affected many of our Christian friends. The first wave came during the fifties when in the midst of the Mau Mau rebellion thousands of Christians were killed because of their faith. The second period came in 1969, when Kikuyu Christians who refused to take a tribal oath were beaten and in some cases killed. Many of our friends had suffered. They knew others who had suffered and died.

I found it sobering to know people who had, in actual fact, risked their lives for Christ's name. At the same time, I was confounded as to why their sufferings were unknown. You cannot buy a book in the United States and read of their testimony. For that matter, their testimony is nearly unknown in Africa. One can explain the lack of accounts of sufferers in China or Iran, for exposure might still put the living sufferers in danger again. But the silence from Kenya or from other African countries can be explained only as a deep lack of interest in suffering for Christ, linked to a deeper apathy toward the body of Christ, our brothers and sisters, who happen to live in a different culture from our own.

Suffering holds a certain fascination for us, as I have noted. But we are quite selective. We are interested in the suffering of certain Christians because we are anti-Communists. We are interested in suffering from cancer because we fear it may strike us. Rarely do we take interest because we believe that through suffering—suffering without escape—the church comes closer to knowing Christ.

The body of Christ is suffering perhaps as much today as during the Roman Empire. Martyrs are to be found if we care to look for them. Only we do not care. Until we recover love for all God's people, wherever they are, and with it a deeper belief in the value of suffering as a means of fellowship with Jesus, we will not be a church of the fellowship of Christ's suffering. Suffering will continue, as it always has, here and there in sporadic bursts, but we will be more interested in our more important concerns — such as physical fitness. Only when suddenly we too are caught up in suffering will it get our attention.

The second thing we must say about our comfort is that it will probably not last. If we suffer in no other way, nearly all of us will experience the crippling incapacities of old age. Forget the rosy Hollywood twaddle about growing old gracefully, curled by the fire. Visit a nursing home. There is a terrible stripping of all dignity and capacity and status, a terrible cauldron of suffering for many. I don't mean indignities piled on by vicious nursing aides; I mean indignities piled on by degenerating bodies and minds. Only in a nursing home can you find ordinary people of all backgrounds openly questioning whether their life has any meaning, whether they would not be better off dead.

But we pay no more attention to nursing homes than we do to suffering in Africa. Our world hums busily along as though the terrible effects of aging have nothing to do with us, are merely an unfortunate accident. Suffering is as much a reality in our time and our culture, drugged as it is, as in any before, but we push it out of sight. We cannot do anything to fix it, so why think about it? Elizabeth Wrightman, a friend who has worked for years in nursing homes, says it well: "Old age is only of value to a society that values poverty. Our society certainly does not."

~⊱~

Suffering is a patient beast. It will catch us. Only it would be far better for us if we would catch it, if we would bend our attention toward the footsteps of Christ. If we track them closely, we will find the Lamb, Jesus himself, still marked by his wounds. He suffered and died *for us*. No fact of his life and character is more personal or more full of love for us.

If we can only struggle and wish and hope to escape suffering, we will never understand him. We need, instead, to count it an honor to walk in his steps, to share in the fellowship of his sufferings, to be like him, and therefore to be bound uniquely to him as fellow-sufferers on our journey to heaven.

16
THREE DANGERS

I hope I have shown that a relationship with God in Jesus Christ is inescapably personal. We have the resources available here and now to grow in this relationship — to grow closer and deeper day by day.

There are dangers, of course, to using the phrase "personal relationship." It can be abused. I think particularly of the person who uses it as a club against those he considers nominal believers. He says, "I have a personal relationship with God," and he implies, "You don't." Used this way, the claim contains an inherent arrogance. It implies that somehow he has an inside track with God — that he has arrived while others are still searching.

Despite this misuse, the words themselves make a much more modest claim. A personal relationship is not necessarily good, let alone perfect. We can have a very bad relationship with someone that is nonetheless personal. Take, for instance, a daughter who has clashed violently with her father. She has stormed out of the house, left town, and broken off all contact. Clearly father and daughter are on bad terms. Yet very likely, though the separation may continue for years, both parties will often think about each other. They will probably have to repress the urge to give up the grudge, to pick up the phone and call. They still love each other. In fact, it is this love that makes them able to obstinately feed their anger. Though they are estranged, they are certainly not strangers. Despite anger and separation, these two still have a personal relationship.

That is not, of course, the normal meaning of the phrase. Usually we use it in relation to someone we are on good terms with—someone we could, at least, call on the phone. I use the example, however, to point out that the words claim something positive, but not purely positive. As a matter of fact, any Christian's relationship with God is largely unfulfilled potential. We do not yet see God or converse with him as we wish to, and there is no use pretending that we can. The Christian gospel does not claim that we know God as we wish to today, but that we will know him fully in the future, on a day determined by God.

I can think of a second group of people who abuse the phrase "personal relationship." They use it carelessly rather than arrogantly, tossing around phrases like: "God is my best friend." They seem to have lost all reverence and awe for God. Someone might ask, Isn't that inevitable when we talk about God in such plainly human terms? Is it properly respectful to expect a personal relationship with the Holy One, whose words made worlds appear from nothing? Men might hope to catch some vibrations from his energy, but how can we know him personally? Thoughtful people respond nervously when they hear people talking lightly of it.

Yet the very fact that we respond nervously hints that such relationship is possible. Our fellow-creatures—the clams, parrots, snails, bears, apes—would not know enough to be nervous. If you told them God was coming, they would neither sing with joy nor shake with fear. They lack the equipment. They have no conscious link to their Creator, so far as we know, and are incapable of longing for him. Whether I have a right or not, I do long for him. The serious mention of his name awakens in me strange and sometimes uncomfortable emotions. Not even atheists manage to wipe out these feelings, as we sometimes see through their bitter response to God's name. We are on a different level from God, but clearly also on a different level from the rest of his creation: we are both self-conscious and God-conscious. So while the claim of personal relationship is daring, it is not ridiculous.

Still we would not dare to claim it if God did not seem to encourage us. Throughout the Bible he stretched himself to appear as a personal God. He told his personal name; he settled down and attached himself to particular individuals and to certain families. He spoke in

꿏

plain words, not as a cryptic oracle. Most remarkably, when he himself came to earth he did so as a one hundred percent human: Jesus. What was his purpose in coming if not to know and be known? "Personal relationship" is a daring claim, but we are not the ones who did the daring. God did. We dare not use the phrase lightly, but we do dare, because we have been invited to dare, to claim it as our privilege.

Presumption with God tends, anyway, to cure itself. Human authorities must keep their distance. If they become too familiar, they lose the mysterious and majestic aura that undergirds their authority. Without their scurrying aides and expensive clothes, what are they but little people all dressed up and acting a part? If they let us get close to them, we will see that they are no better or wiser than we are. But God is different. He is indeed better than we are. The more of his personality we know, the more we will break into astonished praise. Does a "personal relationship with God" bring God down to our level as a sort of cosmic buddy? Only if the personal relationship is just talk. When the relationship is real, it forces us to our knees. The farther in we go, the higher our eyes will be raised.

We see this with Jesus. He was a genuine flesh-and-blood man who walked, slept, ate, and talked with other men. But the more his followers knew of him the more they sensed that they were dealing with someone utterly different. The only point of reference they could find for this man was the holy character of God himself. They began by thinking of Jesus as a great leader; they ended by worshiping him as the one who had separated the first light from darkness. Familiarity did not breed contempt, but reverence.

I have had a similar experience in reading their matter-of-fact accounts in the Gospels: the more I know about Jesus the less I can capture him. He seems increasingly beyond me. It is something like the Pacific Ocean. So long as I am looking at its vast blue expanse on a map, I am not awed. It seems to be merely a fact, a physical phenomenon my mind can contain without difficulty. But when I sit on its margin for a few hours, watch its powerful pulse, stare out to where it meets the sky, I realize that the Pacific is too immense for my mind to contain.

We have no proper scale by which to measure God. He is comparable to nothing but himself; there is no one like him, as the Old Testament frequently reminds us. Thus, a real personal relationship with him will be more, not less, captured by awe and reverence. When we truly meet him, we will truly worship him.

This brings me to a third danger in "personal relationship." Words about God are never substitutes for meeting God himself. Words can only tell truth about him and call us to meet him. I cannot, in a book, produce God for you. I can only search for words that call you to him. God can't be reduced to a mundane level, but our minds can be. Will this nonbiblical phrase "personal relationship" lift us and point us to such a meeting? Will it lift us to the margin of his greatness? Or will it close our minds down to a shallow slit, measuring God on a scale that is too small? Will we end up chatting about God as though we were talking about something ordinary?

That is a real danger that confronts anyone who dares to talk about God. But I hope for the opposite. I hope that instead of making God seem small, it will make him seem big—as big as our minds can go. "Personal relationship" may turn out to be the biggest scale our minds have: both terribly familiar and beyond comprehension.

Outside God, nothing is so mysterious, grand, elaborate, and subtle as the human personality. Our friends and family are beyond understanding. Why is it that when people talk of awesome, mysterious splendor they allude to majestic mountains and atomic power and sprawling galaxies? God has put more splendor in a single human mind than in all the Milky Way. Therefore, much of what I write is devoted not only to the marvels of God but to the marvels of ourselves, for through the lens of the one we must see the other.

PART TWO

THE FACE
OF GOD

❧

My lover spoke and said to me,

"Arise, my darling,

my beautiful one, and come with me.

See! The winter is past;

the rains are over and gone.

Flowers appear on the earth;

the season of singing has come,

the cooing of doves

is heard in our land.

The fig tree forms its early fruit;

the blossoming vines spread their fragrance.

Arise, come, my darling;

my beautiful one, come with me."

—The Song of Songs

CHAPTER
17
SEEING IS BELIEVING

～～

Isak Dinesen's *Out of Africa* tells the following story of her Kenyan cook Kamante:

One night, after midnight, he [Kamante] suddenly walked into my bedroom with a hurricane-lamp in his hand, silent, as if on duty. It must have been only a short time after he came into my house, for he was very small; he stood by my bed-side like a dark bat that had strayed into the room, with very big spreading ears, or like a small African Will-o'-the-wisp, with his lamp in his hand. He spoke to me very solemnly, "Msabu," he said, "I think you had better get up." I sat up in bed bewildered; I thought that if anything serious had happened, it would have been Farah who would have come to fetch me, but when I told Kamante to go away again, he did not move. "Msabu," he said again, "I think that you had better get up. I think that God is coming." When I heard this, I did get up, and asked why he thought so. He gravely led me into the dining-room which looked West, toward the hills. From the door-windows I now saw a strange phenomenon. There was a big grass-fire going on, out in the hills, and the grass burning all the way from the hill-top to the plain; when seen from the house it was nearly a vertical line. It did indeed look as if some gigantic figure was moving and coming toward us. I stood for some time and looked at it, with

Kamante watching by my side, then I began to explain the thing to him. I meant to quiet him for I thought that he had been terribly frightened. But the explanation did not seem to make much impression on him one way or the other; he clearly took his mission to have been fulfilled when he had called me. "Well yes," he said, "it may be so. But I thought that you had better get up in case it was God coming."

In part one, I have written about knowing God through the ordinary opportunities of daily Christian life. God makes himself personally available, I have said, through a variety of means. Each one may appear earthbound and ordinary by itself, but put together these means bind us personally to God.

But that is not all there is. I would be frightened of leaving you with nothing more.

If there were nothing more, Christian lives would inevitably seem insufficient. No matter how sincerely and diligently we pursued the means of grace, we would feel dissatisfied. And we would be right to feel that way.

Kamante, Isak Dinesen's servant, was expressing what some would call a "primitive" view of God when he called his mistress to see God coming. But really, we are all equally "primitive" when we let down our guard.

No matter how sophisticated or religiously well-informed we become, at our simplest, most emotional level we long to see God. Children ask, "How big is God?" and "What does God look like?" until parents and teachers warn them away from these questions. But none of us ever totally shakes the feeling that some dark night we will rise out of bed to see God coming. Indeed, something deeply hungry is touched by the thought of such a possibility. God is always present, we know, but we wish he were visible.

"Seeing is believing," we say, and it is never easy to qualify the sense of sight and "walk by faith" instead. Common sense says that what you can't see may be merely a flight of imagination. To see God is to know that he is real.

But sight is more than mere proof of existence. When I go away on a business trip I never doubt that my wife exists. Nor do I doubt that she loves me and is faithful to me. At any moment I can pick up a phone and talk to her. Yet my eyes remain hungry for the sight of her.

While I'm away I may ask a business acquaintance, "Would you like to see my family?" I pull out little rectangles of colored paper on which replicas of the faces of my wife and children are printed. These are mere representations of their actual faces. A complex little machine focused the light emanating from them onto a piece of plastic coated with light-sensitive chemicals, which was then used to make further duplicates on paper. What my little wallet-sized colored rectangles have to do with my family is hard to specify exactly; physically they are many steps removed. Yet looking at those photographs I long to see my family; I feel a moment of communion, a painful communion of absence and longing. And I show the rectangles to my new acquaintance, feeling quite confident that somehow, something of my wife and children will be communicated.

We want to see. We find it hard to rest in a relationship when we cannot. Anyone who has carried on an acquaintance over the telephone knows what I am talking about. When you have never met the person, only talked on the phone (as often happens in business), there is a dimension of each other you can never quite grasp. Sight takes us beyond speech into a deeper intimacy. And when you already know each other by sight—as in the case of my wife—the phone only accentuates your sense of loss. I long for her tangible presence, for her touch, perhaps even for her scent and other familiarities. But most of all I long to see her.

More specifically I long to see her face. I love her face. When we are separated, I pull out her picture and dream of seeing her again. I have no photos of her hands and feet, though these might prove to be equally individual if I bothered to study them; but they seem to have little to do with her. If through cosmetic surgery she changed her hands it would make no difference to me. Not so her face.

Looked at objectively, of course, a face is a bizarre composite of features. Shiny, watery balls dart in deep sockets, sheltered by crescents of hair. Discolored skin rims a loose, spongy slit that opens to reveal a set of ivory knives. The slit twitches when words come out and occasionally shows, behind the knives, a soft, wet, pulsating mass. In the middle of the face a strangely shaped knob projects outward. And on some faces, hair grows in various patterns and lengths. Yet this messy collection of rather unattractive features is the tangible focal point of any personality.

SEEKING GOD'S FACE

Full intimacy comes between people "face to face." It is no wonder then that when the Bible speaks of longing for God, it speaks in terms of his face. The psalmist pleads with God, "Make your face shine upon us," or, "Do not hide your face from us." David's heart urges him to "seek God's face." And ultimately, "in righteousness I will see your face; when I awake, I will be satisfied with seeing your likeness" (Psalm 17:15).

Such language came effortlessly to the authors of Scripture when they spoke of God, despite the fact that they believed making any image of God's face to be blasphemy. The Jews longed not merely to get along with God and be blessed by him, but to know and experience him. They were hungry for him, not just for his favor. And at a primitive, urgent level, "him" was his face.

The Old Testament, however, is full of anthropomorphic terms for God: "His arm is outstretched," and he puts his enemies "under his feet." Through Jeremiah he even warns his people that he will scatter them before their enemies and "will show them my back and not my face in the day of their disaster" (Jeremiah 18:17). References to God's face are usually taken metaphorically.

Yet some of the records of God's visible presence cannot easily be taken metaphorically. From beginning to end the Bible contains descriptions of strange and unearthly incidents of God's appearing. If we long to see his face, we must look more carefully at the way he shows himself. For he is not content to be, for us, a "spiritual presence."

18

THE GLORIOUS
APPEARANCE

~

I have heard quite a few sermons on God's appearance to Elijah: "not in the wind or the earthquake or the fire, but in a still, small voice." However, that is an entirely uncharacteristic appearance of God, without parallel in the entire Bible. More characteristic were his visible appearances to Ezekiel, to Isaiah, to Jacob, to Daniel, to Moses, to Stephen, and to John. I have not heard as many sermons on these appearances. The reason is obvious: still, small voices we may claim to hear. The sight of God lies outside most of our experience.

But we do not want to focus on our experience. We want to focus on God and on the way he chooses to appear. If we long to see his face, we must look more carefully at the way he shows his face.

God's visible appearances fall into two categories: The first we may call the appearances of the "angel of the Lord." On these occasions God appeared in human form, but no one realized at first that he was anything but a man. For instance, Abraham granted ordinary oriental hospitality to his three visitors in Genesis 18. These men did not seem to dazzle anyone, yet the account makes clear that one of them (or all three as one) was the Lord himself. Similar, it appears, was the Lord's appearance to Hagar in Genesis 16. In this instance it was not his physical appearance that made the event memorable, but his promises.

When the angel of the Lord appeared to Gideon, he plunked himself down under a tree and engaged in a discussion of Gideon's military potential. Quite clearly this "angel of the Lord" was God himself, but Gideon did not realize it. Only after his guest burned up the meal with fire from the tip of his staff and disappeared did Gideon realize whom he had seen. "Ah, Sovereign LORD!" he exclaimed. "I have seen the angel of the LORD face to face!" (See Judges 6.)

When Samson's parents saw the angel of the Lord, they were similarly confused over his identity. He appeared first to Samson's mother, who reported to her husband, Manoah, "A man of God came to me. He looked like an angel of God, very awesome. I didn't ask him where he came from, and he didn't tell me his name." Later, when the angel appeared to Samson's father, he asked, "Are you the one who talked to my wife?" and asked the angel his name. "Why do you ask my name?" the angel said. "It is beyond understanding." Only when they had offered a sacrifice (the angel would not accept a meal) and the angel of the Lord ascended from the altar flames into the sky did Samson's parents fall on their faces. "We are doomed to die!" Manoah said to his wife. "We have seen God!" (See Judges 13.)

These are only a small sampling of the many times God appeared in visible, human form as "the angel of the Lord." They make strange stories, and we often find it easy to ignore them. Indeed, the reflex action of some theologians is to safely relegate much of the Old Testament to antiquity and explain that we should not make too much of events that present so many philosophical and pastoral problems.

We might more easily forget these appearances of God if they were not so similar to, say, the Emmaus road appearance of Jesus. There the disciples did not recognize him. He seemed like just another man, until their eyes were opened. Then, like the angel of the Lord, he disappeared.

In a broader sense, Jesus' whole life followed this pattern. Like the angel of the Lord, he was God in flesh but went largely unrecognized. He looked just like any other man. Nowhere in the New Testament is his appearance thought to be worth a description. (Apparently the writers of Scripture lacked our concern for human appearance, since not only is Jesus not described, but no one else is either unless it bears directly on the story being told, as in the case of Zacchaeus.) Only through the miracles he performed, his kingly bearing, and his words and character did Jesus' divine nature show—and then only to a few. When he did things out of the ordinary, such as walk on water, there is no question that he surprised people. They were not surprised at the idea of God walking on water. What could be surprising about God walking on water, or air, or anything else? They were surprised because Jesus looked like a man while he acted like God.

We can see a consistent pattern here. From the beginning of the Old Testament to the beginning of the New there are stories of God showing himself as a man visibly undistinguished but able to do miracles. These appearances were brief and occasional in the Old Testament, but they anticipated Jesus, who came and stayed and made himself most fully known.

"SHOW ME YOUR GLORY"

A second category of God's appearances is so different that it almost seems to be a different God, filled with radiant glory, dazzling and impenetrable — like what Kamante expected when, from his window, he saw a mysterious fiery figure and thought it might be God coming. Here, there can be no question of God appearing incognito. He is what he appears: absolute, transcendent Lord of all.

Moses occupies a unique position among biblical leaders. By any frame of reference, of course, he was a great leader. He performed remarkable miracles; he instituted the governmental and religious system that many Jews still live by three thousand years later; and he led his people out of slavery into the Promised Land. But the biblical account seems to marvel most over his relationship with God: "The LORD would speak to Moses face to face, as a man speaks with his friend" (Exodus 33:11).

On one occasion this relationship reached a peak of intimacy. In Exodus we find the strange and fearsome details of this event, which began with a request by Moses for help in his role as leader. God's response was to offer himself rather than a set of instructions: "My Presence [literally, 'face'] will go with you, and I will give you rest."

In this offer Moses saw an opening to ask for what he really wanted and what he had not thus far, even on Mount Sinai, seen: "Now show me your glory."

"And the LORD said, 'I will cause all my goodness to pass in front of you, and I will proclaim my name, the LORD [Yahweh], in your presence. I will have mercy on whom I will have mercy, and I will have compassion on whom I will have compassion. But,' he said, 'you cannot see my face, for no one may see me and live.'

"Then the LORD said, 'There is a place near me where you may stand on a rock. When my glory passes by, I will put you in a cleft in the rock and cover you with my hand until I have passed by. Then I will remove my hand and you will see my back; but my face must not be seen'" (Exodus 33:12-23).

This remarkable promise was soon fulfilled on the mountain of Sinai, where Moses spent forty days with God. When Moses came down after this experience his face was so radiant that even his brother Aaron was afraid of him.

Such intimacy with God makes my most inspired time of worship seem like so much smoke. Moses, high on a mountain, actually saw God. God spoke to him. We do well to stand in reverent awe of this. Nothing in our experience can compare even remotely. Moses himself was dramatically affected. This was the man who had seen the burning bush in the wilderness, who had received the Law on the mountaintop, who had talked to God "as with a friend." But this experience so surpassed all those in its glory and power that it had a physical effect on Moses: his face began to radiate reflected light.

Yet it was incomplete; it did not fulfill all Moses' human longing. He was not allowed to see God's face. Thus, though the glory Moses saw transformed him, the effect was temporary. The radiance faded, and he put a veil over his face to hide the sadly fading glory, as Paul explains in 2 Corinthians 3:13. Like the Law, Moses' climactic experience with God pointed toward the future.

Five hundred years would pass before anything comparable happened again. Some great and godly men lived and died without this intimate contact with God. Joshua saw the Lord once, but without the visible glory—he looked like a man. David, a man after God's own heart, recorded no religious experience to match Moses'. Elijah heard the still small sound of God but saw nothing.

Then the great prophet Isaiah had an eyewitness experience of God in the temple. In factual language the prophet describes the sight: the high and exalted throne on which the Lord sat; the train of his robe; the six-winged seraphs attending him; and their awesome, thundering cry of "Holy, holy, holy is the LORD Almighty; the whole earth is full of his glory" (Isaiah 6:3).

People usually say that Isaiah had a vision. What this means (or ought to mean) is that he saw something no one else saw—something ordinarily invisible. God was always to be found in the temple. This truth was foundational to Old Testament religion. But it had been centuries since God's fire flashed out of the Holy Place as it had in the days of Moses. Now Isaiah had seen with his own eyes what people said they believed, and the sight destroyed his confidence in himself and his people. It led to his powerful witness to Israel that God was the supreme reality. For Isaiah everything turned inside out. God was no longer in orbit around human affairs (including religion); he was at the center. God's reality shattered Isaiah's complacency when God came to Isaiah visibly.

It is curious, then, that Isaiah does not say a single word about what God looked like. He describes his garments and his surroundings, but of his face he says nothing. There may be two explanations for this. One is that what Isaiah saw was indescribable. The other is that he did not actually see anything. In view of Moses' experience the latter seems more probable. No man can see God's face and live. Not, note well, because there is nothing to see, but because the sight would kill. The Lord's glorious radiance is too bright for us. We might describe it—as medieval mystics did—as a light that is darkness or as a light like the sun. Nobody has seen the full sun, for it is too bright to see, and those who try will have their sight destroyed. We may say matter-of-factly that we have seen the sun, but we only see around it; we see it filtered through exposed film or the thickness of the atmosphere at sunset. We see enough to know it is there and that it is too bright for our eyes. Perhaps this is the sense in which Isaiah said, "I saw the LORD."

The sight threw Isaiah into despair over his uncleanness and the uncleanness of his people. We have no more magnificent passage on God's incompatibility with sin.

We do not, strictly speaking, eradicate our sins so that we may see God. We see God and then echo Isaiah, "Woe is me!" Our longing to see God is a longing, whether we know it or not, to see our sins exposed and to be cleansed by God himself.

≺≻

The question of whether Isaiah's vision was "real" grows more insistent when we turn to the other glorious appearances of God in the Bible: in Ezekiel, Daniel; and John's Revelation. For the visions they recorded grow increasingly symbolic.

Reading Ezekiel's vision without prejudice is likely to make you think of science fiction rather than allegory. It is simply stunning. The immensity, power, and limitless splendor of God could hardly be better conveyed in words. With detailed care, Ezekiel describes four unearthly creatures, each with four faces (that of a man, an eagle, an ox, and a lion), four wings, and a set of awesome "wheels within wheels" covered with eyes. Words are too weak to describe the sight, especially when Ezekiel's eyes rise to the figure enthroned above the cherubim: ". . . a figure like that of a man. I saw that from what appeared to be his waist up he looked like glowing metal, as if full of fire, and that from there down he looked like fire; and brilliant light surrounded him. Like the appearance of a rainbow in the clouds on a rainy day, so was the radiance around him. This was the appearance of the likeness of the glory of the LORD. When I saw it, I fell facedown" (Ezekiel 1:26-28).

And so may we. The sheer strangeness of this sight makes many read it as either a religious hallucination or as theological allegory. Yet though his vision is often interpreted symbolically, Ezekiel himself offers no hint that it should be taken that way. Rather, he takes pains to establish the location and physical origin of the sight.

He was apparently alone by the Kebar River on the Babylonian plain when he saw God and his helpers approach, looking like a violent storm out of the north. He saw *something*, although "the appearance of the likeness of the glory of the LORD" was evidently substantially removed from the unmediated face of God himself. If Ezekiel saw symbols, he did not seem to understand them as symbols. He did not even realize that the four creatures were cherubim (who were represented around the Ark of the Covenant in the temple) until he saw them the third time (Ezekiel 10:20). Perhaps God surrounded himself with living symbols, as any ruler may do to this day when he makes up his entourage.

Ezekiel's third and fourth visions, on the other hand, clearly came to him while he was in a state of mental transport. He goes to some pains to describe himself as sitting in his own house with the elders of Judah when he saw "a figure like that of a man" who grabbed his hair and "lifted me up between the earth and heaven and in visions of God he took me to Jerusalem" some seven hundred miles away (Ezekiel 8:2-3). There he saw the same sight of God he had seen by the Kebar

River. When it was done, "the vision I had seen went up from me, and I told the exiles everything the LORD had shown me" (11:24-25).

Thus, the distinction between real physical experience and "vision" is blurred. For what he saw on the Kebar River was evidently identical to what he saw "between earth and heaven" while sitting in his own home with others who saw nothing. What someone sees in dreams or visions need not, of course, be simply a flight of imagination. If I dream of a friend it does not mean that the friend is imaginary. In Ezekiel's case at least, the vision corresponded to a more physical reality—a smashing reality that reduced him to a trembling mass. Like Isaiah, he hammered home the message that God is real and utterly authoritative. Fifty times the Lord says through Ezekiel, "Then they will know that I am Yahweh." The awesome reality of God, a shattering sight, dominates the particulars of Ezekiel's messages.

Unlike Ezekiel, Daniel's first vision of God came in a dream— "Visions passed through his mind as he was lying on his bed" (Daniel 7:1)—though the description has some common ground with Ezekiel's. "Thrones were set in place, and the Ancient of Days took his seat. His clothing was as white as snow; the hair of his head was white like wool. His throne was flaming with fire, and its wheels were all ablaze. A river of fire was flowing, coming out from before him. Thousands upon thousands attended him; ten thousand times ten thousand stood before him" (7:9-10). I suspect Daniel has the dubious distinction of creating in the popular imagination the image of God as a white-haired old man. This is not the picture Daniel meant to portray. The white hair is part of a purified, gleaming image: white hair, white clothes, flaming throne, blazing wheels, from which a river of fire flowed.

God's appearances to Moses, Isaiah, Ezekiel, and Daniel remain, for all their brilliance, shadowy and partial. They are fleeting, ephemeral incidents that whet the appetite but do not fulfill. These men heard God's word, saw God's garments, but did not see God's face.

Just as the Old Testament "angel of the Lord" appearances had to wait for fulfillment in Jesus, so these glorious appearances anticipated a later fulfillment. As we shall see, the New Testament writers had not forgotten the physically dazzling glory of God.

CHAPTER
19
VISION OR REALITY?

W hen Saul, a student of the Old Testament, was knocked off
his horse by a blinding light, it did not take him long to
realize what was happening. Lying on the ground, he heard
a voice asking him a question, and he immediately responded, "Who
are you, Lord?" (Acts 9:5). While the word "Lord" is ambiguous, for
it may refer to God or merely to a superior, Saul was surely acknowledging God's presence. Only one voice comes with a light that blinds
the eyes. The light that blinded him belonged to the risen Jesus, but
Jesus looking quite unlike the man the disciples had followed. Saul
had seen (yet not seen, because he was blinded) the Lord of glory —
a sight that could knock a man down.

Jesus had appeared in similar fashion once before: at the Transfiguration, one of the few incidents all three synoptic gospels record.
On a high mountain Jesus' clothes became dazzling white: "whiter
than anyone in the world could bleach them" (Mark 9:3); "as bright
as a flash of lightning" (Luke 9:29); "as white as the light" (Matthew
17:2). His face shone like the sun, and Moses and Elijah appeared
with him. This was a vision of heaven, a visible opening up of Jesus'
God nature. Miracles alone did not prove him to be God, for God
had empowered others to do miracles. But this brilliant appearance
was a sure indication of his heavenly origin.

Jesus appeared in this brilliant form once more in the New Testament. This appearance, however, is not historical (yet); it comes in

a vision of the future recorded in John's Revelation. John describes its beginning as somewhat similar to Ezekiel's third vision; he gives the time and place when, in the Spirit, he heard a voice and saw someone "like a son of man." But this "son of man" did not look so much like a human as the Ancient of Days described in Daniel: "His head and hair were white like wool, as white as snow, and his eyes were like blazing fire. His feet were like bronze glowing in a furnace, and his voice was like the sound of rushing waters. . . . When I saw him, I fell at his feet as though dead. Then he placed his right hand on me and said: 'Do not be afraid. I am the First and the Last. I am the Living One; I was dead, and behold I am alive for ever and ever!'" (Revelation 1:14-18). This is the glorified Jesus, and for the first time someone saw at least part of his face—his eyes.

After hearing Jesus' message to the seven churches, John saw "a door standing open in heaven" and a voice like a trumpet told him to come up and see. There he saw a throne surrounded by four living creatures who were similar, though not identical, to the cherubim of Ezekiel's chariot-throne. They repeated words like the seraphim of Isaiah's vision: "Holy, holy, holy is the Lord God Almighty." And the person sitting on the throne "had the appearance of jasper and carnelian. A rainbow, resembling an emerald, encircled the throne. . . . From the throne came flashes of lightning, rumblings and peals of thunder" (4:1-8).

Suddenly another image appears: a wounded Lamb. He comes to the throne, and the four living creatures and twenty-four elders fall before him in worship, singing. They are joined by thousands and thousands of angels. Then every creature in heaven and on earth and under the earth and on the sea joins the singing: "To him who sits on the throne and to the Lamb be praise and honor and glory and power, for ever and ever" (5:6-13).

At the very end of Revelation we return to this same scene and see around it the new city of God. This city is like the one Ezekiel foresaw, but with two crucial differences: there is no temple, for "the Lord God Almighty and the Lamb are its temple," and there is no sun, for "the throne of God and of the Lamb will be in the city, and his servants . . . will see his face. . . . There will be no more night. They will not need the light of a lamp or the light of the sun, for the Lord God will give them light" (21:1–22:5).

Just as Jesus fulfilled the expectations aroused by the appearance of the angel of the Lord, so he will also fulfill the more rousing expectations raised by the glorious appearances of God in the Old Testament. Jesus himself has appeared in this light on two occasions, but they were partial and fragmentary. The world was not and is not ready for the blinding sight of Jesus in all his glory. But the day will come, says Revelation, when this light will be our only light.

LONGING FOR GOD

Is this merely symbolism? A literary pageant of interchanging images? Can we take these descriptions literally, or are they just fictional devices to tie the descriptions of Isaiah, Ezekiel, and Daniel into John's revelations of the future?

The line between dream and reality is not easy to draw when you are looking into heaven. The line between symbolism and realism is not easy to draw when you are speaking of our Maker, whom we lack faculties to comprehend. But to make such visions mere allegories is, I think, gratuitous. It may be grounded in the incorrect assumption that we can only know God as an ethereal Spirit. This robs Revelation—and all the brilliant appearances and, indeed, the Incarnation—of a powerfully encouraging message.

For us as human beings of God's creation, full personal intimacy comes when we are able not merely to talk, but to see face to face. We hardly dare think such intimacy is possible with God. But the Old Testament witnesses left no doubt that God appeared, tangibly and gloriously. They could not see him face to face and live, but they raised the strange and incredible hope that someday someone might. This hope did not decrease as Israel left its "primitive" stage. The prophetic visions strengthened it.

At Bethlehem this hope took an even more incredible leap. It is true, as John says, that "no one has ever seen God" (John 1:18) and that God "lives in unapproachable light, whom no one has seen or can see" (1 Timothy 6:16). He is invisible according to Paul in 1 Timothy 1:17. He is transcendent, never a part of the creation. Yet he has taken human form; he has shown himself repeatedly. Most significantly, he has come to us as Jesus—Jesus who came to stay. He walked, talked, ate, and slept. He could be touched with human hands and addressed with a human voice.

But even that is not the end of the story. We do not refer back to the days when Jesus was in Palestine for the high point of intimacy with God. Instead, we look forward to the time when Jesus will appear in glory. At that time the same human Jesus who walked our planet will appear, as it were, unwrapped. And when we meet him, it will be not only like the disciples' experience but like Moses'. We will see what Moses was denied—God's glory.

John, who twice says that no one has ever seen God, also says this: "Dear friends, now we are children of God, and what we will be has not yet been made known. But we know that when he appears we shall be like him, for we shall see him as he is" (1 John 3:2). And, says John, "his servants will . . . see his face" (Revelation 22:4). Paul ultimately foresees prophecies, tongues, and knowledge passing away. But the image of a face does not pass away. "Then we shall see face to face. Now I know in part; then I shall know fully, even as I am fully known" (1 Corinthians 13:9-12).

When the Bible speaks of the new age when we will be fully satisfied, when we will be intimate with God in a way that no one on earth has ever experienced, it speaks this way—in terms of seeing God's face.

What this means I confess I do not know; I am not convinced that anyone knows. Our metaphysical speculations are likely to carry little weight at the time when God clears up our confusion. And since we have not seen God, our ideas about his face amount to guesses. We lack more than information; we lack the substance. We must be transformed to see, and we will only be so transformed in the very act of seeing.

Yet we have been told about it in advance. That is the crucial point, focusing our longing for God in the right direction. We hunger to know God personally, not merely to talk about him but to experience him as a living character. He is our father; we long to feel his arms. He has broken down all barriers to love us; we hunger to be in his possession. This hope drives us on, and it also frustrates us because we get only glimmers, nothing solid.

Judging by all human experience, I believe this longing can only be fulfilled when our eyes are opened on the loving and glorious face of God. Such will someday be our joy. But not yet. The Bible does not hint that our intimacy with God can be satisfied through prayer or through ecstatic worship experiences or through the Bible or through spiritual gifts or through miracles or through an attitude of faith. Some satisfaction may come and is not to be sneezed at. But if Moses could not see what he wanted, if Paul and John admitted their global ignorance of the wonderful light to come, then we should not be too surprised at our own sense of incompleteness. Our longing, even our frustration, is nothing to be ashamed of. If anything it is a mark of God's touch. We long to know him completely because we have come to know him in part. Now that we have begun to know him, nothing will satisfy but the sight of his face.

The biblical visions announce the wonderful news that our longing has an answer. We are not condemned to endless searching; God will find us. He will not always be beyond our sight. He will look into our eyes, and all the frustrating limits will be purified out of us just by the searching of those eyes. It will be more than we dreamed of, more than we longed for.

But listen: while delivering this wonderful "Yes," the visions also say a clear, hard "No!" Or at least they say, "Not yet," which is virtually as hard to take. For the visions are not the standard experience of men and women of God; they are rare. And even in their rarity they remain partial—a dream that leaves us troubled, that lifts us momentarily to heaven and then dumps us back to earth. We cannot see God, and even what we can see does not stay with us. We see only through distortions. We see only darkly.

Therefore, the Bible does not encourage us to seek these brilliant visions. It encourages us to wait and to live in Jesus, the "image of the invisible God" (Colossians 1:15).

20

THE PROBLEM
OF INVISIBILITY

⌐⌐

Jesus was God and Jesus was man, and it has never been easy for people to reconcile these two facts. We want to eliminate one or the other—either to consider Jesus merely an inspired man, "the best any of us can hope to be," or to consider him God in a human disguise, not really faced with the weaknesses and temptations of humanity. How can God really be man? The same uneasiness arises when we read the biblical accounts of God's visible appearances. Perhaps you have felt some of this with my references to God's face in the previous chapters. How can God really be seen?

Many people assume that the more "advanced" a religion becomes, the more spiritual it will be. By this they mean intangible, concerned only with some inner invisible essence. They think Christianity took many strides forward when it removed religion from the realm of outward rituals and rules toward inward spiritual or psychological states. They stress God's transcendence as utterly beyond the rational faculties, as impossible to contain in any form.

The God of the Bible does not fit well with this theory of progress. He has no antipathy to flesh and blood; from first to last he has made himself earthly, material, and historical. Heathen gods might be confused with impersonal natural forces, but Yahweh showed a human face; he spoke a known language. The God of Abraham made covenant agreements with a family; he got involved with Israel's politics, with their farming, with the most mundane aspects of their lives. A Jew could conceive of speaking to God "face to face, as a man speaks to his friend," because that is just how Moses spoke to him. Human beings did not leave the earth to encounter God in spirit. Yahweh appeared on earth.

Jesus' life particularly challenges the assumption that God's fullness cannot be material. If progress means leaving bodies behind, then Jesus was a throwback. He was a man, and yet by his own claims far more than a man who knew God or who had received a special message from God. He was the great "I Am" come to earth—a vision of God, if you want to call him that, which lasted for over thirty years, had two arms and two legs, walked and talked and ate, had a mother and brothers and sisters.

This does pose philosophical problems, however. How can God get dirty? Hungry? Thirsty? Tired? How can God die? To the Jewish leaders this was a logical absurdity and a blasphemous one. God, who lived in unapproachable light, could not be imprisoned in a man's body. Centuries before, the Jews had had a sense that God could pitch his tent in the middle of their camp and show his presence visibly. But as years passed they increasingly stressed God's unapproachable holiness, taking it so far that they eventually dared not even whisper his name. How could such a Superior Being come to earth as flesh and blood? Jesus never really answered their question directly. Instead, he challenged them to deal with the facts, rather than their expectations. The outstanding fact he thrust on them was his own life.

If you want a really ethereal religion, you must look to the likes of Buddhism or Hinduism, which work to abstract the spiritual quest from the body or even the mind. Zen, for instance, tells you to ponder the sound of one hand clapping. How does God appear in these religions? Hinduism has a thousand faces for God, some likable, some horrible. You can pick and choose your preferred image. Buddhism does not even have an image of God, but concentrates on man. Its model is sleek and happy, his eyes closed, looking inward. The world outside does not bother him.

Christianity's image is singular and earthly: God on the cross, his arms splayed outward, his eyes wide open in agony. He is a God with a face. He is Jesus.

THE INVISIBLE MAN

While the Scriptures reveal a God who takes the human body as his own, they do not so easily reveal why God should want a body. And we do wonder — we who are more aware of a body's limitations and weaknesses than its advantages; we who are frustrated by sickness, by too little time, by fatigue; we who sometimes wish we could escape the restraints of physical life. What could God do as a body on earth that he could not do as a Spirit in heaven?

One answer is that God could not face sin and defeat it *for* human beings except *as* a human being. "Since the children have flesh and blood, he too shared in their humanity so that by his death he might destroy him who holds the power of death" (Hebrews 2:14). That does not explain, however, why he still had a body after his resurrection, after he had faced death and defeated it for us. So there must be a further reason why, in Jesus and indeed throughout the Scriptures, God shows a face. There must be a further reason why he rose *bodily* into heaven.

Quite simply, I think it is this: *God has a body for the sake of relationships.* An omniscient, omnipresent, omnipotent Spirit has power a body cannot have, but a physical body has the power of human intimacy.

H. G. Wells' famous story *The Invisible Man* brought this home to me. In Wells' fantasy a man finds, through science, a way to become invisible. Who hasn't dreamed it — being able to overhear any conversation, sneak into any private place, do things without being noticed? Who hasn't dreamed of the power of being omniscient, omnipresent, and omnipotent? Being invisible is the closest we can imagine to having such qualities while still being ourselves.

But in Wells' story the dream turns into a nightmare. The Invisible Man may have godlike powers, but he has very human ambitions — and these do not fit well with invisibility. He can steal money, but how can he spend it? He can overhear secrets, but whom can he tell them to? He can see the bodies of beautiful women, but can he touch them? Of course not. He has power over the visible creation, but he cannot enjoy his power. As he confesses, "The more I thought it over, Kemp, the more I realized what a helpless absurdity an Invisible Man was. . . . Before I made this experiment I had dreamt of a thousand advantages. No doubt invisibility made it possible to get [all the things a man reckons desirable], but it made it impossible to enjoy them when they are got. Ambition—what is the good of pride of place when you cannot appear there?"

There is only one way for the Invisible Man to use his powers profitably: he needs the help of visible allies. But the Invisible Man proves unable to make such allies. No one will trust him. All his powers derive from being able to know things that people don't want him to know, being able to do things that people don't give him permission to do. The right kind of allies are repelled by his antisocial behavior—stealing, hurting, sneaking. The wrong kind of allies try to take advantage of him—to lock him up, for instance, and use him as a circus sideshow. An Invisible Man even on his best behavior is an uncomfortable person to be with, but so long as he is on his best behavior his powers are useless. If an Invisible Man respects others' privacy and property, what is the good in being invisible? "Alone— it is wonderful how little a man can do alone!" the Invisible Man confesses. "To rob a little, to hurt a little, and there is the end." So long as he is invisible, he is almost bound to remain alone.

I would not push too hard the analogy between the Invisible Man and God. In most respects they are utterly unlike. The Invisible Man wants to use his powers for his own selfish ends; he has no interest in the good of others. God, by contrast, is love and uses his invisible power to create beauty and blessing.

It is possible to imagine an Invisible Man more like God—philanthropic, secretly helping the needy, and seeking nothing in return. He could do some good, but could he ever be anything but utterly alone in his philanthropy? It is barely possible to imagine befriending such a character. But when we imagine that in detail, it is striking what a nuisance his invisibility becomes. We can imagine being friends with an Invisible Man, but it is much easier to imagine being friends with a Visible Man.

A RELIGION OF PERSONS

God seeks intimacy with human beings. How is he to contact us? For us body-persons nothing happens without a physical act. A pure spirit would miss us altogether. But even a touch or a voice or a pushed neuron, while it gets our attention, is inadequate for us in forming the kind of relationship that God wants to have with us. We want to see and he knows that. After all, he made us as seeing creatures.

Some philosophers have even suggested that "spirit" is a meaningless word, for we can only know of a spirit's existence when it takes on a tangible form, a "body." Other philosophers disagree; they say spirits exist independently of bodies, even if they must always *use* bodies to show themselves. One mental experiment they propose is particularly telling: they ask us to imagine "trading places" with another person's body.

Imagine waking up one day and finding your best friend's face looking back at you in the mirror. You shake your head to clear the cobwebs, but the face does not disappear. Then you notice that you are seeing things from a different angle — you have become taller. You try to shave and cut yourself repeatedly because your facial contours are unfamiliar.

Confused, you walk out to ask your spouse what has happened. She shrieks, turns as white as a sheet, and tries to cover up her nightgown. She calls you by your best friend's name. When you try to explain that you are really yourself, she doesn't believe you. Worst of all, she keeps calling to you for help — to you, but she cannot believe that you are standing right before her eyes.

Using our imaginations, we demonstrate that we can, at least mentally, distinguish spirit — the invisible essence of a person — from body. But the same mental experiment also shows how much we need our body — our own particular body, not just any body. Without it, it seems almost impossible to form relationships.

Imagine switching bodies daily, becoming a dark brute one day, a willowy intellectual the next. We can imagine that for ourselves. But think of our spouse or friends or colleagues. Can we imagine them becoming accustomed to or liking the constant change? They would find it endlessly unnerving to wake up with a different person each morning, to see a different person at our desk each day.

When we really know someone, their person and their body are indistinguishable. Bodies give others a permanent image of us. They also give us a place to stand — a means for reaching out to others and a means for being reached.

We cannot know for certain whether this is why God came to us as flesh and blood. We do, however, know that he came as flesh and blood, and that he did it for the sake of fellowship with men and women.

Christianity is a religion of persons. And persons form real and intimate relationships through bodies. Thus, the Incarnation—God made flesh—is the starting point for the apostle John in all his writings: "That which was from the beginning, which we have heard, which we have seen with our eyes, which we have looked at and our hands have touched—this we proclaim" (1 John 1:1). This proclamation makes fellowship with the Father an open possibility; God has taken form on earth. "No one has ever seen God, but God the One and Only [that is, the Son], who is at the Father's side, has made him known" (John 1:18). Our access to God is through his flesh, his one and only tangible son, Jesus.

Someone may say, "I have never seen Jesus. God has never had a body for me. Yet I have a relationship with him." This overlooks, however, the extent to which our relationship with God through the Spirit depends on Jesus—the tangible, historical person. He who came, who taught, who did miracles, who made disciples, who suffered, and who died and rose again—he is our touchpoint with the Father. This is the Jesus revealed by the Spirit—no other.

21

WHAT DO WE MAKE
OF JESUS?

⤙⤚

"**M**y heart and my flesh cry out for the living God" (Psalm 84:2), said the psalmist, and we agree. Hence the question at the heart of this book: How can we know God personally? So far we have seen that we cannot be fully satisfied with anything less than the sight of God's face. He has promised that one day we will see him "as he is," and that we will be transformed by that sight.

Yet while we wait, we are instructed to live in Jesus through the Holy Spirit and know God through him. In his life and death on earth Jesus was the visible image of the living God, so that he could truthfully say, "Anyone who has seen me has seen the Father" (John 14:9). Even after Jesus left the earth, his life intertwined with people who had never seen him. "Your life is now hidden with Christ in God," Paul wrote the Colossians. "Christ . . . is your life" (Colossians 3:3-4).

If we think about this, however, we quickly come to two problems. The first is to reconcile Jesus' life with the brilliant appearances of God in the Old Testament. God was too bright for the eyes. He told Moses that no man could see his face and live. Yet here, in Jesus, was God on display for over thirty years. Nobody fell down blinded. In fact, few saw that he was anything more than a good, wise man. In what way then did Jesus display God? How can it be true that anyone who saw Jesus had seen the Father and also true, as John wrote after Jesus left, that "no man has ever seen God"?

When we have settled that problem, a second arises: How do we, two thousand years later, relate to God through Jesus? Even if he was God made visible, does he add anything really personal to my relationship with God, since I do not see him but only read about him? I may be informed and inspired by reading about Jesus, as I can be by reading about Winston Churchill or John Wesley. *Knowing* such a person is a different matter. What is the relationship between the historical Jesus I read about and the Jesus who "lives in my heart"? These are crucial questions for Christian faith, for that faith must center on Jesus—the Jesus of the Bible and the Jesus who lives and reigns and will come again.

"He is the image of the invisible God," Paul wrote of Jesus in his letter to the Colossians (1:15). This word "image," I think, holds the best answers to these questions.

"Image" carries a wide variety of meanings. It can mean "representation," such as Caesar's image on a coin. It can mean "mental impression," as when a politician is "image conscious." Paul, however, meant something more when he used the word in connection with Jesus.

"Eikon," the Greek word Paul used, is the source of a word used by Eastern Christianity: the word "icon." From their use of the word we can learn more about its meaning for the apostle Paul.

To us an icon is merely a picture of Jesus that Russians and Greeks hang in the corner. But for the Eastern Orthodox church an icon is more than a picture. It does more than *remind* a worshiper of the historical Jesus. A true icon of Jesus, they believe, embodies him. That is why icons are sacred to them. When they look at an icon in faith, they believe they actually encounter Jesus.

Somewhat similarly the language of philosophy calls an icon a symbol that has something of the original in it, as a straight line on a map has something of a straight road in it. Thus, an icon not only reminds you of something, it embodies that something.

We need not adopt the Eastern Orthodox view of icons or become philosophers to see that Paul used the word "eikon," or "image," in a similar way when talking of Christ. Paul did not mean that Jesus reminds us of God; he meant that Jesus was God himself, of one substance with him.

How then, when we see Jesus, do we see the image of God? I have found the most helpful modern analogy in the science of optics.

Properly speaking, nobody ever sees anything; we see an image of the original. Everything we "see" is really reflected light. When light bounces off an object or a person, its shape and color are recorded in the light. By deciphering this information, we "see" the original. You can get some idea of how difficult it is to decipher if you imagine trying to find out what someone looks like by feeling the water that bounces off his face in the shower. No doubt, if you had good enough instruments, you could determine a great deal from that water. But we lack such instruments. All we would get out of that bouncing water is wet. The light bouncing off a face is similarly chaotic. Fortunately we have a phenomenal instrument for creating order out of that chaos: the eye.

The eye contains a complex, compact pack of astonishingly sensitive rods, cones, and nerve endings. These record light impulses and signal them to the brain much as other receptors in the tongue or the fingertips record taste or pressure. I am told that there are about 107 million such receptors in the eye. Their work is a marvel. Far more marvelous to me, however, is the eye's lens, mysterious and awesome in its simplicity. Were it not for the lens, all those myriad rods and cones would merely record how bright the day is. You would see reflected light much as you would feel reflected water: a complete muddle. I do not mean that you would see dimly, as through a foot of clear gelatin; I mean you would not see anything at all except light and darkness.

If you want to see what the world would look like without the lens of the eye, do this simple experiment. Buy some photographic film, unroll it, and hold it up in front of your family, your home, a flower. Then develop the film. You will have, of course, absolutely nothing on the negatives because you had no lens between the light and the film to sort out the light into intelligible form.

The trouble with light is that it is utterly undisciplined. Suppose that I want to look at my father's face. You would think that the light from his eyes would stay separate from the light from his nose and mouth. It does no such thing. The light from his eyes bounces off in every possible direction. The light from his nose does the same. Light from his various features is immediately so tangled up as to seem impossible to separate. That is why my film, exposed without a lens, shows no image; the images are all there, but like a sand painting that has been shaken until there is no recognizable order.

If we are going to make anything of this mess we need a light sorter. That is what the lens of the eye—or of a camera or a microscope—does. It sorts by bending each beam of light slightly, according to the angle at which it strikes the lens, sending it to its proper destination inside the eye. The subtlety of this process can hardly be exaggerated, for the difference in angle of light from my father's nose and from his mouth as they travel to my eye across a large room may be almost infinitesimal.

In the end I have, inside my eye, a little upside-down mini-replica of my father. All the nose-beams are in one spot, all the mouth-beams in another. They are even proportionately arranged. This is an image. It has nothing of my father's substance to it; it is made entirely of light. Striking where my rods and cones are laid out, this image triggers certain nerves that the brain has learned to interpret, adjusting for size, for instance, so that he looks bigger than my thumb.

Light is naturally unintelligible. An image is light made intelligible—light sorted out for human consumption. Technically then, a photograph is not really an image; it is the recording of an image onto paper by means of chemicals. An image lives in time, always changing as the original changes. A photograph merely freezes one of its moments. The real image lives on as pure light. You cannot save it or store it or stop it. It lives as its original lives and as light shines on the original.

Now let us consider how this applies to Paul's statement that Jesus is the "image of the invisible God." Right away we may notice that Paul is using the word "image" in a different way than I have used "image" in regard to my father. An image of my father is not "of one substance with him." An image is light; my father is flesh and blood. But for Paul, Christ as the "image of God" was of one substance with the Father.

This is possible of God though not of humanity because an image is formed of light, and God is pure light. John describes both Jesus and his Father as light: "God is light; in him there is no darkness" (1 John 1:5). Jesus himself said, "I am the light of the world" (John 8:12). Both Old and New Testaments describe God as light, a blinding light, or a light bright enough to illumine a city. Thus, we can say that God's only son is the image of God's light; he is light sorted out for us to see. This divine light that streams in every direction, filling the universe, is beyond our comprehension. We need it focused in a form that sends comprehensible signals to our brains. This is what Jesus is and does: He makes God known.

A PHOTOGRAPH OF JESUS

To continue the analogy, we might say that the Bible presents a true photograph of Jesus. In the Gospels we see him unchanging, as he was for a moment in time.

The Bible does not automatically bring life and inspiration to everyone who reads it, any more than pictures of my wife and children automatically bring fond thoughts to anyone who looks at them. It is only when we live in relationship to people whose images are recorded on a photograph that we can love them through it. It is only when we live in relationship to the living Jesus that we can see and hear him through the Scriptures.

A photograph cannot be seen in the darkness. It exists in and of itself, but to see it we need light, the same light that formed the image in the first place. Light must reflect from its surface and into my eyes, there to form a new image.

God is light, and he reflects his living light off the pages of Scripture to show the true image of Christ to us. Without that light, for us, the scriptural photographs are in darkness. God himself must enable us through his Spirit to see Jesus. Paul wrote to people who had never seen Jesus, "For God, who said, 'Let light shine out of darkness,' made his light shine in our hearts to give us the light of the knowledge of the glory of God in the face of Christ" (2 Corinthians 4:6). Long before Paul, David noted a similar paradox: "In your light we see light" (Psalm 36:9).

Light, to be comprehended, must be sorted out into an image. Jesus was and is the living image of God. He is the image of unintelligible light. He is the Word made flesh.

Yet for us his image is still blurred and imperfect, for our lens is not very good. We still see "through a glass darkly." It will not always be so. The image outside us, though duplicated poorly within us, is perfect and true. One day we will see him as he is.

THE DARKNESS
OF THE LIGHT OF JESUS

‍

I f Jesus is the true image of God openly displayed, and if the Holy
Spirit carries Jesus' living image into our lives, then why the discrepancy between Christianity's promises and my actual experience? Is something wrong with me? Am I somehow missing the
fullness of God's available light?

Not as I read the Bible. As I look closely at Scripture, I see that
even when God came to earth as Jesus, his light was shaded.

It is tempting to wish we could trade places with the disciples. I
have heard sermons about the marvelous camping trips the twelve
must have had, of their long intimate discussions around the fire. How
wonderful to sit down with Jesus for a face-to-face discipleship train-
ing course! But if the disciples had such a warming experience, we
have absolutely no record of it. Being with Jesus was, by all their
accounts, a wrenching and confusing time. Everything happened too
fast. They knew they were onto something but they didn't know what.
Jesus rebuked them for their lack of vision and comprehension: "Oh,
you of little faith!" "O unbelieving and perverse generation, how long
shall I stay with you and put up with you?" Pasolini's film *The Gospel
According to St. Matthew* captures their situation in one remarkable
scene: it shows Jesus, striding quickly ahead and turning his head to
shout his teachings to a trailing group of disciples, left in the dust.

Nowhere in the New Testament are those years referred to as
"the good old days." None of the apostles said, "How I wish we could

be there again!" They didn't tell new converts, "If you only could have heard Jesus! Then you would understand." Luke 9:45, in its stuttered emphasis, expresses what must have been the disciples' state of mind: "But they did not understand what this meant. It was hidden from them, so that they did not grasp it, and they were afraid to ask him about it." Luke 18:34 repeats the same point: "The disciples did not understand any of this. Its meaning was hidden from them, and they did not know what he was talking about."

If the disciples were confused, think how little the crowds understood. The unbelievable but unmistakable fact is that Jesus went largely unrecognized. Here was God on earth in the form of a man who spoke awesome words and had the power to control nature. He not only claimed to be God, he did things only God could do. He was the image of the invisible God, God's life fleshed out. But the crowds who followed him never saw this. They did not understand what he said or what he did or, most of all, who he was. Occasionally an individual saw the light: the centurion who told Jesus not to bother to come to his house; the leper who returned to Jesus to praise God after his healing; the woman who poured perfume on Jesus' feet. But it is not completely clear how much they understood, and certainly the impact of their insights seemed fleeting. Peter could declare Jesus the Messiah one moment, an insight Jesus said could not come from flesh and blood but only from God, and the next instant give Jesus advice on how to avoid the cross, an insight Jesus said could only come from Satan. Until Jesus' resurrection, not even his disciples, who lived with him day in and day out for almost three years, ever figured Jesus out. They saw and yet they did not see.

It is a fact we need to face: The people Jesus chose to be with in the fullness of time, people who walked and talked with the image of God on the most intimate terms possible, saw only dimly.

You would think this ignorance would have been the first thing for Jesus to clear up. But the Gospels indicate that this was, instead, near the very bottom of his priorities. He was nowhere more obscure than on the subject of his own identity. I cannot be the only reader who has wished more than once that Jesus would simply say straight out who he was. Even at his own trial, in his last public appearance, he resisted saying it with absolute clarity. Jesus came to make God known, but not the way a modern publicity agent would.

Perhaps, we might speculate, Jesus did not want people to respond to his words but to his actions. He wanted to *show* himself to be God. But here too is cloudiness. Jesus walked on water, fed thousands from a few loaves and fish, and raised people from the dead. These miracles attracted people to him by the thousands. Yet the crowds never grasped that someone who so controlled nature was the Lord of nature. They believed in him as a source of benefits but were quick to turn on him when the benefits appeared to run out. It is hard to judge them too severely when Jesus' hand-picked helpers didn't see much more clearly.

The ultimate miracle, of course, was his resurrection. The disciples proclaimed it as though it explained for itself that Jesus was God. Yet nobody actually saw it happen—nobody saw his eyes open, his dead body warm into life. They saw the result: the risen Jesus. And though he appeared to many, he by no means appeared to everybody. Instead of suddenly standing in the courtyard of the temple (where the disciples would shortly proclaim his resurrection) he appeared in a small private room. At one time he appeared to over five hundred, Paul says, which shows his new life was not a question of private illumination but of historical reality. But why not five thousand? Or fifty thousand? He made no public showing to skeptics, and consequently the city of Jerusalem was prey to rumor and public lies. Jesus could have laid these to rest. He did not. Even those who saw him struggled with unbelief. "When they saw him, they worshiped him; but some doubted," Matthew says at the very end of his account (Matthew 28:17).

You cannot escape it: even for his disciples, Jesus' light was far from blinding. They did not gain the insight of faith just by seeing the image of the invisible God. His words, his miracles, his presence— they were not enough.

THROUGH A GLASS DARKLY

To this day people do not easily or often see the glory of God in Jesus. Part of the reason for this is the sheer difficulty of grasping his glory. It is hard enough to know any friend, and Jesus had a great deal more personality than ordinary human beings. He had set the stars flaming.

Part of the difficulty, too, lies in our own sinful natures. If we don't enjoy the full fellowship with God that we want, it is often because we want to see him only on our terms, as a possible addition to the good life we have made for ourselves. But we cannot see him that way. It is an absurd impossibility — like wanting to see the Grand Canyon on a small scale. Either we see God in grandeur and are transformed, or we do not see him at all. "The god of this age has blinded the minds of unbelievers, so that they cannot see the light of the gospel of the glory of Christ, who is the image of God" (2 Corinthians 4:4). The god of this age is a god of self-righteousness and self-glory. We cannot see God's glory through such dark lenses.

If we purified our lives of everything that distracts from God — such as unkindness, anger, greed — and devoted our daily lives to loving and serving him, we would see God much more clearly. Prayer and careful study of the Bible would sharpen our sight further in helping us see and understand Jesus as a real person and the real God.

But something more than sinfulness obscures Jesus. It is tempting to blame all dissatisfaction on ourselves. Heaven knows we have a lot wrong with us; we could make a great deal more of what vision God has given us. Yet though he may become more real to those who devote themselves to worship and prayer and Bible study, he never becomes as real as we want or as real as he is. He remains clouded, just as he was for his disciples: a glorious image seen through a glass darkly.

Jesus warned his disciples, "If anyone tells you, 'There he is, out in the desert,' do not go out; or, 'Here he is, in the inner rooms,' do not believe it. For as lightning that comes from the east is visible even in the west, so will be the coming of the Son of Man. . . . All the nations of the earth . . . will see the Son of Man coming on the clouds of the sky, with power and great glory" (Matthew 24:26-30). The implication of that is unmistakable: *the fullness of Jesus is not yet to be found.* Nor are we to go looking for him. The fullness of Jesus will come to us. He will come to us with glory quite beyond what we see in the Gospels — a glory no one in the universe will miss. Jesus as the apostles knew him — and as we can know him — is still a shadowed image.

Or perhaps we may say, in the terms of our metaphor, that he is a black-and-white image. Not a black-and-white photograph, for he is a living image; not a copy, for he is the same substance as the original. But a black and white image, entirely accurate but without the blinding splendor. Perhaps humanity, as we know it, can only accommodate black and white.

That need not be a completely negative assessment. The general public will take color over black-and-white hands down. Color smacks us in the eye. Nonetheless, many photographers prefer black-and-white, finding the gradations of tone subtler and more artful. Black-and-white photographs require study. They do not dazzle us, but they wear well. We can hang them on the wall and live with them. When we look at it this way, we can say that Jesus displayed God's glory in a form that communicates only to those with the faith to live with him and study him.

In Jesus' life we may see God. But as yet the choice to see remains with us. On any given day we may choose *not* to see God in Jesus. We may, without even sensing our deep and calamitous rebellion, ignore him, act as though he is merely a picture on the wall. I do so often for the simple reason that I have not yet been totally changed by the power of his glory. His Holy Spirit, however, is changing me, teaching me to recognize God in Jesus.

23
THE DARKNESS
OF THE HOLY SPIRIT

~~

Just as it is tempting to want to trade places with the disciples, it is tempting to think of those years when Jesus walked the earth, healing and teaching, as the high point of history. To actually see Jesus! To be able to address our questions directly to him, to look into his eyes! If only we could somehow get back to those days! But that was not Jesus' perspective. In his view we who live without seeing him are better off than those who walked alongside him in Palestine. According to him, his departure from earth was a gift to his disciples: "I tell you the truth: It is for your good that I am going away. Unless I go away, the Counselor will not come to you. . . . He will bring glory to me by taking from what is mine and making it known to you" (John 16:7,14).

The disciples could not understand this. They were distraught. They feared they were being abandoned. Their great gain would be lost; God would be invisible again. Jesus acknowledged their loss but told them he would become intimate with them in an entirely new way—through the Holy Spirit. The Spirit reveals the Son, or as Paul put it even more forcefully, "The Lord *is* the Spirit" (2 Corinthians 3:17).

In *All Things Made New* Lewis Smedes writes that Jesus "is present as the Spirit. There is no touch of the Spirit that is not the touch of the Master's hand." Is this not what Jesus implied when he said of the Holy Spirit, "You know him, for he lives with you and will be in you. I will not leave you as orphans; I will come to you" (John

14:17-18)? Jesus did not say, "I will send the Spirit to you," but "*I* will come to you." And when Jesus says, "You know him, for he lives with you," may we not see in this a reasonably clear suggestion that his disciples would recognize the Spirit as the Jesus they had been living with all along?

At Pentecost the Holy Spirit transformed the disciples' thinking. When Peter stood up to preach in immediate response to the coming of the Spirit, he did not speak of the existential ecstasy we presume he and the others experienced. He never mentioned what it *felt* like to be baptized with the Holy Spirit. He spoke of the past and how the present was connected through prophecy to the past. He spoke of Jewish history and traced a thread through it to the Pentecostal experience. "God has raised this Jesus to life, and we are all witnesses of the fact. Exalted to the right hand of God, he has received from the Father the promised Holy Spirit and has poured out what you now see and hear" (Acts 2:32-33). Jesus' story merged with the Old Testament story, and together they swept over Peter's story. Peter was able to put it all together because the Holy Spirit had come on him. The confusion he had felt while Jesus lived with them was gone.

I have noticed a similar phenomenon in Christians today. They can almost invariably make sense of their own history; they can look back over childhood, over early adulthood, over family troubles, over career choices and say, "I think I see what God was teaching me. I see what he was doing." They can look at the past and see more than change—they can see growth. Christians need never feel lost in the cosmos, because the Holy Spirit identifies for us our place in the sweep of history; the Spirit assures us of our place in relation to God who loves us as his children. This knowledge of intimate love and purpose comes from Jesus through the Holy Spirit just as it came to the disciples at Pentecost, as he had promised: "On that day you will realize that I am in my Father, and you are in me, and I am in you. . . . He who loves me will be loved by my Father, and I too will love him and show myself to him" (John 14:20-21).

Though the disciples had lived with Jesus, they had not understood him. Though they had felt compelled by him, had tried to obey him, they had been confused by him. They had had only fragmentary, momentary flashes of insight. They had hoped, wildly perhaps, that he was taking them somewhere, but where they had not had a clue.

But when the Spirit came, all this was changed—transformed. They began to understand what Jesus' life meant and how he loved them and how their futures were bound up in his.

This explains, by the way, how the Twelve came to accept Paul as an apostle. How else could someone who had never walked with Jesus gain equal authority in interpreting his life with those who had? Could members of John F. Kennedy's inner circle accept contradictions about "the Spirit of Camelot" from someone who never took part in all those events? It only makes sense if, in fact, those long walks and long talks with Jesus were significant to the disciples primarily in the light of what came afterward: Jesus' resurrection and the witness of the Holy Spirit. These experiences Paul shared with them. Through the Spirit, and only through the Spirit, all the earlier events made sense—historical sense and personal sense. Only then, with intimate involvement in Jesus' life, could they go into the whole world and preach good news.

NOSTALGIA FOR PENTECOST

Just as some Christians tend to think of the days of Jesus' physical life on earth as the high point of history, so others think of Pentecost as the ultimate experience of God. Their great ambition is to duplicate whatever happened there. And who can read the second chapter of Acts without feeling some envy? We know the darkness in our own lives. Did not a great light shine there?

Yet the New Testament no more hints of nostalgia for Pentecost than it does for the days of Jesus' corporeal life. Pentecost was definite progress, but those who experienced it looked for even more progress. They were not satisfied with what Pentecost had given them. The New Testament view is not focused back into history but forward into the future: "For you died, and your life is now hidden with Christ in God. When Christ, who is your life, appears, then you also will appear with him in glory" (Colossians 3:3-4).

The New Testament makes us sense the powerful forward surge of history directed by God. These are, it says, the last days. Because of our faith in Christ, we have the Holy Spirit. He has lifted us onto the crest of a wave, unstoppable, unfathomable. Only when it washes us up on shore will we feel solid ground beneath our feet and see, finally, how all things come together.

The Spirit is not a force or a principle; he is the person of God shining Jesus' personality into us. Through him we can "taste and see that the Lord is good." But the entire Bible points toward a better and brighter revelation of this light. And that implies, necessarily, that we are still partly in the dark.

The history of the Spirit's life in people is light and shadow, illumination and darkness. He is proof of the kingdom of God in our midst—the first installment of our redemption. But he too remains invisible. He is hidden from the world and sometimes from us. Wherever we look for the life of the Spirit, we will find this mixture of light and darkness. We never find the fruit of the Spirit without finding, at the same time and in the same people, some of the fruit of the spirit of this age.

How do I know? After all, some people speak about the Holy Spirit as though they have no sense of darkness. They tell us that they converse with God just as they talk with a friend, that in prayer they are regularly overwhelmed by a physical sense of God's presence. They speak of verbal promises God has made to them: "God spoke to me and told me that the house belonged to me."

I can't see inside people to know what really goes on between them and God. I can, however, look for secondary effects or signs of that relationship on their lives. There are consistent, recognizable patterns in the way the Holy Spirit works.

First of all, the Holy Spirit always works in conjunction with the truth—God's Word. The Reformation recognized this formally as the principle of "Spirit and Word." If people say, "We have the Spirit," but do not exhibit reverent and accurate proclamation of God's Word, they are wrong. If they say, "We preach the Word," but do not evidence such fruit of the Spirit as love and self-control, they are wrong. You cannot have true Word without true Spirit or true Spirit without true Word. They are indivisible.

Second, the Holy Spirit always produces the fruit of the Spirit, such as love. Where love is lacking, the Spirit must surely be darkened.

And third, the Holy Spirit always produces power. This power is not aimless, for show, like a fireworks display. It is power to do work, to spread the name of Jesus. The Spirit moves, as he moved in Acts, toward the furthest, most remote people, and so will the Spirit's people. They will always be missionary-minded. His mighty power works miracles and breaks down barriers to spread God's kingdom.

None of these effects is individualistic. The Holy Spirit did not come upon certain individuals at Pentecost; he came upon the church and its entire leadership. When a group of people is adopted by the Spirit, they are called in Scripture, "the body of Christ." A body is, as we have seen, a personality's point of contact with other people. The church is Jesus' point of contact; through it the world meets Christ, and Christ meets the world.

One person can never say that he is the body of Christ; he is always just a member of that body. The Holy Spirit does not fill us to isolate us from our brothers and sisters; he fills us to make us a part of something much larger. When the Holy Spirit lights the church, every member shares in the light. This is not just religious rhetoric. We can see it most practically if we think of the Bible.

The Bible, on which we are so dependent for our life in the Spirit, is a thoroughly corporate production. It depended first of all on the Spirit's inspiration of a collection of writers, but the Spirit's work did not stop there. Through nineteen centuries the Bible has been painstakingly copied and recopied with remarkable care for accuracy. Protestants tend to disparage the monks of the Middle Ages, but we had better not disparage them too much. Monks had no Xerox machines; they did not even have typewriters. Try taking down even one page of the Bible with pen and paper, and you will have a greater appreciation for the unbroken string of faithful, careful, inspired workers who preserved and disseminated the Bible throughout the centuries. In more recent years Christians have translated the Bible, printed it, and sold it. These may all seem mundane activities, yet they are essential to the work of the Holy Spirit. Without the church— the whole church of the centuries, including some people very unlike ourselves—we would have no Bible. In the most practical of ways we depend on others for our life in the Spirit.

But when we look closely at this church that we are so dependent on, we see most clearly how clouded the Spirit has been. It started right at the beginning with the early church. We must study the New Testament church, for they were given truth to pass on to us. From them we get the teachings of Jesus and his apostles. But we make a grave mistake if we want to become like them. Nothing in Scripture encourages us to imitate the church itself, except in the specific things they did right. Practically as often they were wrong. Wracked by dissension, by doctrinal aberrations, by sexual sins, by lukewarm spirituality, by legalism, by proud and divisive leaders, the New Testament church testifies not only to the truth but also to man's disobedience. Living in the shadow of Pentecost, they ought to have been overwhelmed by the witness of the Spirit. The evidence says they were not: "I am astonished that you are so quickly deserting the one who called you by the grace of Christ and are turning to a different gospel—which is really no gospel at all" (Galatians 1:6-7). We are certainly like the New Testament church in this. God forbid we should try to be more like them!

But what about individuals? May not some individuals show the fruit of the Spirit far more than the corporate church? Some of the New Testament leaders certainly did, and they deserve to be imitated in their faith. But even the best of them showed times of darkness. Peter was caught in an act of blatant hypocrisy regarding the Gentiles. Paul fought with Barnabas and could not resolve the quarrel. When Paul was imprisoned, other leaders stepped up their evangelism because of envy and rivalry. These were great men of faith, worthy of imitation, but they had not been utterly washed clean by the coming of the Spirit. They, like us, looked forward: "Come, Lord Jesus."

WALKING IN SEMI-DARKNESS

There is no Golden Age of the Church. In our two-thousand-year history we have wonderful moments, but that is all they are: momentary, fragmentary. The church has never been altogether pure, altogether faithful to God's Word, altogether powerful. Neither have its leaders. The Spirit always promotes love, does works of power to spread the good news of Jesus, works in and through God's Word. But the darkness in which we experience the Spirit is obvious when you see how much the people of the Spirit have mixed love with hatred, have lost power to witness, have forgotten the Word of God. After the Reformation, the great triumph of the Spirit and Word, it took a century and a half for Protestants to realize the Spirit and Word were concerned with reaching out beyond Europe with the gospel. We have in our history inquisitions, crusades, witch trials, and wars. And before you suggest that none of this was done by "real Christians," make sure that you track the path of the Spirit through a good church split in your town. The path of the Spirit through history, ancient and modern, is light clouded by darkness.

How should we feel about this? One temptation is to feel relieved. We can read church history to find that the great saints were no better than we are, just the way some people take delight in learning that a famous evangelist has left his wife. It lets us off the hook. We may be a mess but so is everybody else. But with such thoughts our darkness grows hopeless.

The proper response to darkness is grief—and hope. Today the world may be divided between those who pretend they are all right and those who don't pretend, but tomorrow is a different matter. Tomorrow, for believers, all darkness will be dispelled with pure light. This is our hope and our focus: the light that has begun to break.

Through God's Spirit we have access to the One who made the heavens and the earth, and in the first part of this book we explored his resources in some detail. But let us keep today in proper perspective. Let us not make the mistake of thinking we have arrived. Let us not focus on what we can see and experience. For "the man who thinks he knows something does not yet know as he ought to know" (1 Corinthians 8:2). "But our citizenship is in heaven. And we eagerly await a Savior from there, the Lord Jesus Christ, who, by the power that enables him to bring everything under his control, will transform our lowly bodies so that they will be like his glorious body" (Philippians 3:20-21).

We are waiting—waiting like Paul to see the unrestrained, purifying, fiery glory of God "face to face." Until then we walk in semi-darkness, by faith and not by sight. Our semi-darkness is the half-light of dawn.

CHAPTER
24
THE AGE TO COME

⚜

W hen I was a teenager, I would have been happy to do away with heaven. To my pragmatic mind the concept seemed disreputable. I was disturbed by the idea that Christianity's value depended on someplace vaguely celebrated as having golden streets. I remember questioning a Sunday school teacher closely on the subject: "But even if there were not a place like heaven, even if life ended at death, don't you think Christianity would be worthwhile?" I got, as I recall, a hesitant yes, and I felt better. I wanted a faith that was practical and valuable here and now. If I got a bonus after this life, that would be fine, but it was not the reason for my faith.

When I read old Christian books I found them often, in their loftiest passages, telling of Christians who had deathbed visions of angels, or of martyrs who faced torture and death without fear because they longed to be with Jesus. These were not to my taste. They seemed old-fashioned and sentimental, carrying the musty scent of mildewed bindings and great aunts. I wanted a modern, realistic, stainless-steel faith. Had I heard Bonhoeffer's phrase "religionless Christianity" then, I would have liked it.

I think the period of my youth, in the sixties, had a great deal to do with the way I felt. Through its events we lost any sense that we were part of history. The moon walk, the Kennedy and King assassinations, the pill, the Vietnam nightmare, the new math, marijuana and LSD, encounter groups—all these were, it seemed to my

208

generation, a departure from everything that had ever happened. We had no certainty where they would lead us. To heaven on earth? To hell on earth? Both views had their partisans. We were often told how unusual we were; I remember several teachers who said we were the smartest class ever. Those were days when everything was shooting upward—crime, consciousness, rockets, and test scores. What had happened twenty years before seemed absolutely ancient, no guide whatsoever to what would happen in the present. What might happen in heaven, after death, lacked the excitement and tension of what seemed to lie just around the corner. I do not think I am the only one who lost a taste for heaven and "the age to come." Our generation lost it. We lived in a vivid present.

Once lost, a sense of history—the continuity with and importance of time out of reach, forward and backward—is very hard to regain. Thus, for my generation Christianity has focused around two poles. We want at one pole a practical Christianity that will help us establish sound marriages, raise well-adjusted children, form healthy friendships, and contribute positively to our community and the world. That is the outside of life. At the other pole we want a faith that cures loneliness, disperses anger, and fills our God-shaped vacuum with a "sweet, sweet Spirit." This is the inside of life.

Our churches work hard to help both poles. For the outside they hold seminars on family life, "God's will" (which means vocation and marriage), and simple living. For the inside they bring in inspiring teachers on "how to be filled with the Spirit," "how to have a quiet time," and "true spirituality." Both inside and outside are "practical." They make sense to us and sometimes even to our nonChristian neighbors.

But our "practical" Christianity has neither past nor future. It floats in an existential present. What happened in biblical times is relevant only as it helps us *now*, while the future kingdom of Christ is a blurry theological detail.

We assert that the Bible is history, that Jesus really rose from the dead in time and space. But we do not approach history with the same concern we give to present-tense events—we merely tip our hat to it. We study the Bible, but primarily the "nonhistorical books" like Paul's letters and the Psalms. The Old Testament becomes a hunting ground for inspirational stories and poems, rather than a library of an ancient people whose history we are invited to continue. Some of us even have trouble appreciating the Gospels, finding them just "one thing after another." And once past the apostolic age most of us know next to nothing. Protestants see Christians between the time of Christ and the time of Luther as largely misguided, as though Jesus, having promised to be with his church continuously, let a thousand years slip by before recalling his words. Catholics, while theoretically putting more weight on God's past work in the church, often have no better sense of unity with the church that happened to die before they were born. If the Holy Spirit has been alive and active all this time, then church history must contain a record of God's work; but our interest in that record has been very limited.

On the other hand, evangelicals have had a long-standing interest in eschatology, the study of the future as the Bible predicts it. For a while, with the publication of *The Late Great Planet Earth*, this was on the increase. Yet I doubt that that book or others like it left a firm deposit of understanding behind. I think it might be fair to say that eschatology has become a rather arcane subspecialty for the minority of church members who enjoy getting jots and tittles straight. To them, trying to line up and synthesize all the numbers and symbols of Daniel, Ezekiel, Matthew, and Revelation is a mental discipline akin to solving advanced crossword puzzles.

The problem is that eschatology has become a question of timing, a question of "who" and "when." The Antichrist has been incorrectly identified several times in every generation and the date of Christ's return falsely predicted. But even if the guesses had not been wrong, this use of eschatology would be. "Who" and "when" are not the primary issues. Our first question must be "why"—why should we care about ten horns or apocalyptic beasts? What do they have to do with life? With faith? With knowing God?

JESUS IS COMING

I have come a long way from my early antipathy to heaven, a distrust and distaste that easily extended to eschatology and stories of martyrs. I have even reached the point where I feel some sympathy for people who guessed Christ's return-date wrong, for I suspect that some of their errors were errors of enthusiasm. Perhaps some had their eyes fixed so completely and longingly on another world that they strained their eyesight.

I realize now that you can't cut heaven out of the Christian faith. It is a lining bonded onto the whole garment. Tear it out and you tear the garment at every point. It is not an arcane specialty, nor merely a blessed hope after death. It is also our only hope before death. I have been told that about one out of nine New Testament verses refers to the second coming of Christ, and I don't doubt it. But even more significantly, these verses are not segregated; they are bonded onto everything else. We may manage to read through them without noticing their sense, but logically and theologically the whole house depends on them as a foundation. Without them Christian faith is a house of cards; the slightest wind blows it down.

Theologians and scholars know this well. You find heaven considered in all the weighty tomes. It is a vital part of the historic doctrine of Christianity. Jesus taught us to pray to our Father in *heaven* that "thy kingdom come, thy will be done on earth as it is in heaven." The Apostles' Creed declares that Jesus "ascended into heaven" and from there "will come to judge the living and the dead." There is no chaff in the creed, only the fundamentals all Christians believe essential to the faith.

Unfortunately I did not rediscover heaven as a result of reading the Bible, the historic creeds, or the great theologians. What led me to care about heaven was the exploration I have taken you on so far, my search for the answer to the questions at the heart of this book: Where is God? and How do I know him personally? I realized, when I asked those questions most frankly, that while God was with me, he was also absent. I lived in darkness as well as light. I could not see his face; I could not carry on a real conversation with him. This was more than a theological problem; it was a personal problem. I missed God.

When I admitted that to myself, I began to feel a passion for God I had not been aware of. As I have mentioned, I am not by nature a particularly emotional person. My faith had been rather matter-of-fact, and I had assumed it always would be. After all, what was there to be emotional about? I thought without thinking, that the relationship I had was all I ever would have. But when I admitted my emptiness, I found I was not as religiously neutral as I had thought. I found that I missed God, wanted God, craved him. My emotions did not center on his presence so much as on the hope of his presence. And it was then I began to pray with true urgency, "Come, Lord Jesus. Come to *me*."

Then I found that I was not the first person to feel that way. The Bible contained the same expression, "Maranatha!" People in New Testament times knew that the kingdom had still not come in its fullness. They felt pain and longing at its partialness and unfulfillment. They also lived in expectancy and hope, believing that what they wanted was on its way.

Paul wrote in Romans 8:24-25, "Hope that is seen is no hope at all. Who hopes for what he already has?" That fact was so obvious to the biblical writers that they seldom mentioned it this plainly. When they signed up to be Christians, they joined a group of men and women waiting at night, lamps ready, for the bridegroom to come. It was no party. They were waiting for the party. They stood teetering on the brink of a new age. They were citizens of an emerging country. They knew that the full glory of following Christ was yet to come.

Christian hope is the realization that our current world situation is, without Jesus, hopeless; it is the expectation that Jesus is coming—may come at any minute. This is what gives our faith meaning. It is what makes our "personal relationship" ultimately personal.

I longed to know God intimately, to know him as the kindest and grandest of friends. The Bible told me wonderful news: I would know him that way, and beyond anything I could dream of. Someday my longing to know God intimately would be satisfied. But not yet. Not in this age. In heaven. In the age to come.

⇥

My grandparents were missionaries to India and Pakistan, and because they came home only every five or seven years, I did not see them often. Their picture was prominently displayed in our dining room, and I remember that picture as clearly as any of my childhood. To me their faces looked soft and gentle, like old pieces of brass polished so often that the sharp corners have rubbed down. They were very real to me. I felt a personal attachment to them even though I actually had no memory of seeing them. This was possible because we talked about them frequently, and because my parents read their letters to us. Most of all it was possible because I believed the promise: "Grandpa and Grandma will be coming back." I knew that someday I *would* see them.

When I finally did, at the age of eight, I got a jolt: they did not look exactly like the picture. They were not frozen in time. They lived; they moved. In fact, they were harder to relate to than they had been as pictures and mental images because they were so much larger and so much more alive. Yet in every way that counted, my image of them had been quite accurate. My faith in them had not been misplaced. They were kind and gentle and generous to little boys. They were the same people whose letters I had read. I knew them; they knew me; and we belonged to the same family. It was just that I had a lot more to learn about them when their presence overwhelmed my mental picture.

So it is with God. We know him, though in a limited way. More importantly, he knows us. And he is coming. He will come to us, and he will never go away again. This hope lets us call him, with personal assurance, our Father; it lets us believe that we have a personal relationship with him. If he were not coming back, we would have a poor claim. If he were not coming back we would be, to paraphrase Paul, of all people most to be pitied.

A VIEW FROM THE END

So far our life here and now sounds grim. We live as aliens in "this wicked age," and we wait to see Jesus in the age to come. Everyone must chose which to build his hopes on: the present kingdom of this world or the coming kingdom of Jesus. There is no in-between. In light of this, then, it seems our practical, sensible, helpful-for-now faith must go out the window. Only the future counts.

But the Bible also offers a subtler view. The "age to come" has already come in seed form. The kingdom of God is already "in our midst" as well as "at hand," and it has been ever since Jesus came to earth. We are "in Christ," and Christ is in us, while we wait for him to come to us.

This dual perspective makes a most confusing situation. It reflects not only an intellectual difficulty, but a living paradox. On one hand we have the undeniable satisfaction and joy of living as Christians; on the other we have a strong sense of our own sinfulness and the sinfulness of the world around us. Paradoxically, the greater our joy in Jesus, the more we long for purity and love. The better we know God, the more we miss him. To judge by the saints who feel it most, this sense of loss is a mark of God's grace.

"Well, which is it?" someone may ask impatiently. "Is life in Christ joy or hope? Do we have Christ, or do we *expect* him?"

It is hard to answer, for it is a question of timing, and time is slippery stuff. Sometimes it seems to move quickly; sometimes it moves slowly; and sometimes both at once. (It seems, for instance, only a short time since I moved into my house, yet I seem to have been there forever.) It all depends on our perspective—where in time we are looking from.

Perhaps we can make a little more sense out of the Christian dilemma if we consider the way we normally remember history—that is, how we look at events that have already blown past us. The past always looks different than it did when it was the present. For memory selects from all the things that happened only the few that prove of lasting importance.

The world of science may serve as a good nonreligious example. Most textbooks chart the history of science as a steady march upward. Knowledge gradually increased, one discovery building on top of another, reason inevitably triumphing over superstition and error. From our perspective every great scientist stood on his predecessors' shoulders, passing the bag of knowledge up to the next level where, as though by a prearranged signal, another scientist carried it on. Einstein could not have written his general theory unless Newton had first written his localized theory; $E = mc^2$ depends on $f = ma$.

As we look backward, scientific knowledge seems to flow smoothly, almost inevitably forward. The timing may be delayed a few years or even decades, but sooner or later someone will make the next jump. The church may have threatened Galileo with the stake, but his clear vision triumphed, for he saw things the way they really are. Progress does not even ultimately depend on the rare genius. An Einstein speeds things up, but as long as there are real scientists practicing real science, man's knowledge must expand, his mastery increase.

Historians of science, however, have discovered that the truth is not nearly so neat to those living in the middle of the events. For every scientist who made a crucial discovery, ten made "discoveries" that turned out to be irrelevant or even false. Fairly often those in error were more renowned as scientists than the true discoverers. And even the true discoverers did not always realize what they were doing; they may have made half a dozen "discoveries" before they got to the "real" one. To them they were all real.

Only by looking backward can we separate the wheat from the chaff; as a matter of fact, the chaff utterly vanishes from history as though it had never existed. The unsuccessful scientists are nameless. Their insignificant or incorrect theories are unknown. It is the same with any series of events: a courtship, a career, a war. In the middle of life we see only confusion; we are mainly aware of *looking* for paths, not of finding them. But from the perspective of the end, all confusion vanishes like a shadowy memory. Only the results endure: the successful marriage, the rewarding career, the martial victory. When we look back, it all seems to have been inevitable.

Now let us apply this to our Christian dilemma. Our problem is that Christ lives in us and that at the same time we wait for him to come. According to the Bible we are children of God, yet we often feel like orphans. Which perspective is the Bible speaking from, the middle or the end? Scripture, I believe, mainly presents us with a view of life from the end—"the eternal perspective," we might call it, or even "the heavenly view." It is a voice telling us, "This is how it will seem when it is all over." This view separates what is real from what is unreal. What is real is what will last. Everything else, no matter how real it seems to us, is treated as insubstantial, hardly worth a snort. That is why Scripture can seem at times so blithely and irritatingly out of touch with reality, brushing past huge philosophical problems and personal agony. That is just how life is when you are looking from the end. Perspective changes everything. What seemed so important at the time has no significance at all.

Have you ever tried to explain some aspect of mathematics to someone—long division, or square roots, for instance? It can be maddening. You cannot begin to understand the muddle in the student's mind, even though you once had a similar muddle of your own. Often there *is* no answer to the muddled person's questions: he does not have any idea what he is really asking. A gulf divides student from teacher until through a mysterious process the student steps forward into the answer. Now he can see quite clearly what he ought to have seen all along, but he can no longer remember what kept him from seeing for so long. I simply cannot recall what made algebra so difficult; it seems as natural as breathing now. So it will be with Christians who enter the "end perspective" God offers. The old profound dilemmas will not even make good questions any more.

Pain and sorrow are also transformed by the view from the end. If we walk through a hospital, we can encounter a practical example of this. There is one particular ward where moans are most likely to assault our ears. Young women writhe in severe and helpless pain. Their problem is obvious to the eye: their stomachs have swelled to the size of beach balls. The taut skin glistens. As the hours pass, the women's faces grow increasingly worn with pain. If they were there with any other diagnosis, say cancer, the scene would cut our hearts.

Instead, we feel great joy in a maternity ward. The women there may be feeling as much pain as women with stomach cancer, but they look confidently toward a different end—a joyful end. Later, they will not even remember much of the process. How often have we heard a mother say, "Isn't it strange how you can't remember how much it hurt?" The pain that seemed so terrible has faded away because it came to its proper end: she holds her baby.

The Bible is constantly trying to get us to see things this way— problems erased by a greater understanding, pain eclipsed by a greater result. Psalm 73 is a good example. The psalmist presents a frightening view of the wicked: "They have no struggles; their bodies are healthy and strong. They are free from the burdens common to man; . . . They say, 'How can God know? Does the Most High have knowledge?'" Materialism throws up an impressive facade of success and permanence. Seeing the view from the middle, the psalmist ponders this with a bitter spirit. Then, in a moment of insight, he realizes the eternal value of God: "God is the strength of my heart and my portion forever." The wicked will someday vanish like shadows: "You destroy all who are unfaithful to you." Thus, the frustrations of the psalmist's life are put into perspective by a glimpse of the future, and his bitterness evaporates.

A great deal of Jesus' teaching emphasized the view from the end. How do you tell a good tree from a bad tree? By the harvest that comes at the end of the growing season. Jesus told us to store up treasure in heaven—treasure that is indestructible, that has lasting value in the perspective of history. He told us to build our foundations on rock, not sand. Only a house that endures the flood is a good house. What seems important and valuable to us must be tested by the view from the end of time.

So how do we answer the original question? Is Christ here or yet to come? He is here, coming. Amid the mess of our lives, amid the broken experiments and the mistaken theories, the joy and the sorrow, is a vein of pure gold. Sometimes it surfaces. Other times it lies buried. But ultimately the whole mess will be purified with fire, and when that furious burning is over we will look at the shining gold that is left and say, "So you were there all the time!"

CREATING THE FUTURE

By now some readers will have begun asking an awkward question: "If the 'view from the end' is so important, why did God take so long to give it?" For in the Old Testament we find no clear idea of life after death. Of course the idea peeks through here and there, especially in the Psalms, but generally death leads only to Sheol, the grave, where no one can rise up and praise God. Old Testament Jews were practical people who cared about what happened here, in flesh and blood. The mysteries of the grave made them uneasy.

Yet their ignorance of life after death does not mean they lacked a "view from the end." God gave them a clear picture of the future. To the Jews, "afterlife" would come through their corporate life as a people. Most of the great covenant promises offered blessings after death through their descendants. Old Testament Jews found great personal satisfaction in thinking of the future of their nation-family, though it was a future they did not expect to see. The Day of the Lord and the triumph of the Messiah were realities they looked forward to whether they would live to enjoy them or not.

Abraham, like us, built his life to prepare for a coming kingdom. Thus, he left his home and became a nomad preparing for "the city with foundations, whose architect and builder is God" (Hebrews 11:10). He did not expect the city of Ur to last; it did not have a permanent foundation in God. In Palestine, where he owned no land, he saw a future. He died owning only a burial plot there.

Nonetheless he believed, through faith, in the end God had told him about.

We can only guess why God did not tell Abraham that he would live to see this future. Perhaps, had Abraham believed in survival beyond death — and many of his contemporaries in Egypt did — he would have lost interest in the dirty hard work of herding sheep and managing a contentious family. He might have separated his faith from the world, dreaming only of some ethereal, spiritual life to come. Whatever the reason, Abraham did not think of God's promises as a vague future unrelated to the here and now. God's kingdom was quite literally the culmination of the family he was building.

The real mystery to me is not why Old Testament Jews were kept in ignorance about life after death. After all, they got the view from the end, which is all they needed to live. The real mystery is why we, of all people, have been informed. Considering how often we abstract the coming kingdom from the here and now, making it an irrelevant dream "way beyond the blue," we might question whether it has been useful information. We need to care about the future in the same way Abraham did — care about it in a way that makes us care more, not less, about the present. For in a real sense we are creating the future; it is straining to get out. "I consider that our present sufferings are not worth comparing with the glory that will be revealed *in us*. The creation waits in eager expectation for the sons of God to be revealed" (Romans 8:18-19, emphasis added).

What will be revealed? *We* will be revealed. We are already chosen and have begun to dress for the celebration. We have seen the future, and it is us — Christ and us, and Christ in us.

25

WAITING IN HOPE

~+~

S ay that you put your hope in the Second Coming of Christ, and you will inevitably meet disdainful skepticism. "An escape from reality," people will accuse. Marx called religion "the opiate of the people" with this very point in mind; by promising "pie in the sky," faith pacified the masses. They cared less about this world because they counted on another.

Christians today are tolerated, even valued, as long as they maintain charities or demonstrate on popular ethical issues such as, depending on your political loyalties, abortion, human rights, or nuclear war. But let them begin to talk about heaven and hell and Jesus' return, and they lose their audience. The problem is not just that people don't believe in eternal life; they may not believe in prayer either, but that doesn't prevent them from keeping respectful silence when invocations are offered. Prayer, if not helpful, at least does no harm, they think. But eternal life — that kind of dogma drains away commitment to this life. In extreme form it may make people spend their time banging tambourines instead of working. Citizens of another world are naturally less committed to this one.

So our critics complain, and unquestionably they are sometimes right. The Jesus Movement of the late sixties and early seventies was a case in point. In a spasm of apocalyptic enthusiasm, many "Jesus People" quit school, quit work, quit protesting the Vietnam war, quit everything except worshiping God and trying to convince other people to join them as they waited for the world to end at any moment. Like similar spasms before it, this one faded away, and most of those who were involved went back to "normal" living—to honoring their parents, loving their neighbors, and building families and careers and churches. For most of them Jesus' arrival became a much more distant prospect.

Luther said that worldly reform is like a drunken peasant trying to get on a donkey: he climbs up on one side and falls off on the other. Perhaps that is the case here. In wanting to avoid overenthusiasm, some of us have lost a fundamental insight into our world's future—and our relationship with God.

This problem of too much enthusiasm about the Second Coming does not seem to have occurred to the apostle Paul—or to any New Testament writer. In Paul's letter to the Colossians he refers to "the faith and love that *spring from* the hope that is stored up for you in heaven" (1:5, emphasis added). He is talking about very practical and this-worldly faith and love, which create "a life worthy of the Lord, [pleasing] him in every way: bearing fruit in every good work" (1:10). Not only did he consider the Colossians' orientation toward heaven no obstacle to good works; he thought of it as their source.

Paul thought of the Second Coming in a different way than most of us do. We think of it mainly in terms of cataclysm: war, resurrection, judgment. Paul thought of it primarily as a personal encounter. To Paul and to all the first-century Christians, Jesus was before all else a human being. There were men and women around who remembered him, who had taken trips with him and shared meals with him. So when they talked of Jesus' return, they thought of the return of a particular person. They did not think first and foremost of the cataclysm that would come with him. They thought of *him*.

What is the end of this world all about? It is about Jesus, and it is about his people living in intimate love with him. "You eagerly wait for our Lord Jesus Christ to be revealed," Paul writes (1 Corinthians 1:7). He refers to the end of our history—and the goal of our lives—as quite simply, "the day of our Lord Jesus Christ" (1:8).

Paul longed for this full, personal encounter with Jesus—and he assumed that all real Christians did: "Now there is in store for me the crown of righteousness, which the Lord, the righteous Judge, will award to me on that day—and not only to me, but also to *all who have longed for his appearing*" (2 Timothy 4:8, emphasis added). Paul could not have conceived of a Christian who did not long for Christ's coming or who hoped (as I have heard some hope) that Jesus delays his return until they have time to enjoy married life.

Christian futurology is simple and personal. It is like saying to my children, "Grandpa is coming." Yes, Grandpa will arrive at a certain time via a particular means of transportation, but that is secondary. We can think about that later, if we need to at all. What matters is that Grandpa is coming and that we will enjoy him.

Paul put our situation most clearly in 2 Corinthians 5:6: "As long as we are at home in the body we are away from the Lord." That is as clear as, "As long as we are in San Francisco, we are not in Boston." We may long for the fall colors of a Boston autumn, but we are not going to see them—at least not more than a hint—in San Francisco, which is not a natural environment for fall leaves to show their colors. Similarly, this world is not the place where we can see God in all his glory.

That does not give us the right to give up on this world, however. In fact, Paul brackets the verse with his sense of confidence: "We are always confident. . . . We live by faith, not by sight. We are confident, I say . . . So we make it our goal to please him, whether we are at home in the body or away from it" (2 Corinthians 5:6-9).

I believe that the Jesus People and others like them went wrong because they expected a kingdom quite disconnected from this world. They did not see that the kingdom that is coming is already here, at work, visible for those with eyes to see. They could not imagine how to please the coming Jesus through any means other than warning people that he was coming. Who can blame them? The way Jesus' return is commonly talked of, you would never make any connection between our life in the future and our life today. The identification of the Antichrist? The role of computers in numbering people? The revived Roman Empire? What do these have to do with my life? But the Bible anticipates something far more personal: Jesus himself, coming to his family. When we concentrate on this perspective, we are in no danger of abandoning this world. For Jesus, in his healing compassion, has not abandoned this world he created. Rather, he holds it together; he has great plans for it.

When eschatology is used evangelistically, it capitalizes on the urgency of fear: "God is coming to judge and you are not ready." But most of the New Testament proclaims the Second Coming to *Christians* and with a different urgency—an urgency of expectation, not of fear. It is the expectation of seeing a loved one again, of being embraced in loving arms, of being rescued from darkness. And with this urgency of expectation comes a desire to please the long-awaited loved one. Thus, we work to prepare for his coming.

POSITIVE EXPECTATION

There is another kind of response to be considered, however. Some Jesus People, hearing that Jesus was coming, overreacted drastically. But many other people who say they believe that the kingdom of heaven is coming go right on living just as they always have. The good news seems to make no difference in their lives.

A friend, Jack Crabtree, has suggested an illuminating illustration of this. Suppose, Jack says, that you are a sixteen-year-old practicing basketball in your driveway when an angel appears to you and delivers a message about the future. "Good news! You are destined to be a great basketball player. You will one day be Rookie of the Year in the NBA. You will go on to be recognized as one of the greatest players who ever lived!"

"So what's the catch?" you ask.

"Nothing. This is a free gift from God."

Suppose that the angel managed to convince you that he was a real angel and that the message was absolutely unconditional and supernatural. Would it make you practice basketball more, or less?

That would depend on what your heart longed for. If the angel had merely happened to find you practicing basketball out of boredom, if you didn't really care much for the game, his message would have little impact. In fact, it might make you less interested. "Hey, great. That'll be fun. I'll look forward to it." And you'd go off and do the things you really wanted to do. After all, you were guaranteed success whether you practiced or not.

But suppose you lived and breathed and dreamed basketball. Suppose the greatest joy you had ever dared imagine was being NBA Rookie of the Year. Then how would the message affect you? It would, I believe, release you to work harder at your game. You would

lose that sense of discouraged uncertainty that afflicts people: "What's the use? I'm just kidding myself that I can be good at this." Instead, you would know that every moment you practiced was preparation for the very thing you longed for. When you made a basket, you would say, "I'm on the way!" When you missed one, you could shrug your shoulders, grin, and say, "Well, I still have a way to go, don't I?" Because your mistakes were merely transitional, you could forgive yourself for them.

I once heard an Olympic swimmer define the difference between a winner and a loser this way: "A winner dives into the pool excited about the chance to win. A loser dives into the pool afraid that he is about to lose." Positive expectation does affect the way we compete, but only if we first care deeply about the game.

For example, I expect that I could be a good bridge player. I have a mind for the intricacies of games and learn them quickly. But nothing in all the world—even promise of a world championship—could induce me to practice bridge, because I do not care for card games. I am not interested in changing my life to be successful at something I care nothing about.

Plenty of people are in just this situation. They have been told they can go to heaven to be with God forever. They are glad to hear the news; after all, it is good insurance coverage for the future. Now they can stop worrying and get on with whatever they really care about—making money or becoming admired or outdressing their neighbors or hunting and fishing. They do not really long for Jesus, so the promise of meeting him in heaven has little effect on their lives.

But the promise should have a far deeper effect on those who long for God. It should catch and hold their attention, forming a burning, joyful expectation that overshadows everything else. If they really believe that Jesus is coming—and I am not sure most do really believe it—it should make Christians devote themselves to love because they believe that the King of Love is coming.

Rather than providing an escape from reality, the Second Coming clarifies the very nature of reality. Much of what we call "real" becomes insubstantial when seen in the light of Jesus. What will fame be worth for those whom the Everlasting One dismisses with, "Go away; I don't recognize you"? The enduring things will be those that have already the quality of heaven: love, and service, and especially adoration of the Lord. Some actions, seemingly insignificant, will prove to have been part of the secret thread of history in service of the unrecognized king. "Whatever you did for one of the least of these brothers of mine, you did for me" (Matthew 25:40).

Not only does this have very practical implications here and now, but it helps us as we deal with the question I have been discussing throughout this book: How do we resolve our double vision? How do we reconcile our longing for God with the dull facts of where we are? Now we can see that we cannot reconcile it and ought not try. Our unfulfilled desire has a point: it will motivate us to care about living faithfully. For only those who ache to be great basketball players will practice more, not less, as they see their greatness on the horizon. Only those who ache to be with Jesus will do his will more, not less, as they wait for his arrival.

Here and now we do not have Jesus as we want to have him. But rather than trying to do away with our uncomfortable unfulfillment, we should let ourselves feel most deeply what we miss. We should allow ourselves to dream of Jesus' full presence as we prepare for his coming.

The Second Coming is not the end of history; it is the fulfillment of history—a history we are now making. The King is coming. Let the kingdom prepare.

CHAPTER
26
UNTIL THEN

～

W e have covered a lot of ground. We began in the first chapter with my worried gropings as a college student. I wondered whether I had something wrong with me since I could rarely feel God's presence as I thought I should. Now I ask myself, if I could go back in time to speak with that serious, cautious young man that I used to be, what would I say? Or what would I tell my fellow-student who left the faith because "it wasn't working"?

I would point out, first of all, that a sense of God's absence is not foreign to the Bible. The Psalms are filled with expressions of this painful longing: "My God, my God, why have you forsaken me? Why are you so far from saving me, so far from the words of my groaning? O my God, I cry out by day, but you do not answer" (Psalm 22:1-2). And these are not just Old Testament words. Jesus himself spoke them, taking them as his own. Even Jesus' followers felt incomplete and alien: "Meanwhile we groan, longing to be clothed in our heavenly dwelling, because when we are clothed, we will not be found naked. For while we are in this tent, we groan and are burdened" (2 Corinthians 5:2-4). A spiritual man such as the apostle Paul could cry, "I want to know Christ and the power of his resurrection. . . . Not that I have already obtained all this, or have already been made perfect, but I press on. . . . Brothers, I do not consider myself yet to have taken hold of it . . . I press on" (Philippians 3:10,12-14).

But in the New Testament, something greater outweighs the groaning frustration over the human condition: anticipation. And this is the second thing I would tell my younger self. No, you will not solve this discrepancy here and now, but God will solve it in the age to come. For some reason—we may only dimly understand why—the state we are in is necessary to create the state we want. Our unsatisfied passion for God is not to be played down or "solved." Our pain and longing make sure we will never remain content in our current situation. It is to our benefit that we cannot grow comfortable in a city fated for destruction. We wait for another city, a better city where God is the light.

Third, instead of trying to dull my desires, I would tell my younger self that I should fan them up. The pain is good for you; it enlivens your mind, sharpening your sense of need for God's goodness. It can help shape you into a proper ambassador of the age to come. You cannot be a good representative of a country you have forgotten how to love. Through worship, through prayer, through reading and meditating on the Scriptures, through all the means of grace that part one discussed, a deeper longing for God will be stirred up that can keep you from settling for anything less than God himself. If your emphasis is on Jesus' coming, you will not be abstracted from this world. You will work to prepare for his arrival, for you will want to please him. He came to our world in flesh and blood. He cares for it; he sustains it; and he wants to redeem it.

And finally, I would tell my younger self that God does, here and now, give himself in a totally personal way. He simply does not do it the way we want or the way he will someday. Sometimes our frustrations and our desires cry out so loud that we cannot hear his voice. We must shut them up with a very loud no before, in the quietness, we may hear a more quiet yes.

Picture children waiting for Christmas. In November Christmas is just a word to them, vague and far off. But by December, events conspire to make Christmas real and terribly desirable. Tantalizing packages begin to arrive after every shopping trip. The house smells of pine and candlewax, and bright decorations catch their eyes. Television ads stir their desires for toys and dolls—always barely under control—into a fever. Parents ask children what they would most like to have. Uncles, aunts, grandparents, friends of the family join in this merry horror, like asking a man dying of thirst what sort of drink he would like, and then withholding it from him. The children are certain the brightly wrapped packages under the tree contain the very things they want so badly. Yet for some perverse reason they are not allowed to have them—not even to touch them.

There is a simple solution to this agony, of course. The parents could let the children rip open the presents and get what is inside immediately. But this would only spoil Christmas. In trying to solve the problem they would spoil the fun. So the children must learn to wait. They must learn that every day is not Christmas and that Christmas is worth waiting for. When they come to this realization—and it is not an easy leap to make, as parents of small children know—then they can begin to enjoy the whole Christmas season.

Anticipation is part of celebration. The days leading up to Christmas have their own special loveliness because they lead to the event itself. Then all the pretty packages will be unwrapped.

In the same way, Paul wrote that if there were no Resurrection, Christians would be of all people most pitiable. This age, too, has its loveliness—the loveliness of anticipation. We may not *open* our presents now, or not all of them anyway, but we can see them wrapped up and waiting for us. God speaks personally to us—softly, but he can be heard if we have ears to hear. We can see his glory—dimly, if we have the eyes. These sights and sounds are never enough to satisfy our desires, but they are enough to help us find our way on the journey. They are enough to even give us joy, when we know for certain that the fog will lift and we will make it home.

ENGAGED TO CHRIST

Would these answers have satisfied my younger self? I suspect I would have accepted them somewhat grudgingly. I wanted something solid to hold on to—something tangible now. I wanted to see God, to feel his presence, to know in such a way that I could never doubt again. I wanted certainty, and I still do. But that kind of certainty is not available in this age of anticipation. A certain sense of longing remains inevitable. "Who hopes for what he already has?" says Paul (Romans 8:24).

Any good speaker knows that you communicate through stories and examples; they are what people grab onto. But I can't even offer tangible "success stories." Where would I get them? I can offer plenty of examples of people frustrated by their longings, but none of people completely satisfied. We are all caught in the same dilemma. We all wait together. None of us has seen God face to face, and we do not know what it will be like to see him that way. We have only metaphors to help us understand.

But metaphors are not bad—the Bible is full of them. The one that helps me most in this instance is the metaphor of marriage.

In the Old Testament the prophets spoke of Israel as an unfaithful bride, as a marriage partner who preferred prostitution. Paul adapted this comparison to our more hopeful age, referring to the church as the "bride of Christ." The church was not by nature a more faithful bride than the nation of Israel, but her husband had purified her by his own sacrifice.

The marriage of Christ and his church is usually interpreted (in my experience, anyway) as something already complete. But some New Testament passages make me think that this marriage is yet unconsummated—that we are engaged to Christ and waiting for the wedding ceremony.

I hurry to say, however, that Jewish engagement was nothing like our modern engagements. For us, an engagement is tentative. The couple can break off at any time, and many do. For a Jewish couple, however, engagement was as firm a commitment as marriage. In fact it was the same commitment. The man had paid the marriage price in the presence of witnesses, and the woman was his, and he was hers. She was even called his wife. Unfaithfulness during the engagement period was considered adultery and punished as such. The engagement, or "betrothal," could not be broken except through the same provisions as for a divorce. In the eyes of others the betrothed couple were husband and wife. The only reservation was that they did not yet live or sleep together. In that sense the engagement period was a time of waiting for the proper celebration and consummation.

Certainly when Jesus used marriage as an illustration of the kingdom of God he did not speak of the daily routine of marriage, but of the dramatic circumstances that usher it in: the preparation for the wedding, the maids waiting for the groom to come, the invited guests, and the wedding feast itself. It was not marriage of which he spoke, but the preparations for its celebration. Revelation 21:2-3 puts this celebration at the end of our age: "I saw the Holy City, the new Jerusalem, coming down out of heaven from God, prepared as a bride beautifully dressed for her husband. And I heard a loud voice from the throne saying, 'Now the dwelling of God is with men, and he will live with them.'"

Through this metaphor we learn several things about our intimacy with Christ. First, we learn that intimacy begins with a shared purpose. An engaged Jewish couple did not have the intimacy of living together, yet they were absolutely committed to a future of living together. They walked in the same direction, their thinking pointed the same way, they made preparations for the same joint future. They were married; they could be called husband and wife in the Jewish context because their hearts and their wills had called them together. There was no way back; they could only go forward.

This kind of joint preparation and anticipation brings a special closeness. I remember this very tenderly from my own engagement. We knew we were in a passing stage. In fact, its joy came from the fact that it was passing; we were committed to enter, together, a new world that we knew next to nothing about. So Christians may experience a tender, passing joy with Christ as we prepare to enter the home he is preparing for us.

The analogy shows, secondly, how foolish we would be to try to force premature intimacy. I confess that in my more desperate prayers to God I have sometimes sounded like a teenager demanding that a girl "prove her love" by going to bed with him. I refused to take God's word for his love; I wanted him to prove it to me in drastic fashion. But the partner who insists that his fiancée "prove her love" is, at best, immature and unworthy. The couple who cannot wait for the wedding bed merely cheat themselves; in a sense, they deprive themselves of what they want by taking it prematurely. The fullness of consummated love can only come at the end of a courtship, when the couple has fully experienced the preparation, longing, wondering, waiting, and lastly, celebration. This is hard to understand (as I know too well, having spent many hours trying to explain it to sex-hungry teenagers). But the whole human family—Christian, Buddhist, Hindu, Muslim, or animist—knows it is so of human marriage, and Christians know it is true of marriage to God.

The engagement metaphor also reminds us that we have the very real and important privilege of communication with God. Oriental fathers kept their daughters secluded from the world. A young girl might not even see her prospective bridegroom until they were actually betrothed. Then, once the commitments were made, they were allowed a wondrous, unprecedented privilege. Neither had, since childhood, talked freely to any potential lover. Now they could, in prudent circumstances, meet, talk, and get to know each other. Those times must have seemed like an incredibly joyful freedom—at first. Inevitably, the initial joy would wear off, and since the betrothal period usually lasted a year, both would begin to take their privileges for granted and feel the frustrations of waiting for their wedding day.

We too have unbelievable freedom with God—unbelievable in comparison with the darkness of life outside Christ. To someone newly initiated into this freedom, the joy is palpable. Many new Christians simply would not know what most of this book is talking about, speaking of frustration and groaning and longing to see Jesus. But after a few months and years they will know. We easily forget how bright the light seemed when we first stepped out of darkness. To those who have spent their lives hanging around God (I am one of these—a church kid) the freedom and joy of life in Christ may even seem minimal and be taken for granted.

Getting tired of the engagement period is natural, for the engagement is not an end in itself. In fact, when an engagement lasts for several years and the couple are in no hurry to marry, it seems unnatural. Friends and relatives get nervous, wanting them to get on with the program. In the same way, our engagement to God is not meant to make us comfortable. It is meant to lead to something better, more complete.

Finally, the analogy of engagement reminds us that two persons do not come together just for their own pleasure. A Jew simply could not think of marriage that way. Two individuals were to become one blessing for their parents, their relations, their community, their children. So we ought not to think of our relationship with God as primarily for our benefit. God seeks a fruitful unity. Knowing him is the beginning of creating with him a new family and a new world.

BARELY TOUCHING THE SURFACE

When I think of my own engagement, I primarily remember my intense desire to be with Popie. I wanted to know all about her. I was, I think, oblivious to circumstances and people whom I would otherwise have considered quite important. I was oblivious because my thoughts and emotions were focused on her.

The days are never long enough for engaged couples; they want so much to learn about each other. No longer are they just "trying out" the relationship to see how they like it. Now they are building it, from the ground up. They not only want to know each other, they need to.

And how do engaged people get to know each other? There is nothing mysterious about it. In fact, it is very much like getting to know any other person. Yet however unmysterious it may be, it remains difficult. Those I know best of all—my wife, my family members, my most intimate friends—sometimes seem quite beyond me. There is a deep interior to their hearts, like a vast cave with countless tunnels and interconnecting caverns.

I thought I knew Popie well during our engagement, though I was (I now see) barely touching the surface. The further I go, the more I see the immensity. Even in a lifetime I cannot explore all the chambers of her personality.

It is not even easy to know myself. As both the Bible and Sigmund Freud have taught, the heart is deceitful. I cannot understand why I do the things I do. I think that I know myself, but then I find myself angry for no apparent reason or moved to tears of joy by something very small. In truth I see myself through a glass darkly.

If this is so with human beings, it is infinitely more so with God. When we speak of a personal relationship with him, we are speaking of a relationship with a personality totally different from any we can know here on earth. What I know of him can only be the tiniest fraction of his fullness. Yet what I know today is real, it is deep, and it is entirely significant, for it lays the foundation of a relationship that will last forever.

So the phrase "a personal relationship," which we began by questioning, turns out to be a good way to speak of God. Knowing God is in some ways as simple and as familiar as knowing a friend. It is also as complex, as endless, as infatuating, and as frustrating as trying to understand those we love—or even ourselves. For the more we know, the more we are called to explore farther in and higher up. And in the immense echoing splendor of God there is much more to know than we can ever comprehend.

27
FROM HERE FORWARD

In one of his letters to Arthur Greeves, C. S. Lewis remarked about the danger in thinking about spiritual things, particularly for imaginative people: "We read of spiritual efforts, and our imagination makes us believe that, because we enjoy the idea of doing them, we have done them. I am appalled to see how much of the change which I thought I had undergone lately was only imaginary. The real work seems still to be done. It is so fatally easy to confuse an aesthetic appreciation of the spiritual life with the life itself—to dream that you have waked, washed, and dressed, and then to find yourself still in bed."

Lewis's comment puts the fear of God into me, for I know how susceptible I am to just what he is talking about. Mental discoveries elate me—a fact that this book reflects. In it I have tried to excite your imagination by exploring familiar corners and shining a new light into them. Believing that faith begins as a way of seeing, I have been trying to help you see that the God of the Bible is inescapably personal. More than that—he offers his personality to us.

But these are really only ideas, and we do not come one inch closer to God merely by knowing them. They must be acted on.

It is possible for God to shape us without our awareness. When we were babies, after all, our parents' personalities shaped us without our conscious understanding. We had no idea what they were doing, yet we felt their influence. Often we grow in Christ while similarly unaware. At our best we see him dimly, but that does not diminish his influence on us. He knows us perfectly, though we know him partially, and he is always with us. He can move us in any direction without our cooperation, just as he did Pharaoh or Cyrus, whom he used without their knowledge.

God wants more than this from his children, however. Like our earthly parents, he does not want us to remain babies. He wants us to become his responsive and thankful grown-up children. He desires not merely to change us and use us but to live in reconciled fellowship with us. For this he must open our eyes to himself as a person so that we can live closely with him, walk with him as with a friend, and be shaped by his character. Holiness is not some intangible stuff. It is the influence of God's entirely pure person on our lives. When we live closely with him, we become like him; his personal goodness suffuses us.

This book is an attempt to wake you up to the glorious privilege of being a child of God—the privilege of knowing him. But after waking we must still get out of bed and go to work. And make no mistake about it: Knowing God is work. Any deep relationship takes great effort. No good marriage or friendship is ever formed by people who do strictly what they want when they want. It is harder yet when the person is out of sight. (Think about how well your friendships survive with those who have moved to some distant place.) Life by sight is considerably easier to us weak-willed, temperamental characters, but God calls us to live with him by faith and not by sight.

"DON'T YOU KNOW ME?"

Before he left his disciples the last time, Jesus spoke about the physical separation that was coming. The Twelve were distressed by Jesus' talk of leaving, and they grappled to understand how they would live without him. John 13 and 14 record their conversation.

As usual, Peter was the first to speak: "Lord, where are you going?" His question represents the concern of all who want to be with Jesus in flesh and blood—to see his face, to feel his touch. Peter did not want to let Jesus out of his sight. If Jesus was leaving, Peter wanted to go with him.

Jesus' answer was hard and direct: "Where I am going, you cannot follow now." He offered no religious sentimentality about a "spiritual" relationship. "But," he told Peter, "you will follow later." Thus, he introduced Peter to the "last days," the in-between era of waiting to see Jesus.

Peter's second question speaks for many believers who have not been content with this in-between era, but have tried to earn their way into Jesus' presence by convincing him of their utter commitment. "Lord, why can't I follow you now? I will lay down my life for you."

At this, Jesus delivered another hard blow: "Will you really lay down your life for me? I tell you the truth, before the rooster crows, you will disown me three times!"

Why did Jesus foretell Peter's denial? He was not warning him away from failure; he was assuring him that he *would* fail. I think he said it because he wanted Peter to understand, at least partially, why he was being left behind. Peter was not as pure and fearless as he thought. Because he was not, he was not ready to go with Jesus. Not yet. He had lessons, hard lessons, to learn on earth. Like Peter, we remain on earth because we have unfinished business here. God is not done working on us. Nor is he done working, through us, on the world. We must wait and work.

Thomas asked the next question: "Lord, we don't know where you are going, so how can we know the way?" That is to say, how can we know the route if we don't know the destination? Won't we be left adrift? How can we work toward a future we only see in the vaguest outline?

Jesus' answer is one of the most remarkable in his career of remarkable sayings: "*I am the way* and the truth and the life. No one comes to the Father except through me." In one stroke he changed the focus from the geography of Palestine—for the disciples must have thought, until then, that he was talking of going somewhere on earth—to the geography of our relationship with God. "If you really knew me, you would know my Father as well. From now on, you do know him and have seen him." Jesus claimed to be, himself, both the destination of life and the way to get there. In relating to him, in following him, the disciples were on the way to the only destination worth reaching: God himself. And when they got there, they would find a familiar face: the face of Jesus.

The disciples did not immediately grasp what Jesus was talking about, and Philip's next question reflects their disbelief: "Lord, show us the Father and that will be enough for us." As a student of the Hebrew Scriptures, Philip could not easily believe that he had seen the Father whom Ezekiel and Isaiah had described as living in awesome splendor. Perhaps, Philip suggested, Jesus could show God to them. Certainly he had not yet done so.

Jesus answered with a reproach: "Don't you know me, Philip, even after I have been among you such a long time? Anyone who has seen me has seen the Father. How can you say, 'Show us the Father'?"

With these words, Jesus reminded Philip—and us—of his words and the miracles he had done. He wanted Philip to look back at their years together and realize that God had been with them in the person of Jesus. God had appeared, not in blinding splendor, but in the secret revelation of God to those who had faith to see.

Jesus also pointed Philip toward the future. The disciples would not need to depend only on their memory of Jesus' life to know the nature of God's personality. Jesus would send the Holy Spirit to be with them forever.

To those without faith, however, the Holy Spirit would be no more obvious than Jesus had been. "The world cannot accept him, because it neither sees him nor knows him." He would give the world no proof of his existence. But to the disciples the Spirit would be a recognizable character. "You know him, for he lives with you and will be in you. I will not leave you as orphans; *I* will come to you. Before long, the world will not see me anymore, but *you will see me*. . . . On that day you will realize that I am in my Father, and you are in me, and I am in you. Whoever has my commands and obeys them . . . I too will love him and show myself to him."

The Spirit would come as something better than Jesus-on-earth; he would be Jesus within. The disciples would recognize in the Spirit the Jesus they had known and in recognizing him would begin to understand that their personal contact with Jesus on earth had given them access into something bigger and better: Jesus-in-them, and through him, life-in-the-Father.

The disciples had only one more question after that, and Judas (not Judas Iscariot) asked it: "But, Lord, why do you intend to show yourself to us and not the world?" This too is a question many believers over the centuries have echoed. Why is the light of Jesus only for those who follow him in faith? Why not show it to everybody? Why not devastate the world with his glory, leaving no doubt of his power? Why not light up the sky with fireworks? Why not suddenly appear on everyone's television screen? Why keep himself a secret?

Jesus answered Judas' question by pointing to a division between people. There are those who love Jesus and thus obey him. There are others who do not love Jesus and thus do not obey him. The former group God will love and will establish intimacy with. As for the latter, their fate is not mentioned. But the implication is clear: God will not establish intimacy with them. They will be left on the outside, for they will have chosen to be there.

God's purpose in the universe is to establish intimacy with those who love him. A display of his power and glory is secondary; it only comes when it serves that primary purpose. It seldom does, however. Love cannot be coerced through a display of power.

God is not playing a game of hide-and-seek. He gives himself to anyone who will love him and obey him. But he will not show himself to anyone who is not serious. Obedience, Jesus said, must go with love. Though crowds followed him, claiming to love him, he knew the truth about those who called on his name. He knew their hearts. Because he wanted them to recognize the truth, he continually asked: Are you serious about God? Serious enough to obey? For those with serious love—love willing to work—he would return love beyond all they could ask or think.

God has put into our hearts the longing for him, just as he put it into the hearts of those disciples. He has given us the witness of his life on earth, recorded in the Scriptures to show us as clearly as possible what he is like. He has given us his Holy Spirit, tying us to Jesus through various means, some of which we have considered in this book. We have not been abandoned. Far from it.

Like the disciples, though, we wait. We have seen a great light but not clearly. Only dimly do we see what makes it shine. Jesus has promised, however, that someday we will see perfectly. And when we see that light most clearly, we will see his face, for that is its source. Face to face, we will need no other light.

What will it be like? We do not know. But we will. And that is what we look toward and long for. We will know, just as we are presently known, and we will be changed.

ETERNITY BEGINS NOW

In the meantime we have work to do, learning to know God and allowing him to change us in preparation for the great, final revelation and transformation. We need time, for there is much to learn and much to change.

I think of my own adolescence as a period of bewildering, painful confusion. I did not understand myself. I was in the process of forming my own identity, but the process went on over my head. Why did I act moody? Why did I resent my mother's advice to smile and shake hands with strangers? Why did I so admire and yet despise the "popular" kids? Why was I shy with girls? I did not know the answers to those questions. I did not even know enough to ask the questions. I just lived and reacted. Since I did not know myself, I naturally did not really know others. I could not put myself in other people's positions nor wonder how something felt to them. I could not empathize.

One big step out of this agonizing age came from a summer job. I was responsible for moving about two miles of irrigation pipe twice each day on a big corporation farm in California's San Joaquin Valley. I did one move just after sunrise and another in the scorching afternoon. The six-inch aluminum pipe came in thirty or forty-foot break-apart sections. To move it, I had to turn off the water, wrestle a section of pipe away from its mate, carry it through twenty yards of mud to the next setting, and then go back for another section. I worked alone and rarely saw another person. Sometimes weeks went by before I even saw my boss. He would leave my paycheck in the front seat of my car where I had parked it on the dusty farm road. It was exhausting, lonely work, but it paid well.

The most frustrating part of the job, however, was its mindlessness. After a week or two I could do the work without the least conscious involvement. Often after a day's work I could not remember a single detail of what I had done. But I could not turn off my brain. If the work gave it no grist to grind, it would look for other things to think about. After only a few weeks it seemed I had worked my way through every mental topic I knew: every relationship, every dream, every book I had read, everything under the sun worth consideration. I did not particularly want to think about these things. It was as though my mind were a mechanical sorter, tirelessly working its way through any material thrown into it. And when the sorter had thought through all my topics, it began working through them again, and then again and again. I did not choose to think. I had to.

The temperature exceeded one hundred degrees most days, the sky was deep blue right to the horizon, and the fields were so flat and large that the distant power poles were the only visible objects breaking the line between earth and sky. Nothing distracted me from my relentless mental churning. Slowly but surely I began to discover myself. I found in myself a great deal of anger and sadness and fear. I realized that I had developed a hardened, cynical manner. I realized that I wanted friends, good friends, friends of a kind I did not have. As I thought through my relationships and my behavior, I began to understand myself a bit—how I was and how I really wanted to be.

That summer was, of course, only a beginning. It introduced me to myself and taught me that my life was worth thinking about, that it could be thought about, and that choices could be made. I hated that job as I have never hated any other work. Yet I have always been grateful for its impact on my life, for the time it gave me to know myself. There is, I concluded, no substitute for time.

It takes time, too, to know other people. It is no accident that many people make their best lifelong friends while they are young and have uncrowded hours to spend together—almost unlimited time. When will we again have time like the days of childhood when we played together from dawn to dusk? When will we again get time like high school or college days when we sat for hours and talked about "life"? Those friendships endure beyond school because we keep piling more time on top of our initial investment. We may feel a more immediate and powerful bond with new friends, but it is the old friends we know most fully and who most fully know us.

A mind like Einstein's may master calculus in a day, but it cannot by the same pure power master another human life. We cannot plow through a person's life the way a graduate student plows through his subject in a few semesters. Human lives, being fragile, characteristically hide. Only love, patiently applied, can bring them out. Only a lifetime of love can understand them.

How then can we expect to know God with our finite minds and within our earthly time frame? Maybe we cannot yet fully know God because we are too young. Maybe in our seventy or eighty earthly years there is simply not time to master the subject. The young are characteristically impatient, and that is certainly true of us. We become terribly worried because we don't know God as we wish to. Do we sound to him like children fretting that they haven't yet grown up?

We must have unlimited time to grasp God's infinite personality, and that sounds strangely like eternity. If certain theologians are right and eternity is a timeless state, a beyond-time in which a changeless God lives and contains all the changes of time, then we can imagine (faintly) the continuous rolling over of knowledge we will experience there. We will discover and rediscover, find and forget and joyfully find again the many aspects of our God. This infinite variety will be bound together into a single Möbius strip that turns over and over on itself without beginning or ending.

But I must come down to earth. This vision is far from anything I know. What about the time I do have? The trouble with wishing for heaven is that life on earth may seem hardly worth bothering about. I cannot moon about endless time so much that I neglect the bits of time at hand, inadequate as they are.

Eternity begins now. This is what John's gospel promises when it says that "whoever believes in the Son has eternal life" (John 3:36). In time, here and now, we set our direction toward infinite time.

We need time to know God, and he has given it to us. Hebrews refers to God's time as Today: "Today, if you hear his voice, do not harden your hearts" (4:7). Today is always a day of opportunity. Hebrews urges us to enter God's rest Today. God's rest I take to be the state in which everything else stops and we have the opportunity we need to know God. It is not sandwiched into small slots of time. It is a river from heaven flowing through our normal events.

God gives us the time we need to know him. But do we take it seriously? We have seen in chapter after chapter the opportunities we have to know him personally in a multitude of ways: in conversation, in meals together, in visits with his family, in stories, in sacrifice, in praise, in work, to name a few. Time is the medium in which we use these avenues of God's grace. He makes himself available through them, here and now in time. Are we living through our God-given Today in a deadened stupor, stumbling from one activity to the next? Or are we using Today to begin our relationship with God and enjoy it to the utmost? Do we give God our time? Do we use our time to explore his personality? How does our use of time today predict our use of eternity?

28

WAKING TO THE LIGHT

~

I began this book with a very personal dilemma. I had double vision. I was unable to resolve the world I saw with the world I thought Christianity promised. My difficulty could be summed up in a single question: Where is God? Where, in shopping malls and carpeted offices and freeways and all the busy, irreligious organization of modern life? Or for that matter, where in church services or my own personal prayers, which are at best sporadically glorious?

Has this question been answered? It has been for me. I am no longer troubled by the fear that I am missing some secret technique of Christianity that will make God tangible to me. I know now that Jesus, God in the flesh, is not on earth but in heaven preparing a place for me. As long as we are physically separated, there will always be an incompleteness to our relationship. My true life, as Paul wrote the Colossians, is hidden with Christ; only when he appears will my life appear.

I can live with this, though waiting is hard. It is hard, when you are engaged, to wait for the wedding day. But you can do it if you know that you have found the partner you want and need, and if you are sure that the fullness of marriage will eventually come. I have no doubt that in Jesus I have found someone who can fill every emptiness, and I believe his promise that our day together will come.

I also know that Jesus offers himself to me here and now. But I cannot pin him down to just one way; the fullness of his personality requires many means. Where do I find God today? In Scripture, where he tells stories about himself and where Jesus' personality is exactingly described. In the body of Christ, where he invites me to share a meal and asks me to meet his family. In prayer and praise and work. Through these and other means I may find God, as the Spirit of the Lord Jesus opens my eyes and teaches me to see him there. The opportunities may be mundane, but so are the opportunities through which I know any person. I have experienced far more richness in these means since realizing that Jesus is in them.

My problem is not a lack of access to God. My problem is my deep residual aversion to God and his light, my lack of faith that keeps me from pressing on to know him. Since Eden, men and women have been hiding from God. We have been doing it so long and so thoroughly that we could do it in our sleep. It has become natural to us—but remains utterly unnatural to God.

He has gone to pains to nurture a relationship with us, even sacrificing his son to break down the barriers that keep us apart. He is not hiding from us; we hide from him. Isn't this the constant message of the Bible? Does it not suggest, repeatedly, that our sinfulness keeps us from the full blessing of God's presence? Yes, we want him, but only on our terms—and that is not to want him at all. "Surely the arm of the LORD is not too short to save, nor his ear too dull to hear. But your iniquities have separated you from your God; your sins have hidden his face from you, so that he will not hear" (Isaiah 59:1-2).

When I was in college, I said to God, in some desperation, "If you would just show yourself to me, show me that you are unquestionably and absolutely real, I would be able to love you forever without any question." God knows that was pure self-deception on my part. Every time he has shown himself to men and women they have eventually spurned him. They have reveled in the momentary splendor of his glory and then gone stubbornly like sheep in their own direction. Would I be any different? I have no reason to think so.

If God does not yet show himself in full radiant glory, it must be because in his exquisite timing he has other plans for the human drama before he comes finally into it and, by coming, judges it. The author never comes on stage in the second act; he waits for the curtain call at the end of the play. How much more this applies in God's case, for he has serious and redemptive intentions in this human drama. He intends to train the players.

ENDURE AND ANTICIPATE

If the part we have been given in this human drama is a relationship to a living God, what are we to do with our aversion to him? I believe that Jesus is risen from the dead, that he is alive and accessible. I confess that he is Lord, that my only proper vocation is to know and obey him. But when I wake in the morning, other realities are on my mind. I do not leap to fellowship with him. Sometimes his life is vital to me, but I fall back into dullness of mind and heart. I live, sometimes, as one who does not understand at all. For if I understood, would I not tremble with anticipation and joy and awe?

In Romans, Paul summarizes his situation in a way that sounds familiar. "So then, I myself in my mind am a slave to God's law, but in the sinful nature a slave to the law of sin" (7:25). What can I do about this? Paul's answer is twofold. The first, great, overwhelming answer is that I can and need do nothing about it; only Jesus can and does rescue me from this body of death. I am forgiven. "There is now no condemnation for those who are in Christ Jesus" (8:1). "If God is for us, who can be against us? . . . Will he not also, along with [his Son], graciously give us all things? . . . [Nothing] will be able to separate us from the love of God that is in Christ Jesus our Lord" (8:31-32,39). I will see Jesus face to face because, in his love, he will come to me. His love, not mine, links us together indissolubly.

The second answer—small though it seems after the first—is that I must act as I am able. I can overcome my aversion, day by day, because God will enable me to do so. "We have an obligation—but it is not to the sinful nature, to live according to it. For if you live according to the sinful nature, you will die; but if by the Spirit you put to death the misdeeds of the body, you will live, because those who are led by the Spirit of God are sons of God" (8:12-14). Living as one of God's children requires action; to live as a child of God, I must stop living by sin.

James, who stresses action, puts it this way: "Come near to God, and he will come near to you" (James 4:8). In my experience, the only cure I can work for my residual aversion to God is to move toward him, to spend time getting to know him by the means he has given me. As David said, "Taste and see that the LORD is good." When I taste, the sweetness increases my appetite for more.

But I must apply this cure again and again. Time after time I slip back into forgetfulness. God is easy to forget because he is out of sight. He has gone to prepare a place for me, and he has been gone a long time. Even when his sweetness is a most distinct and sharp reality, I miss him. The more I know of him, the more keenly I feel his absence and the more avidly I wish to see him as he is, face to face.

This play we are in seems like a long run. Often our role seems tedious and difficult. We long for it to end in ovation and celebration. We long to see the author. But we cannot hurry God's timing; we can only endure and anticipate and make the most of the joy we now possess. We ought to say, like Paul, "I want to know Christ and the power of his resurrection and the fellowship of sharing in his sufferings. . . . Not that I have already obtained all this, or have already been made perfect, but I press on to take hold of that for which Christ Jesus took hold of me. Brothers, I do not consider myself yet to have taken hold of it. But one thing I do: Forgetting what is behind and straining toward what is ahead, I press on" (Philippians 3:10-14).

We are invited to the wedding of heaven and earth; we are in the bridal party. In fact, we are the bride. Nothing is lacking, except this: we must be ready. Wake up. Get out of bed. Wash yourself. Clothe yourself. Sing joyfully as you prepare to meet your love—the Love who formed you, the stars and the sun.

> For you were once darkness, but now you are light in the
> Lord. Live as children of light. . . . This is why it is said:
>> "Wake up, O sleeper,
>> rise from the dead,
>> and Christ will shine on you." (Ephesians 5:8,14)

THOUGHTS ON THE HISTORY
OF SPIRITUALITY

~⁌

Everything I have said in this book is, as much as I can make
it, orthodox Christian truth, generally agreed on for the past
two thousand years by believers of all kinds. I suspect, however, that many readers will be struck by the combination of familiarity and strangeness in my words. Everything is just as we know
it—and yet why have we never seen it this way before?

It is a question with personal implications. Is it possible that we
have overlooked the personal focus of the faith we have known and
loved for so long? If so, how did it happen?

It seems to me that we have inherited a historical accident that has
made it seem strange to us. To explain, I must sketch a little history
of the Christian church.

In the years after Christianity was accepted as the official religion of Rome, a new way of seeking God became prominent. An
early believer in Egypt named Antony left a home of considerable
wealth to spend much of his life in a desert cave. He was the pattern
for the early hermits who fled society to confront the powers of Satan
and win through to a dramatic encounter with God. Nowadays we
think of hermits as cranks, but for the early Christians their writings
and personal testimony had an immense influence. They had not set
out to be influential; they set out to know God, and the purity and
wisdom of their lives attracted others to them. In a decaying society,
a world where decadence and an official Christian faith grew side by

side, these men represented a truly radical alternative. They sought to know God.

Fairly soon these hermits learned that a life in solitude was often unstable; they required periods of fellowship and an ordered, disciplined existence. This discovery brought about the establishment of monasteries. At first they were relatively informal groups of radical Christians joining together, often in a remote area, to help each other find God. Gradually more formal and institutional rules were adopted, and patterns of spiritual disciplines were encoded. Monasteries became, over the centuries, the highly institutionalized orders that we think of today. Their purpose, though, remained essentially the same: they assumed that a person called to know and experience God required a radical break from ordinary life. Everything had to be bent toward the highest calling: to know and love the Holy One. These Christians developed highly articulated spiritual programs that were designed to purify a man's or woman's heart from every love but love for God.

You can argue over whether their methods and ideas (which varied considerably) were correct. But you can hardly argue over the holiness and goodness of some of their leaders. In the chaos of the fall of the Roman Empire, the monasteries and convents held men and women of evident godliness, unafraid of the fall of civilization, anxious only to know and love God. They had fled civilization; now when civilization (art, universities, industry) fell, they were little moved. Until that time, the monasteries had been one alternative for those who wanted to know God. After the fall of Rome they were, for a long period, practically the only alternative.

By the time of the Reformation the monasteries were badly diseased, despised by the ordinary citizens of Northern Europe. Stories of sexual promiscuity were common. Monks were not subject to ordinary civil law, and some badly abused this privilege. While all monks supposedly lived by the rule of poverty, some monasteries had become fabulously wealthy. For these reasons, and other more theological ones, the Reformation did not reform the monasteries; it destroyed them wherever it had the power. Some of the Reformation leaders were themselves former monks. Martin Luther, in particular, knew the monasteries from the inside, for he had slaved for years to find the peace of God there. He and other Protestants closed the monasteries and convents and sent the monks and nuns out to earn their bread by "honest" means, rather than by prayer. Over a thousand years of thought and experience about how a person can pursue a relationship with God was simply done away with. It survived, of course, wherever Roman Catholicism survived, but Protestants soon knew little about it.

Outside the monasteries, deep spiritual piety had been little cultivated. "In the fifteenth century, despite the general decadence of religious houses, fervent laymen scarcely conceived that one could respond fully to the call of interior grace except in the cloister," writes Catholic historian Dom François Vandenbroucke. So the Reformation did not inherit a well-formed, systematic tradition of lay spirituality, not even a tradition to reform. The only serious practical approach to spirituality was the monastic one, and the monasteries, with all their tradition, simply went out of existence for Protestants.

Protestant Christians have not, it seems to me, ever quite managed to fill this void. Our history is full of avid concern for a personal confrontation with God. The "devotional classics," the Wesleyan revival, the Great Awakenings, the Pentecostal and charismatic movements, the writings of, to cite only two, A. W. Tozer and Watchman Nee—all these testify to a continually renewed search for God's personal presence. The power of God's Word has never let us remain apathetic. The book of Acts has disturbed our complacency. Paul's passionate and personal letters have challenged us to press on to Christ.

Our spiritual practice, however, has been underdeveloped. There has been very little institutional or theological continuity from one revival period to the next. The charismatic movement, for example, grew up almost without reference to hundreds of years of kindred piety that went before. It was as though some of its leaders believed they had to reinvent the fellowship of the Spirit. They were not the only ones. Each generation has had to rediscover the practice of the presence of God for themselves—not necessarily a bad thing for vitality, but a bad thing for stability.

Theologians have generally spurned these intense movements of spirituality. Our seminaries to this day focus primarily on forming their students' intellectual life, not their spiritual life. Some of the devotional manuals would hardly stand theological scrutiny, but our theologians have offered few alternatives that communicate to laymen. (It was not always so—read Augustine.) Thus, for many if not most Protestants, spirituality amounts to "pray and read your Bible," and those who don't find sufficient satisfaction in that may go hunting for more among the many Christian groups that promise more—that promise, in some cases, everything, and that sometimes become unbiblically fanatical, disturbing the unity and the good reputation of God's people.

Recently many serious Christians have carried their search all the way back to the Catholic monastic movement, trying to take insights from the medieval spiritual masters and translate them into a form that makes sense to busy laymen of the twentieth century. Such a translation is not easy, and there is much from those medieval Christians that is extremely difficult to reconcile with Protestant theology and with life outside a monastery. At least in the monastic disciplines, however, these seekers find a consistent, reverent, and durable way of life that takes the knowledge of God as its reference point.

Yet even there they do not find a satisfactory biblical or theological basis for their life with God. In the centuries after Augustine, the pursuit of God and the pursuit of theology became increasingly split. The spiritual masters wrote allegories of the encounter with God or practical manuals for spiritual growth. The scholastic theologians, for their part, dissected theological questions to the point where they held quite serious discussions about whether more than one angel could occupy the same space at the same time. The two areas—theology and spirituality—were rarely integrated. They are not integrated today. Theology, as most people think of it, deals with ideas and facts, while piety pertains to emotions and supernatural encounters. The two don't mix.

I have wanted to mix them, to draw from the Bible and from experience a basis for spiritual life that makes sense for laymen today. That is why I suspect much that I have written sounds novel, though it is not; I have mixed things that are not often mixed.

I have tried to build a basis for spirituality on the understanding that God, as he presents himself in Scripture, must be known as a person. Here theology and piety must mix, for in all personal encounters emotions mix with ideas, hard facts with inclinations of the heart.

We cannot and must not intellectualize a personal relationship; but we must not, either, get lost in emotions.

I have tried to express the biblical message about this personal relationship in a way that would both comfort and challenge. A biblical spirituality must make clear what wonderful resources for knowing God we already have, and also how much we lack. We have come, by God's grace, amazingly far, but we have much further to go before we know God as fully as he wants to be known.

I have also tried to look at spiritual life in a way that is essentially democratic, in a way that neither lends itself only to a small, self-selected elite nor reacts to the common institutions of the church as being "second rate." There will always on this earth be variations in individual levels of personal Christian commitment. But every Christian has full access to God through Christ, and every Christian living a life of faith must experience, however dimly, his personality. I have looked to the means of grace we all have available. In them I have seen not just grace, but personality.

The phrase "a personal relationship with God" implies that each person will build a relationship with God in a way that is uniquely suited to him or her. Personal relationships are not built by blueprint, like tract houses. No two of my friendships are exactly alike, though they all share common ground. I do not expect, therefore, that any two persons will have the same kind of relationship with God, and I do expect that different kinds of spiritual programs will be helpful at different times and places to different people. Certainly history indicates that this is so. This diversity of approaches, unfortunately, has often led to quarrels and distrust among Christians. I hope this book will help many believers to see that different emphases and styles are quite natural, even healthy, in relating to a personal God. If two men have grown enviably close through playing golf every Thursday, I do not have to take up golf to learn from their example. I may take up golf, or I may adapt their pattern to tennis, a sport I like better. Even if I take up no sport, their closeness encourages me to deepen my own friendships according to my own pattern and the general guidelines for building sound relationships. So I hope this book will encourage many Christians to deepen their relationship with God according to a pattern that fits their personality and within the general guidelines set by God himself.

I have not gone into the "how-to's" of prayer and meditation, of praise and worship and community life, of political involvement and innumerable other practical affairs that affect our life with God. I have not discussed gifts and callings, such as tongues, healing, preaching, chastity. I have not discussed the place of religious experiences, such as feelings, visions, voices, and miracles. All these concern us as we walk with God, and some Christians believe one or more of them is crucial. This book has not settled anything about any of these, but I hope that I have built a basis for considering them.

I would like to think that spiritual pathways will be discussed always within the knowledge that we are not experimenting like scientists with a Force; we have to do, in whatever we do, with a personal God whom we will one day see face to face.